The Construction of Period Country Furniture

The Construction
of
Period
Country
Furniture

V. J. TAYLOR

Former Editor of *Woodworker*

ILLUSTRATED BY THE AUTHOR

Stobart Davies Ltd

Copyright © 1978 by V. J. Taylor

Published 1978 (Hardcover) and 1985 (First paperback edition, with minor amendments), reprinted 1986, 1990, 1991, 1996, 1998.

ISBN 0 85442 029 0
Stobart Davies Ltd, Priory House, 2 Priory Street, Hertford SG14 1RN

Printed in Great Britain by BPC Wheatons Ltd, Exeter

Contents

List of Period Furniture Designs

Introduction

The designs of the classical pieces of furniture which have come down to us over the past centuries have a touch of eternal beauty about them, and their grace and elegance often surpass the best that modern designers can achieve. Further, such designs have the happy attribute of being able to blend in with modern decoration and enhance it.

The first step when thinking about making up any design, whether it is in this book or not, must be to give thought to your materials. Luckily, brassfoundry such as handles and knobs of authentic period designs are quite readily available, as are the various types of hinges and stays. Advertisements appear regularly in woodworking magazines and those dealing with antiques and architecture. Many firms offer a mail order service.

If your aim is to make an authentic reproduction either for sale or because you wish to approximate to the genuine as nearly as possible, then there is no doubt that solid timber is essential, but of course it is possible to economise by employing man-made boards such as blockboard, chipboard, and plywoods.

Obtaining suitable timber will probably be your biggest problem. As we all know, the choice veneers and woods so freely used in the past are now difficult to obtain, but in many instances they can still be found. Readers who live near the coast will find that boatyards still use choice timbers for fitting out; another source could well be architectural woodworkers or shopfitters who specialize in fitting out banks, hotels, and the like.

Another interesting and often intriguing way to acquire well-seasoned prime timber is to buy old furniture at auction sales. It's quite surprising what bargains turn up, often at knock-down prices, but keep a watchful eye for woodworm infestation. There is also the chance that you will come across useful antique handles or fittings.

You should also get to know the home-grown timber merchants in your area. Frequently they are asked to clear an estate or a coppice and after they have earmarked the timber they want there are often some small trees left over which have no commercial interest for them. Such trees could include fruit woods like apple, cherry or pear, all of which are good turnery woods; laburnum, which when cut transversely yields the well-known "oyster shell" veneer; alder, too, can be used for drawer stuff on small pieces.

Most readers will already have the woodworking machinery to take the slogging out of ripsawing, crosscutting, and planing. Actually, very little extra machinery is needed for reproduction work, nor is it desirable.

What is needed is plenty of patience and resourcefulness, and willingness to make up unconventional tools for specific jobs. The old-time craftsman assembled a vast array of scrapers, scratch stocks, and plane irons over the years and most if not all of them were home-made, and we could well follow his example.

Almost any period design carries, perhaps, half a dozen completely different designs of moulding. To this end it is better to spend money on a good quality moulding plane with a full set of cutters than twice as much on expensive mechanized accessories.

As you will be using hand tools to a larger extent than is usual today, a selection of home-made gauges is highly desirable. Such a selection could include a simple shooting board with a mitre planing attachment, a mitre box, and a hold-fast.

Most craftsmen will want to polish their handiwork in its authentic period finish, and in almost every case this will involve french polishing, linseed oil, or wax polishing. A book such as "Staining and Polishing" by Charles Hayward will prove invaluable as these forms of polishing are dealt with in detail.

Remember, too, that the workshop will need to be well heated, as french polishing cannot be undertaken successfully unless the temperature is at least 20 degrees C. Also, using Scotch glue will entail warming up the wooden pieces to be joined as otherwise the glue will chill and lose its strength.

The aim of this book is to present a range of designs, none of which should be beyond the scope of the average woodworker who seriously aspires to reproducing simple classical pieces.

CHAPTER 1

Cabinet Work

DRAWER CONSTRUCTION

In the type of work we are doing, which involves using natural timber rather than man-made materials, the traditional method of drawer construction gives the best results.

This did not come about haphazardly, but is founded on tried and proved ways of minimizing shrinkage. Fig. 1A shows a typical example of traditional construction, and the first point to notice is that both the

which spread any strains due to shrinkage over the entire width of the drawer side. Additionally, it is extremely strong and positive, and is also attractive to look at when made well.

Lap dovetails are used at the front so that no joint is visible when the drawer is viewed face on. The pins between the dovetails run almost to a point at their roots, thereby giving the joint an elegant appearance.

Looking now at Fig. 1B, you will see that the drawer front itself is grooved to accept

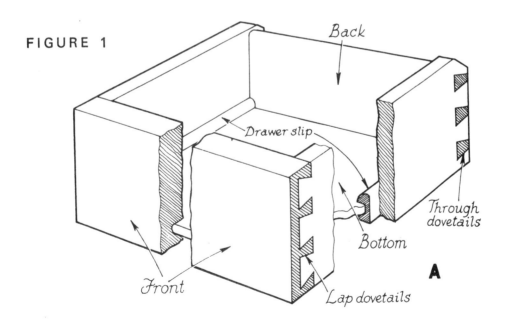

FIGURE 1

Back

Drawer slip

Through dovetails

Bottom

A

Front

Lap dovetails

drawer front and the back are dovetailed to the sides — the front is lap-dovetailed, and the back through-dovetailed.

The old-time craftsmen were, of course, working with natural woods and found that the dovetail joint was basically the only one

the drawer bottom, and the point to watch for here is that this groove must be positioned to be above the bottom pin and wholly contained in the bottom dovetail, otherwise it will show.

The drawer bottom itself is worthy of

mention, as there are several characteristics which must be borne in mind.

First, the grain of a solid wood drawer bottom (as opposed to one made of plywood) runs from side to side, and not from front to back as you might suppose. Again, this shows the craftsman's concern to reduce the effects of shrinkage as if the grain

of the bottom, and is secured by screws (no glue) from underneath. As we have seen, the drawer bottom enters a groove prepared for it in the drawer front, and ideally the front edge of the bottom should be ''fielded'' — that is, the underside is tapered back as shown. As the bottom is a dry fit in the groove it is free to contract by shrinkage and

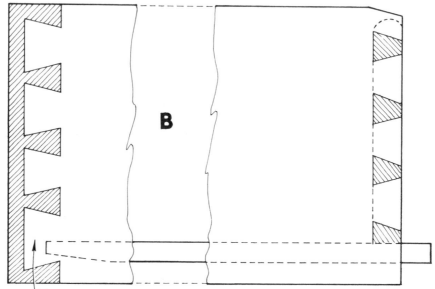

Note how groove for bottom is located in lowest dovetail

did run from front to back, any shrinkage would take place across the width with the likelihood of the bottom shrinking away from the sides and losing support. And showing ugly gaps, of course!

Shrinkage can, and may well, take place across the width when the grain runs from

the effect will not be seen. This also explains why the bottom is only screwed, and not glued as well, to the drawer back — it means that in extremity you can withdraw the screws and use some of the surplus drawer bottom.

The drawer sides also have to include

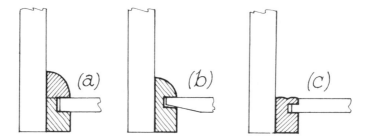

side to side, but this is allowed for by making the bottom half-an-inch (12 mm) or so oversize and allowing the surplus to project at the back.

To accommodate this extra width of the drawer bottom, the drawer back sits on top

some provision for taking up any shrinkage of the bottom, and you can see how this is provided for in Fig. 1a, b, c. Either you can use lengths of drawer ''slip'', which is a rabbeted moulding screwed and glued to the bottom edge of the drawer side, or a grooved moulding which is fixed in a similar manner. Note, too, that the drawer slip has a quadrant beading pinned and glued to it to mask any gaps caused by shrinkage of the drawer bottom. Needless to say, the drawer bottom is set in dry (no glue) and has fielded edges. Whichever way you do the job, it's interesting to observe two things – one, the

except for the method of inserting the bottom. On the assumption that in such a small drawer (say, 9 inches or so (230 mm) or less in width) shrinkage will be so small that it can be ignored, the bottom is rebated in all round, as shown, except at the back. The bottom is, in fact, slid in from the back and can be pinned and glued in place at the

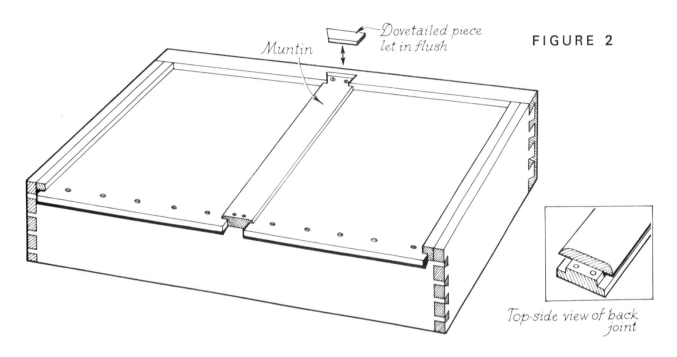

—Dovetailed piece let in flush

Muntin

FIGURE 2

Top-side view of back joint

drawer side is not cut into and so retains its strength, and, two, the slip provides extra sliding surface.

Coming now to the two extremes – large drawers and small drawers, Figs. 2 and 3 show you the best methods to adopt.

A large drawer, which would be one over, say, 30 inches (760 mm) wide, is dealt with by incorporating a centre muntin, as in Fig. 2. Two views of this muntin are shown, one with the drawer upside down to show the dovetailed piece let in at the front, and how the muntin is chopped out at the back to accept the drawer back itself. As for the muntin, you can either cut the grooves as such, or rebate it and plant the strip on to it. Bear in mind that the edges of this strip have to be well rounded off so that any clothing placed in the drawer will not be snagged. I should have mentioned, of course, that such a drawer has two separate pieces to form the bottom.

The small drawer design, Fig. 3, follows the construction we have been talking about,

front and on the sides, and screwed to the edge of the back.

Again, you'll have to bear in mind that you will have to set out your dovetails so that the rebate is wholly contained in the side and does not involve any cutting away of the dovetails on the front.

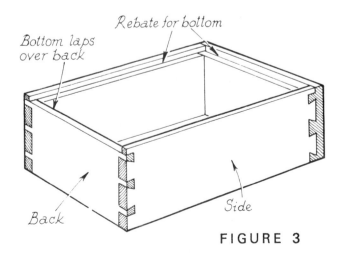

Rebate for bottom

Bottom laps over back

Back

Side

FIGURE 3

To prepare the stuff for a drawer, begin by truing up the bottom edge of the front, and face-mark this edge. Follow on by making one edge true to the drawer side, but if you want your drawer to close with an almost imperceptible gap between it and the side of the surrounding framework, bevel the edge of the front a trifle. It only needs the merest shaving taken off – just enough to give a wedging effect.

At this juncture, I should mention that you may find it useful when planing the end grain, to start with a piece about ⅜ inch (10 mm) wider than the finished drawer front. If you then chamfer off one corner, you'll be able to plane right along the end grain without any splitting out.

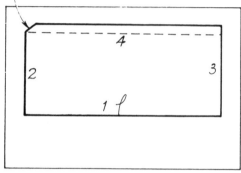

Bevelled off to allow planing without splitting end grain

FIGURE 4

Fig. 4 shows the sequence of planing. Preparing the back, sides, and bottom parts is quite straightforward. I have dealt with dovetail joints elsewhere, but before leaving the subject of drawers, look at Fig. 5. There you will see a handy way of supporting the

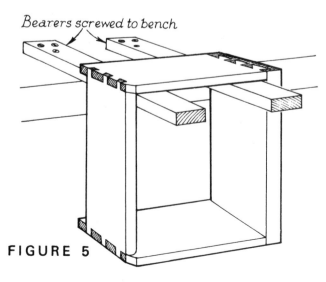

Bearers screwed to bench

FIGURE 5

drawer frame while you true up the dovetails by planing across them; normally, this would impose a severe strain on the strength of the frame but the method shown avoids this.

I see that I have written, rather glibly, that you can true up the dovetails by planing across them. This is perfectly all right if you are using animal (Scotch) glue, but if the joints are glued up with a modern PVA or UF adhesive which sets rock hard, then your plane iron will suffer! Although the suggestion may provoke shudders of horror among some traditionalists, I would strongly recommend that you use a Surform or Aven shaper tool instead. These can cope with hard or brittle substances with no trouble at all.

CARCASE CONSTRUCTION

This naturally divides itself into two types – either a carcase using solid ends, or one in which panels are employed.

Dealing with the solid-end carcase first, a typical form of construction is shown in Fig. 6. It's worth studying because not only is it extremely strong, but also because careful provision has been made to accommodate shrinkage as far as possible.

To this end, we can see once again that dovetails are utilized to secure the front and back top rails to the end, and their use equalises out any strain as far as possible. In addition, triangular corner fillets are also dovetailed and glued in for added strength.

There is an interesting feature on the runners which is often adopted by professionals, and that is to groove the runners as shown and to cut the tenons to line up with the groove. The grooves are, of course, central in the thickness of the runners and normally serve no other purpose than to ensure uniformity of the tenons. However, if you have an accurate sawbench to cut the tenons on and you can guarantee accuracy, this procedure would not be necessary in the normal way.

What does call for such grooving, however, is whether or not you intend to fit dustboards under the drawers – this was always done, I might add, in best class work.

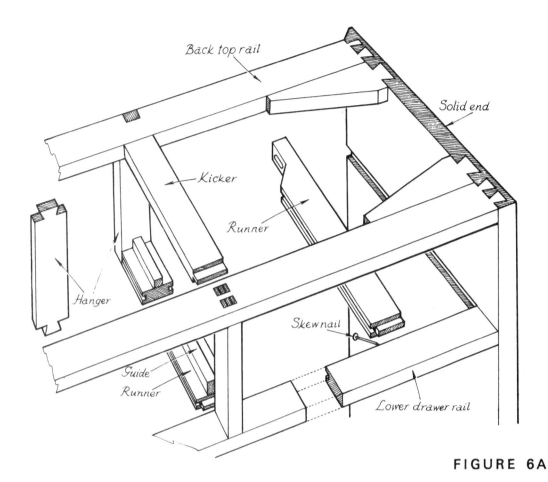

Back top rail

Solid end

Kicker

Runner

Hanger

Skew nail

Guide
Runner

Lower drawer rail

FIGURE 6A

If you do fit dustboards, then you will need to groove the runners, and also the back (inner) edge of the lower drawer rail, as shown in the section. This will use the same settings as for the grooves on the runners. When all are done, the dustboards can be slid in from the back.

Now to consider the runner next to the end. As you can see, this is housed in its entire width into a channelling cut for it in the solid end itself. This channelling runs out at the back and it is stopped about 1 inch (25 mm) back from the front edge and the lower drawer rail is notched round as shown so that the major part of it is supported in the channelling.

To allow for movement in the end, glue is only applied to the end of the drawer rail and to the tenon on the front edge of the runner. This tenon, of course, fits into the dustboard groove on the back edge of the lower drawer rail and it's a good idea to tap in a nail on the skew to hold the tenon in place. The runner is not glued into the channelling but left dry; its only fixing is by

means of a slot screw at the back end where the wood is notched out to allow a screw of reasonable length to be used.

Slot screwing is a handy dodge to know about and is shown in Fig. 6B. As you can see, the screw is inserted in a slot rather than a hole, the slot being made by boring two holes side by side and joining them up. Although many woodworkers use countersunk head screws for this fixing, I prefer round-headed ones, as they seem to function better. When you are thinking about driving the screw, remember to put it at the correct end of the slot to allow movement to be taken up! I should add that such fixings are meant to provide support only, and not to provide a positive fixing all round.

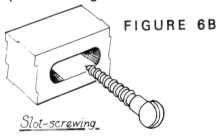

FIGURE 6B

Slot-screwing

Next, the centre runner. If, as is most probable, you have a central muntin, then you can cut a groove across it for the runner to lie in – a dry joint, of course, without glue.

However, if the job is not wide enough to warrant a centre muntin, then we have to think of other means of support. The traditional way is to use a "hanger", as shown, which is dovetail-housed into the top back rail and also to the runner itself at the opposite end. Glue can be used on both joints. Because of the grooves on both edges of the runner, the lower dovetail on the hanger has to be small enough to be located between them with plenty of spare wood each side.

Again, glue is used only where the stub tenon of the runner enters the groove in the drawer rail, and a nail is driven in askew as before. The drawer guide and its fixing is straightforward enough as it is simply screwed and glued to the runner, as shown. The professionals make it very slightly wider at the front than it is at the back – only by the proverbial whisker! – and this does give a wedging effect which prevents the drawer shooting out at the merest touch.

If your carcase has a solid top which is fastened directly to the end, you can dispense with kickers as the top itself will prevent the drawer tilting downwards as it is opened. But if the top is mounted on to the carcase rails you will need a central kicker; the triangular corner fillets will keep the drawer from tilting at the end, and, of course, the central kicker does the same job.

The fixing of the solid back is interesting. As you can see, the rear edge of the end is bevelled off at an angle of 45 degrees. This means that the back, which should have its grain running vertically, also has its corresponding edges bevelled so that, once again, when the back is offered to the carcase, it should fit in with a slight wedging action.

Of course, no glue but screws only should be used for fixing the back. And it would be advisable to ensure that the back is bone-dry when it is fixed in – that way, any movement will be due to swelling and will simply push the back outwards so that it stands slightly proud of the carcase.

Before we go any further, it would be as well to mention two points about inserting and driving screws. First, always push the tip of the screw threads into a piece of candle, or a cake of soap. This will ensure that a thin film of wax or fat is distributed along the screw threads. The results? – your screw will go in much easier without loss of holding power, and it will be easier to remove after a lapse of years as the threads will not rust so quickly.

But I must warn you not to overdo it. Don't use oil or grease as both can migrate into the surrounding wood and ruin any attempts at gluing or polishing.

The second point is that professional craftsmen always align the slot in the screw head along the grain when they finish driving it home. This is not just for neatness' sake (although it does look better) but to help the polisher. As you will know, the polisher always works along the grain and if his rubber meets a screw-slot at right-angles two things happen – his rubber is likely to be snagged, and also there will be a build-up of polish left in the slot which will look unsightly and which could need cleaning out should the screw need withdrawing at a future time.

FRAME-AND-PANEL CARCASE

With the scarcity of well-seasoned solid timber being what it is, not to mention the price, it's very likely this is the kind of construction you will use.

The panels will almost certainly be veneered plywood and before going on to the construction of the framework proper, there are several matters worth mentioning, as follows:

(a) If you are veneering the plywood yourself, don't omit to lay a "balancer", or compensating veneer, on the back. If you don't do this, you will be imposing a strain on the plywood and in time it is almost inevitable that it will "bow". The balancer need not be the same veneer as on the front, but can be a less expensive one. And, of course, both veneers must be laid at right angles to the grain of the ply faces.

(b) Whenever you groove ply into a frame, always leave a deliberate break between them. Fig. 7 shows what I mean. In one instance, the ply is set back about $\frac{1}{16}$ inch (2 mm) or so from the face of the framework; in the other case, the ply is tongued into grooves on the framing but a tiny gap of 1 mm or so is intentionally built in.

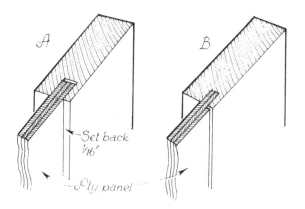

FIGURE 7

Both of these features mask any slight movement in the framing — without them, the smallest gap or discrepancy would stick out like the proverbial sore thumb.

If you are using a solid timber panel, then really the only way to ensure that any shrinkage will be concealed is to "field" the panel in. We have already seen how this can be done on the back of the panel, but the classic type of fielding is shown in Fig. 8. Note that the wood is not simply bevelled away; there is a small vertical quirk which defines the exact limits of the fielding.

Instead of this quirk, you could insert a small beading — in fact, this was a favourite trick of the old craftsmen when they wanted

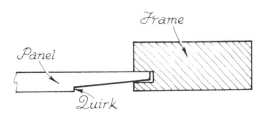

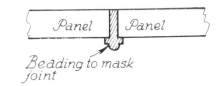

FIGURE 8

to mask the joining of two panels which were side by side and butted together.

Fig. 9 shows a typical framed-up carcase. Note, first, that the end includes stout posts both at front and back; the front drawer rail has twin dovetails, one of which enters the post and the other, the end rail. At the back, the end rail and the back rails also are tenoned into the post — all joints are glued as the likelihood of shrinkage is small and can be ignored.

Another feature of note is that the runners are grooved and tenoned into the lower drawer rail; the latter is notched round the corner post.

Not having a solid end to slide against, the drawer requires the provision of a guide to be glued and screwed to the runner, and this guide fits between the posts. But do not glue the runner to the panel in case the latter tends to shrink.

At the back end of the end runner you can see again how one side of it is cut away to allow a comparatively short screw to be used. But this time you can see that it is also notched on the other side to fit into a channel cut to accept it on the post.

Although quite a small point, it does illustrate a useful procedure when screwing one part to another. This is that whenever possible, it is good practice to recess the face of one part to receive the other part rather than to have two perfectly flat surfaces screwed together. A moment's thought will tell you that the shoulders of a recess will provide much more resistance to a turning or racking movement than the mere purchase of the screw, or the additional strength of an adhesive.

Getting back to the carcase, you will see that the central runner is similar to that previously described, except that if there is a muntin in the back, it can be notched and glued to it. Otherwise, you can use the hanger already shown in Fig. 6.

The back is screwed (but not glued) into a rabbet all round the back frame, and can also be screwed to the central muntin, if there is one.

It is often helpful to lubricate the underedges of a drawer to ensure that it slides smoothly, and the best lubricant to use is ordinary candle grease. Resist any temptation to smear on any kind of oil or grease.

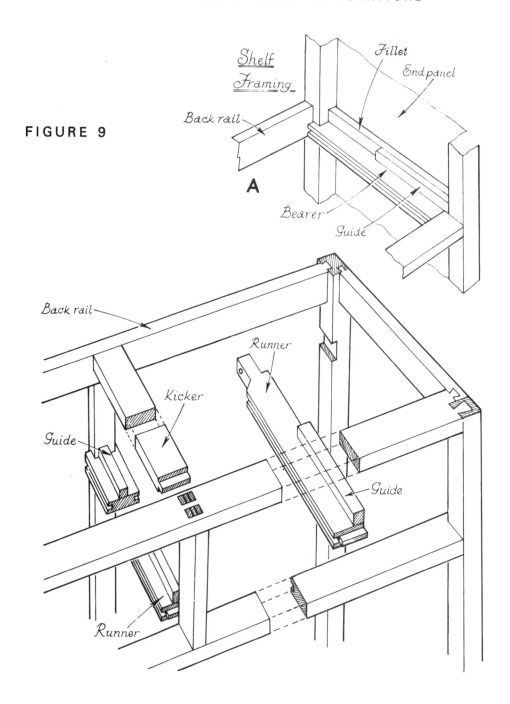

FIGURE 9

JOINTING, FRAMING AND FIXING TOPS

Undoubtedly one of the most rewarding sights to a woodworker is that of a vast expanse of gleaming table top with the grain perfectly matched, and this can only really be achieved by using solid timber.

As we are only too well aware, solid timber of the requisite choice grain, width, and stability is becoming increasingly scarce.

But this can be overcome by jointing comparatively narrow strips together, side by side, to make up the required width.

With the advent of man-made boards, the old-fashioned method of rub-jointing boards seems to be falling into disuse, which is a pity. Properly done, it can enable you to make up a beautiful top out of what would otherwise be odd strips.

There are several provisos which must be observed before you decide to go ahead.

First of all, the method can only be used on woods which hold glue well, such as mahogany, walnut, and the pseudo-mahoganies. Spruce and birch, if good quality, are also good. Teak, rosewood, oak, or resinous woods are not, either because they are too close-grained, oily or liable to exude resin.

Next, the length of the pieces is a major factor. You'll find it difficult to handle pieces much over 3 feet (915 mm) long although longer pieces can be managed if you have an assistant. Remember, though, that you will require a long (jointer) plane, or it will be difficult to plane the edges straight and square.

Again, the thickness can also pose problems as anything under $\frac{1}{4}$ inch (7 mm) is really too flimsy.

Obviously, accuracy of planing must play a large part in jointing. For thin stuff, say $\frac{7}{8}$ inch (22 mm) and under, it would probably be best to do the job on a shooting board. Or you may care to make use of a little dodge I learned a long time ago.

This is to take two thin strips of any wood, 1 inch by $\frac{1}{4}$ inch (25 mm by 6 mm) would be a good size, and longer by a few inches than the piece you are about to plane. You must be sure that at least one edge is

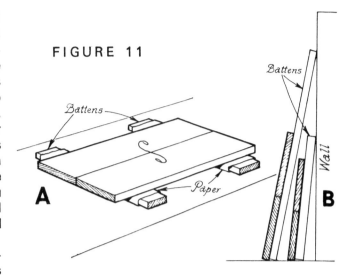

FIGURE 11

Battens

Battens

Wall

Paper

A   **B**

FIGURE 10

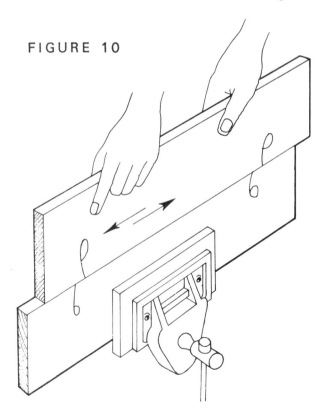

dead flat and true, and this should be smeared with a little French chalk. Then cramp one strip on each side of the piece you are going to plane so that the edges of the strips coincide with your marked line.

No doubt you can see what comes next! The strips act as guides and your aim should be to plane down without removing any of the French chalk.

Having finished the planing, put a face mark exactly halfway along each edge. Cramp one piece in the vice, planed edge uppermost, and then apply glue to both edges.

Pick up the loose piece with a hand at each end and place the glued edge on the one in the vice. Move it from side to side three or four times, as shown in Fig. 10, and then bring the face marks to coincide. Then lean the pieces against the wall as near vertically as possible (Fig. 11B) and the job is done. By the way, there's no reason why you shouldn't rub-joint several pieces together, and you don't have to use Scotch glue as most of the PVA and other synthetic resin adhesives will do. The only ones you cannot use are casein glues and impact adhesives.

One point I have overlooked so far. When you are rub-jointing thin wood it's often difficult if not impossible to do the job with one piece held in the vice and the other in your hands as everything wobbles too much!

The best way to overcome this is shown in Fig. 11A. A couple of battens (they must be of identical thickness) are laid on the bench with strips of paper over them to prevent the glue sticking. Wrap the paper right round and Sellotape it so that it cannot move. Then lay your pieces on the battens and move them as required.

Before we leave this particular subject, I would like to remind you that if you are making a top from cramped and jointed pieces (*not* a rubbed joint) then you should make a definite effort to plane the edges to be jointed slightly hollow. It need not be much of a hollow — say, $\frac{1}{16}$ inch (2 mm) in 3 feet (915 mm), or $\frac{1}{8}$ inch (3 mm) in 6 feet (1829 mm). The idea is that the joint at the ends, where it is weakest, is kept together by the natural springiness of the wood.

Of course, you may be lucky enough to have a piece of solid timber that can be used as it is. However, it sometimes happens that although wide and long enough, it is too thin.

In such cases, you can visually increase the thickness as shown in Fig. 12 — note that the end pieces are cross-grained so that the grain of all pieces runs in the same direction, thus reducing the effect of shrinkage. Although the front thicknessing piece can be glued and screwed, it would be better to slot-screw on the other pieces, without glue.

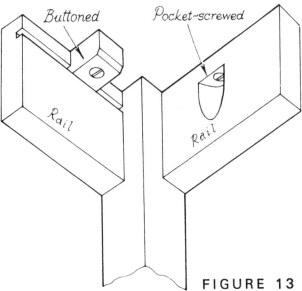

FIGURE 13

FIGURE 12

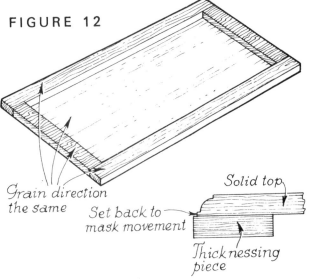

Grain direction the same

Set back to mask movement

Solid top

Thicknessing piece

Again, dealing still with solid tops, the method of fixing is normally to pocket-screw the front rail to the top while the other three rails are fixed by means of buttons as in Fig. 13. Note that there should be a slight gap at the top of the tongue so that when the screws are driven home the top is brought hard down, yet it is free to move in the event of shrinkage.

CHAPTER 2

Veneering

GENERAL PRINCIPLES

Before we can begin considering the actual process of veneering, it would be as well to deal with groundworks first.

If you have to use solid wood as a groundwork, it has to meet the following requirements:

(*a*) It has to hold the glue well. This rules out woods of a greasy nature such as teak. It also precludes oak because of its coarse open grain which can eventually show through the veneer.

(*b*) It should be straight-grained and free from knots or patches of wild grain which might be slow to absorb glue. In other words, the rate of glue absorption should be pretty constant over the whole groundwork.

(*c*) It should be dry and well-seasoned. This brings up the familiar old problem of shrinkage. If you do have to use strips with

FIGURE 14

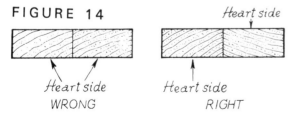

Heart side
WRONG

Heart side
RIGHT

heart grain showing as in Fig. 14, then joint them together with the heart side alternately up and down, as this will minimize movement.

(*d*) Softwoods, if they are of good quality, are perfectly all right for the job — Parana pine in particular. But any knots even the small ones, should be cut out and the holes plugged, otherwise glue absorption could be uneven and you might get resin bleeding through. Also, the knot does not shrink at the same rate as the groundwork. In any case, give all softwoods a coating of glue size before applying the glue proper, or you'll find the wood drinks up the glue.

A word about the plugging referred to above. Whatever you do, avoid dowels as their end grain will run at right angles to the grain of the groundwork. So, if the groundwork shrinks, they will stand proud of the surface with startling results.

The best things to use are plugs made by a plug-cutter. Cut them from an offcut of the same wood as the groundwork and make sure their grain direction runs to match the groundwork. For small holes, Polyfilla mixed with a little PVA adhesive makes a good filler. But however you plug the holes make sure they are sanded perfectly flush before you get on with the gluing.

(*e*) A good quality plywood also makes a suitable groundwork, as does a laminboard. Be sure to lay both the face and the compensating veneers at right angles to the grain of the exterior faces of the groundwork. Blockboard and battenboard are not so good, as the wider core strips have a potentially higher warping factor and this can show up as "telegraphing", when the surface develops a series of ripples.

(*f*) Chipboard: This is quite satisfactory as a ground-work, and the smaller the particles of which it is made, the better. It needs counter-veneering, that is, a compensating veneer on the back; this "balancer" should be at right angles to the face veneer.

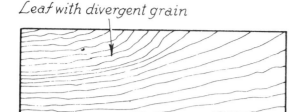

Leaf with divergent grain

Type of panel which results from using such a leaf

FIGURE 15

QUARTERED PANELS

Quartered panel veneering is not so straight-forward as it may at first appear. To get perfectly matched quarters you need to cut one piece from each of four consecutive leaves, and the result should be as in Fig. 15.

Of course, this is expensive, and very often all four quarters have to be cut from one leaf. The thing you must watch for in this case is that the grain must be regular, straight, and evenly spaced.

Trouble sometimes occurs when trimming edges, as the edge persists in crumbling or splintering away. To overcome this, cramp the edge of the veneer between a couple of battens with thumbscrews and trim the lot, veneer and battens, on a shooting board. It will mean taking a shaving off the battens, so they had better be scrap.

The problem of "flatting" veneers can keep you awake at nights, particularly such awkward customers as elm burr or burr walnut.

Probably the best way to deal with it is to give the veneer a light dampening with thin glue size and leave it overnight between two boards with weights on top. Put a sheet of greaseproof paper either side of the veneer, and interleave each piece if you are dealing with more than one. If it should require to be done again, do not use more glue size but merely damp the leaves with lukewarm water.

VENEERED PATTERNED PANELS WITH CROSSBANDED EDGES

This is a standard job in veneering as the number of doors, fronts, and panels

veneered in this way must be enormous.

In principle, the technique (in small shops, anyway) is to lay the main panel with cauls, trim the edges when the glue has set, and then lay the crossbandings with the hammer. On reflection, you will see that this is, indeed, the only way to do it when only one or two jobs are needed. If the whole thing was laid at once, main panel, crossbandings and all, everything would be all right provided the panel was exactly true and not even a trifle out.

But this is very difficult to achieve, and any error, however slight, could only be corrected by trimming the edge of the banding.

The procedure starts by drawing out the pattern on to a flat piece of paper or card, and this is, in fact, standard practice for pattern veneering. Spare ends of wallpaper rolls are handy for this and can be pasted down to a sheet of hardboard. Bear in mind that the board has to be dead flat, however, so paper both sides. When all is dry it can be pinned temporarily on to a flat surface.

Next, you will have to draw the pattern on to the papered board in pencil taking your time and making sure everything is accurate. Be warned — do not use a ball point pen for the drawing as it can leave ink traces which can be disastrous to some finishes! As you complete the drawing it's a good idea to mark in, very roughly, the grain direction for each piece.

The next step is to cut the veneer to match the pattern exactly, and for this it is absolutely essential that the veneer is dead flat. You can imagine how any buckled pieces would behave when under pressure — the buckling would flatten outwards, moving the adjacent pieces and ruining the work. And remember that all veneers must be the same thickness; if they are not, abandon the idea of using a caul and employ the hammer method instead.

To accomplish this, damp the veneers with glue size (a piece of plastic foam makes a good applicator) and place them between two stout boards. Cramp the boards together, or place them under weights, and leave overnight. In the morning, the pieces will be dry and flat and, what is more, they will stay that way. Don't make the glue size too strong, though, as you do not want the leaves sticking together. If you're worried about this, interleave them with a single sheet of plain paper — if this sticks, you can always damp it slightly to remove it.

Incidentally, it is often recommended that veneers should be interleaved with news-papers before being put under pressure. I am never very happy about this as I have had printing ink transferred to the veneer in the process. Perhaps the newspaper was too fresh — anyway, I play safe and use ordinary brown paper.

Although professionals have specially shaped knives for cutting and trimming veneers, a good sharp craft knife will do the job well. Once you have got the pieces

Fig. 16 shows a typical caul arrangement. The bearers have a slightly convex curve on the bearing side so that when the cramps are tightened down, the pressure is exerted from the centre outwards.

For panels up to, say, 3 feet long (915 mm), three bearers should suffice, with cor-respondingly more bearers for larger panels.

There are one or two points to note which can make all the difference between success and failure. Gluing down veneer is not (in the home workshop, anyway) an exact science and a little know-how is worth a great deal.

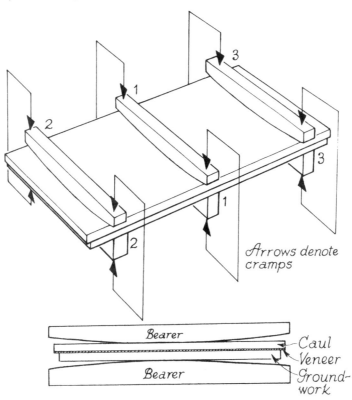

FIGURE 16

cut and arranged to your liking, hold them together with strips of gummed brown paper tape. In addition, you can put a dab of glue on the back of any recalcitrant pieces which will not stay in place.

As we have seen, the crossbandings are laid later by hammer, so the outer edges of the main leaves can be allowed to run over the edges.

Now the set-up is complete, it can be lifted off the board. You can remove any dabs of glue by damping to loosen them with warm water — not too much or it may cockle the veneer.

First then, recruit a helper. It's rather like learning to drive a car — everything needs to be done at once and you seem to need at least four hands!

Get the cauls well heated. This may mean leaving them stacked near some kind of heater for several hours, but they must be hot right through.

Collect all your G-cramps and/or hand-screws and open them to the approximate gap so that you don't have to waste valuable time feverishly adjusting them.

Mark out, with pencil lines, the exact position of the veneer on the groundwork.

It helps here if you can drive in a few veneer pins partly home so that the veneer butts up against them and is thereby prevented from shifting. Nip their heads off and position them somewhere in a waste area — in this case in the margin left for the crossbanding.

Have your glue freshly made to a consistency of thin cream. Apply it to the veneer and to the groundwork but do not be in a hurry to put the two together.

Let it get quite cold and firm, and then lay the veneer in position. This may seem a paradoxical way of going about things, but there are reasons!

If you lay the veneer on the groundwork while the glue is hot, it is very liable to float about and be ruined when pressure is applied. And if the glue is still tacky when you do the job it will act just like an "impact" adhesive and grab the veneer so that you have no chance to make any small adjustments to its position.

You will have to put the hot caul on quickly and then the bearers, tightening the cramps on the centre one first. Leave the assembly for a couple of hours and then slacken the cramps off.

We now come to laying the crossbandings. Remove the completed panel from the cauls and dab over the brown paper strips lightly with a piece of plastic foam moistened with warm water. This will loosen the glue and allow you to peel them off readily.

Cutting the excess veneer away to expose the margins comes next and this is shown in Fig. 17. A cutting gauge is illustrated as doing the job but if you feel happier using a

FIGURE 17

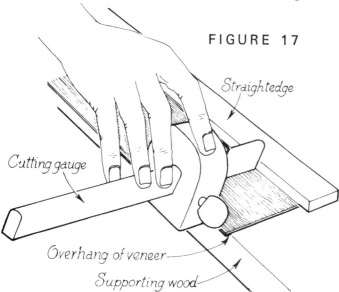

Straightedge

Cutting gauge

Overhang of veneer

Supporting wood

metal straightedge and a sharp craft knife, by all means do so.

If the glue has not set hard you will be able to lift and peel away the offcuts: if it has, then you will have to resort to the plastic foam and warm water to loosen it.

The veneers for the crossbanding should be cut about $\frac{1}{4}$ inch (7 mm) or so oversize in the width to allow you enough to trim back.

Begin at one corner and work round the job; any joints should be taped with gummed brown paper tape. You don't need a special veneering hammer for the job although it is the best way to do it; the cross pene of any hammer will suffice.

If the glue is hot and no delays occur, the work can be completed with the hammer alone. But if something does go amiss you may need to use an iron to get the crossbanding down.

The type of iron used in veneering is the old-fashioned flat iron and it should only be warm, not hot. If you can hold it about 2 inches away from your cheek and feel a pleasant warmth, it's hot enough. Hotter than this may well scorch the veneer, and in any case the veneer should be dampened slightly to prevent any damage.

Probably an ordinary thermostatically controlled electric iron would also do the job if at a low setting, although you would have to press harder as it is lighter in weight.

The last job will be cleaning up, and we will deal with this in detail now.

Cleaning up veneer One of the most essential things to do before cleaning up is to allow as much time as possible for the glue to harden and any sinkage to take place. Forty-eight hours is a minimum, and a week is better.

However, one thing you can do a few hours after laying the veneer is to remove any tape and sponge away excess glue with clean warm water. Such glue can be a real nuisance, as when using a scraper it will clog it in no time — the same goes for glass-paper, too.

For straight-grained plain work, a scraper can be employed, using it in the normal way. However, built-up patterns and crossbandings present a problem because of the opposing grain directions and it is advisable to hold the scraper at a pronounced angle so that the cut slices more than it would normally do.

Another problem arises when dealing with a burr veneer where the grain is completely random. The only thing to do here is to use a fine/medium glasspaper wrapped around a cork block or a block with a felted face. Employ a circular movement, and finish off with a very fine flour-grade glasspaper.

Needless to say, it is imperative that you use a very light hand when cleaning up. Veneer is necessarily thin, and it is quite easy to scour right through, particularly at the edges.

Hammer veneering This method of veneering is restricted to knife-cut, thinner veneers, as thicker saw-cut varieties tend to be springy and will not lie properly unless considerable pressure is applied.

The hammer itself bears little resemblance to a conventional hammer and is usually home-made. Fig. 18 gives details and sizes which do not have to be followed slavishly. It should be made in hardwood, the blade being $\frac{1}{8}$ inch (3 mm) thick brass.

Perhaps the most important part is the blade, as the edge must be perfectly smooth and rounded off with a file and emery paper.

We have seen that with caul veneering, the pattern is assembled and then laid as a whole. But with hammer veneering only a restricted range of simple patterns can be laid as the veneer pieces are laid to overlap, the joints being cut afterwards.

Fig. 19 shows the way to use the hammer. Start at the centre of the work and follow the grain as much as possible, working from the centre outwards so that the glue is squeezed outwards. Keep a damp rag handy to wipe the blade clean from glue.

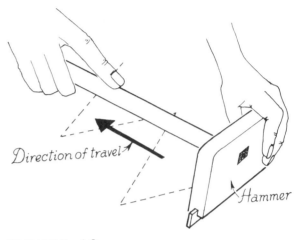

Direction of travel

Hammer

FIGURE 19

If you have a groundwork on which the veneer has been laid to overlap the edges, manipulate the hammer as shown in Fig. 20 so that the overlap does not get broken off.

All of this process takes place while the glue is still setting and you will have to heat the veneers with an iron to reliquefy the glue.

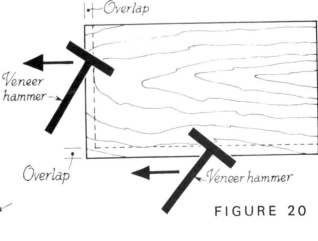

Overlap

Veneer hammer

Overlap

Veneer hammer

FIGURE 20

Fig. 21 illustrates the procedure for cutting a joint between two pieces of veneer, one of which overlaps the other by an inch (25 mm) or so. Lay a straightedge along the overlap and cut through both thicknesses with a really sharp craft knife.

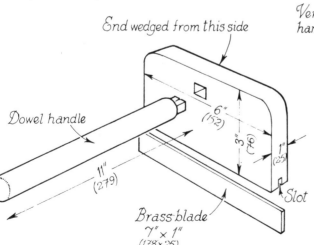

End wedged from this side

Dowel handle

6"
(152)

3"
(76)

1"
(25)

11"
(279)

Slot

Brass blade
7" x 1"
(178 x 25)

FIGURE 18

FIGURE 21

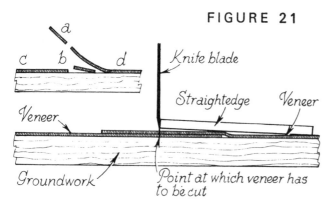

FIGURE 22

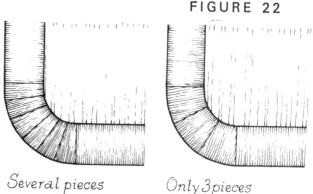

Several pieces   Only 3 pieces

You can then peel away the top strip of waste. Lift the veneer up and remove the waste strip beneath, let it fall back and you will have a perfect joint, which should be taped to prevent it opening.

Crossbanding with curved corners This is a perfectly straightforward hammer-veneered job, the only problem being how best to negotiate the corners. It's best to use a multiplicity of wedge-shaped pieces as seen in Fig. 22; to use only 2 or 3 tends to catch the eye, because of the glaringly obvious changes in grain direction.

The face veneer is then laid to lap over the beading and then a veneer strip is laid on the beading to cover both it and the edge of the face veneer. It is essential that the grain of the beading itself runs crosswise to minimize splitting.

Bubbles These can sometimes be troublesome. To test for them, tap your fingernails over the surface, which should feel solid. If you do feel a bubble, re-heat the spot locally with the iron (moistening the veneer

FIGURE 23

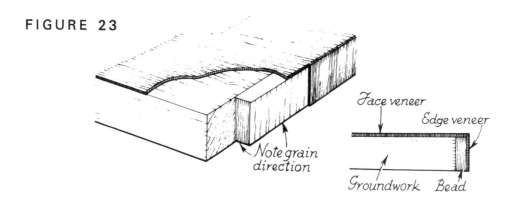

Treatment of end grain A very tricky job because of the tendency of the grain to absorb large amounts of glue. Further, there is always the alarming possibility of splits developing if you are using solid timber, and no veneer can stand up to the stresses imposed.

The answer, really, is to apply beadings, or slips, to the edges and veneer them. Fig. 23 illustrates the method. As you can see, the beading is glued direct to the panel edge or, better still, it is recessed into it.

slightly) and go over it again with the hammer.

If this does not cure it, and it is near to the edge, try fixing a heated wooden block over it and cramping it down as in Fig. 24. Don't forget the interleaved paper.

Not all bubbles are so obliging, however, and if it is near to the centre of the panel you'll have to adopt the set-up as shown in Fig. 25. The stout bearer is essential to prevent the groundwork bending under pressure.

FIGURE 24

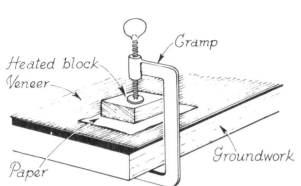

FIGURE 25

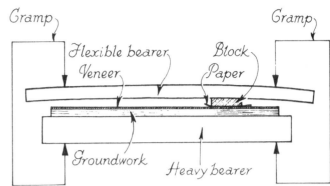

Scotch glue The glue I have been mentioning throughout this section on veneering is Scotch glue. As we have already noted it is indispensable for this kind of work due to its ability to reliquefy under gentle heat and then re-set. Actually, veneering is the one aspect of woodwork where it does not matter if the glue *does* chill, as it can always be revived by the application of heat.

A word of warning about the use of water to dampen veneer for the various purposes outlined above. Such water must be used as sparingly as possible to avoid diluting the glue too much and thereby causing bad bonding.

SHAPED WORK

Veneering shapes is quite fascinating because, although there are standard ways to tackle the various jobs, you can make up your own methods which are just as effective.

Basically, there are four ways to make up a curved (or "bow") front, as in Fig. 26. Little explanation is needed. A curve cut from the solid is expensive and wasteful of wood; if you do use one of these methods, remember to save the off-cuts as they will be invaluable for cauls.

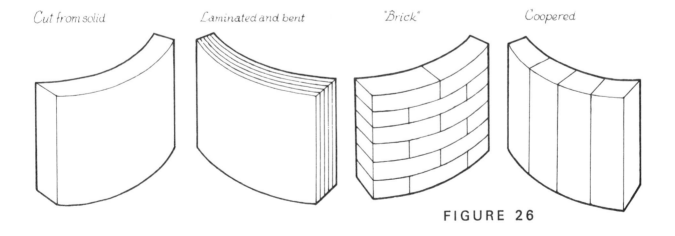

FIGURE 26

Scotch glue can be coloured by the addition of a little precipitated chalk, well stirred in; use this when working with light coloured woods such as holly, sycamore, and so on to prevent discolouration.

The "brick" idea is the one I favour as there's the least risk of movement — further, there is not likely to be much waste. Before starting, cut yourself two templets of the curve from hardboard and use one as a base on which to lay the "bricks" — the other one can be used for checking as you proceed. If you are going to true the whole assembly up on a bandsaw after gluing, it will be necessary to make the bricks over-size to allow for the width of the saw cut plus a margin for small errors in cutting. Cleaning up by hand, however, will only call for the usual allowances.

(5 mm) plywood, this should be well steamed and bent as far as possible by hand round the former. They can then be glued and placed in the set-up shown in Fig. 28 where they should be left for at least 48 hours. To allow for any natural tendency to "spring" when released from the cramp, the formers should be of a rather more acute curve than required.

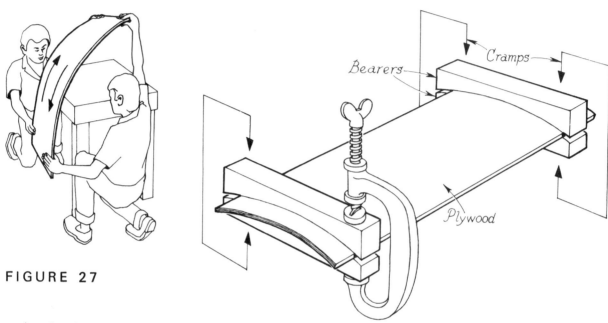

FIGURE 27

Laminating is the modern way of bending difficult shapes by means of several layers glued together and then bent in a large press with heavy formers. We can, however, imitate the process in a small way, see Fig. 27. Assuming the laminations are $\frac{3}{16}$ inch

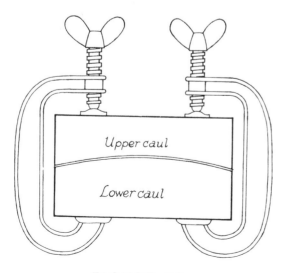

FIGURE 28

The last method, coopering, is particularly suitable for making up serpentine doors. The principle is that a number of strips are jointed together side by side, their edges being planed at an angle so that the completed assembly can be planed and scraped to the final shape. Obviously, the stuff has to be considerably oversize and you should certainly draw out a full size plan of the work so that you can determine the angles and the thickness of the pieces.

Small shaped work It is in this type of veneering that you can adapt old methods, or invent new ones, to deal with the particular problems you have.

In some cases it's possible to use the off-cuts as ready-made cauls, while in others the old-fashioned sandbag comes into its own (Fig. 29). Although I have not used them myself, there are three other ways for applying pressure that you might care to try.

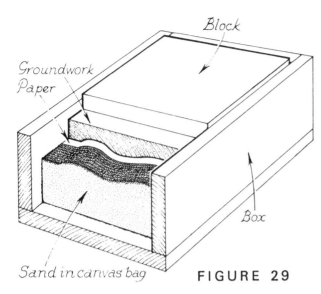

Block
Groundwork
Paper
Box
Sand in canvas bag

FIGURE 29

special plastic mix through a pre-bored hole. All interior surfaces should be well coated with grease or wax to prevent the mix sticking to them. This mix comprises two liquids which, as soon as they contact each other, solidify and expand enormously to fill any cavity available. It is most often used for providing buoyancy in boats and is readily available from marine supply stores.

Its final texture and hardness is governed by the amounts used, and I have seen large cauls made by this method which are quite as tough as wooden ones.

Whatever method you use, however, please don't forget to use an interlining of something reasonably thick and soft which will distribute the pressure evenly. Felt is an obvious answer; odd strips of linoleum or thin carpet could be utilized, too.

First, there is the adaptation of the vacuum bag principle used in industry. In this, the work, plus the veneer, is placed in a heavy gauge plastic bag and the air is exhausted by means of a domestic vacuum cleaner. This is very quick and surprisingly effective. The veneer and groundwork are pre-glued, of course, before being placed in the bag, and rubber bands hold the veneer in position until the vacuum is applied. Quite primitive means can be used for holding the plastic bag round the nozzle of the cleaner — usually rubber bands or several turns of string are sufficient.

Next, there is the employment of exactly the opposite principle — expansion of air instead of extraction. For this, you will need to build a box-like container similar to that in Fig. 29. Instead of sand, however, a bicycle tyre inner tube is crammed into the box with its adaptor nozzle protruding through a hole in the side. The set-up is shown in Fig. 30 and you can vizualize what happens — as the tube is pumped up it exerts a quite exceptional pressure which is easily capable of holding the veneer down to the shaped groundwork.

Lastly, there is a quick and effortless way to make intricately shaped cauls. In the traditional way, these were built up from softwood laminations and could take on massive proportions. I remember them stacked up in the cabinet shop like so many enormous Dutch cheeses!

If you temporarily fix the groundwork in a box similar to that shown in Fig. 29, and then screw on the lid, you can pour in a

ADHESIVES

If you intend to do much veneering, you'll want to know how to make up Scotch glue. Although it has the disadvantages of neither being waterproof nor water-resistant, these same defects bring with them the ability to correct errors. No other adhesive has this characteristic, yet all you have to do with Scotch glue is to dampen the area around the mistake with a rag wrung out in hot water, and the glue will loosen, allow

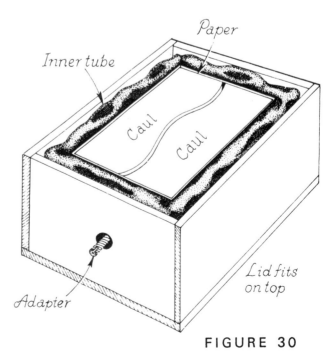

Paper
Inner tube
Caul
Caul
Adapter
Lid fits on top

FIGURE 30

the mistake to be rectified, and the area re-pressed. A thin-bladed knife dipped in hot water is also a useful tool for this purpose.

Another big point in its favour is its initial tackiness which is just right for holding down one part of the veneer while you work on another. Apart from contact and impact adhesives, which have too much of it for our purposes, no other adhesive possesses this attribute.

It is, however, temperamental in its reaction to heat. Deterioration sets in well before boiling point in the glue pot, and boiled glue is useless except as a fertilizer for the roses! But you have to be equally careful not to chill it when working, and to prevent this you'll need a comfortably warm workshop and all pieces to be glued should be thoroughly warmed. This includes wooden cauls which should be warmed as long as possible to retain their heat.

This does mean, incidentally, that the expanded plastic foam cauls we have dealt with cannot be used with Scotch glue, only with adhesives used cold.

Scotch glue is sold either as granules or in "cake" form — if the latter, put it into a sack and break it up into small pieces (say, thumbnail size). The glue should then be put into the pot, just covered with water, and left overnight to soak.

I use a device which is, I believe, rather more convenient and easier than the conventional glue pot. A "Pyrex" type glass container is my glue pot and I stand this on a couple of small wooden blocks in a saucepan. Pour in water (hot water from the domestic supply) until it reaches a level about ½ inch (12 mm) below the level of the glue mixture in the container.

This way you'll find it only takes a couple of minutes to heat up the glue to the correct working temperature — to judge this, stir the glue all the time it's being heated and lift the stirrer a few inches above the surface at frequent intervals. When the glue runs down freely with no lumps and without breaking into drops, it's ready.

Don't practise false economy and keep re-heating the glue — once or twice, at the most — so only make up as much as is needed for the job in hand. I am rather fussy about allowing metal to touch the glue because of the possibility of rust staining later. I use a piece of dowel as a stirrer and as an applicator for dowel holes, and a brush such as pastry cooks use in which the bristles are bound to the handle rather than held in a metal ferrule.

I hope the "old hands" will forgive me for dealing with Scotch glue at such length, but with the advent of synthetic adhesives it has been rather neglected. This is a pity, and I hope some of the up-and-coming craftsmen will consider using it in the right context.

Characteristics of the various adhesives are shown in the chart below:

CHARACTERISTIC	ANIMAL	CASEIN	CONTACT	EPOXY	PVA	RF	UF
General strength	Good	Good	Very fair	Excellent	Good	Excellent	Excellent
Water resistance	Nil	Poor	Fair	Excellent	Poor	Excellent	Good
Damp resistance	Poor	Fair	Good	Excellent	Fair	Excellent	Good
Mould resistance	Poor	Fair	Good	Excellent	Good	Excellent	Excellent
Heat resistance	Nil	Good	Very fair	Excellent	Poor	Good	Good
Gap filling	Nil	Slight	Nil	Good	Nil	Good	Good
Hardening time	6–8 hrs	4–6 hrs	10–30 min	5 min to 48 hrs	20–40 min	6–8 hrs	6–8 hrs
Colour when dry	Light brown	Clear straw	Clear pale straw	Yellow	Clear	Opaque white	Opaque white
Liable to stain	No	Yes	No	No	No	Yes, some woods	Yes, some woods

CHAPTER 3

Fittings

LOCKS AND THEIR FITTING

The three principal locks shown in Fig. 31 are the Cut Door Lock, the Cut Drawer Lock, and the Mortise Lock.

There is also another lock in common use known as the Straight Cupboard Lock. This has not been illustrated, as it is simply screwed on to the door, no recessing or other work being needed.

Dealing with the cut door lock first, you will note that it is "handed". To determine which "hand" you require, face the door: if the lock is to be fitted to the right-hand stile, then a right-handed lock will be needed,

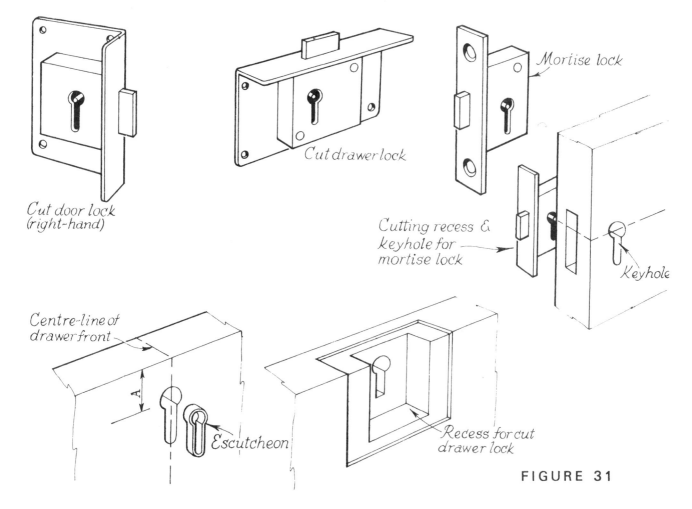

Cut door lock
(right-hand)

Cut drawer lock

Mortise lock

Cutting recess & keyhole for mortise lock

Keyhole

Centre-line of drawer front

A

Escutcheon

Recess for cut drawer lock

FIGURE 31

and vice-versa.

Actually, the principles involved in fitting all three locks are very similar in that the first job is to mark where the hole has to be bored for the key to be inserted.

The centre of this hole coincides, of course, with the centre of the pin of the lock. After the hole has been marked, you can use the escutcheon as a template to guide you when cutting the keyhole. Just stand it on the wood so that the centre of its hole corresponds to the centre mark you have made and tap it lightly with a hammer to make an impression. Remove the escutcheon and pencil round the impression.

In the case of the drawer lock you should mark the centre line for the key hole to correspond to the centre line of the drawer front. A point to watch here is that the pin of the lock is not necessarily at its centre so the recess for the lock does not fall equally about the centre line of the drawer. The distance (A) is found from measuring the lock itself. You should finish up with a recess similar to the one illustrated. Next comes the task of marking the position of the slot into which the bolt engages. To do this, screw the lock into its recess. Then lightly smear the tip of the bolt with a drop of white paint, or dirty oil from your oil-stone – anything, in fact, which will leave a mark.

Turn the key and the bolt will leave a mark on the rail, and you can cut a slot accordingly. Don't forget to wipe the paint or oil off the bolt!

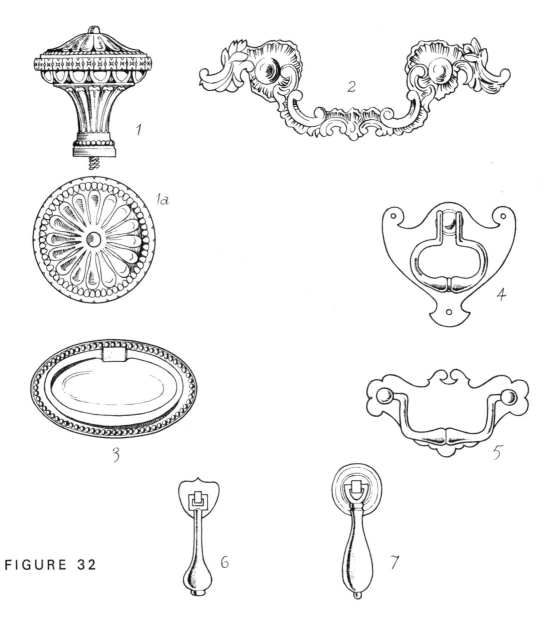

FIGURE 32

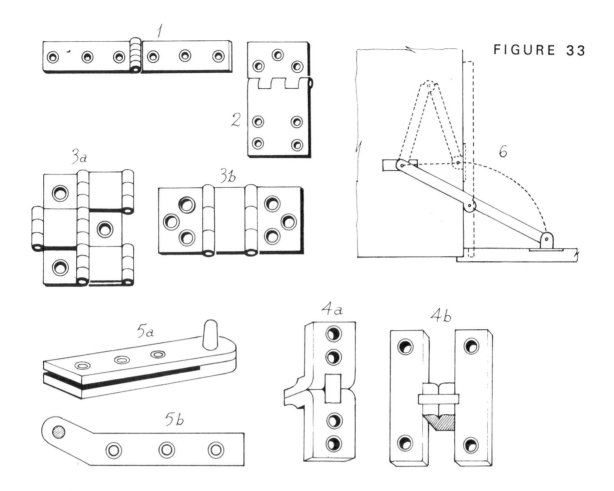

FIGURE 33

Fixing the mortise lock is virtually the same. Start by marking the keyhole position, using dimensions taken from the lock itself. Bore the hole but only take it halfway through the thickness of the wood — or even a little less than halfway as it only needs to penetrate as far as the recess for the body of the lock.

Again, the dimensions for this recess can be taken directly from the lock itself. While you are cutting the recess, remember that the body of the lock should be a push-fit into the recess, otherwise all the strain will fall upon the fixing screws.

HANDLES AND HINGES

Up to the seventeenth century most of the metal fittings for furniture, such as handles and hinges, were made of iron and probably wrought by the local blacksmith. Although many were both decorative and ingenious, the use of woods other than oak brought brasswork into prominence to offset the beauty of more showy timbers like mahogany and walnut.

Designs of handles have varied from one furniture period to another, and can be subdivided into French and English styles. Thus, those shown in Fig. 32 numbers 1 and 2, are both French, Louis XVI style. The knob is circular, with a back plate to match as illustrated in number 1a and was the type of design much favoured by eighteenth-century designers, particularly Adam. Number 2, which is more rococo in style, is the kind sometimes copied by Chippendale.

A very delicate handle is shown in number 3, and such designs were quite often made of silver in the early part of the nineteenth century. The two handles depicted in numbers 4 and 5 are both eighteenth century-style, and the "drop" handles at number 6 and 7 are the kind widely used on Queen Anne furniture.

All the designs shown were fixed in the same way, the spindle (or spindles) being threaded and inserted through holes provided in the drawer front, and nuts screwed on to provide a fixing.

The only exception to this general rule of fixing drawer handles was the turned wooden knob which was so popular (in many guises) from the middle of the nineteenth century onwards. These had a wooden thread worked on them which fitted a correspondingly threaded hole, the job being done with a screwbox and tap.

There is a vast number of types of hinges on the market today, many of them having specific applications to a particular material such as blockboard or chipboard. However, space does not permit me to deal with the full range of reproduction-style hinges let alone their modern counterparts, so those examples shown in Fig. 33 numbers 1 to 5 are the ones you are most likely to need. Straightforward butts and backflaps are not included as they are so well known as not to need mentioning.

Number 1 shows the strap hinge, used for locations which allow little fixing room as on desks and the like.

The rule-joint hinge Number 2 is noteworthy because of one leaf being longer than the other so that it can bridge the gap of the joint (a glance at Fig. 33 where the rule joint is illustrated will make this clear).

Numbers 3a and 3b are both hinges for folding screens; the former is for reversible screens, the latter for non-reversible.

Two patterns of card table hinges are shown in Numbers 4a and 4b for edge and top use, the purpose being that a flush surface is presented on either face rather than the unsightly knuckle which would result from using a conventional butt hinge.

Numbers 5a and 5b are both centre hinges, and are employed for heavy doors on such pieces as wardrobes or for doors fitted with plate glass, the plate with the holes being fixed to the carcase while the pin plate is fitted to the door. 5b is simply a cranked version of 5a and is used where the door needs to clear some projection (e.g. a moulding) when opened.

The rule joint stay (Number 6) is a standard fitting for flaps on bureaux or similar work, and derives its name from the joint used with it, which is similar in principle to a rule joint. Fixing the stay is accomplished as follows: measure half the length from pin to pin and mark it off from the centre at A to B and C. Screw on the flange at C, and then mark a line at right angles from B — the centre on the remaining flange must be on this line and will automatically locate itself when the flap is in the horizontal position. The dotted lines show the stay when the flap is closed.

CHAPTER 4

Carving Details

LINENFOLD PANELLING

There are many designs of linenfold panelling, quite a few of them being little more than travesties of the magnificent examples seen in ecclesiastical work or old houses.

can check the depths to which the wood has to be removed. Most of this can be taken away with a variety of planes and gouges although it's best to leave any undercutting until a later stage. You should now have the block in the state shown at (c).

Next, the groundwork has to be cut back

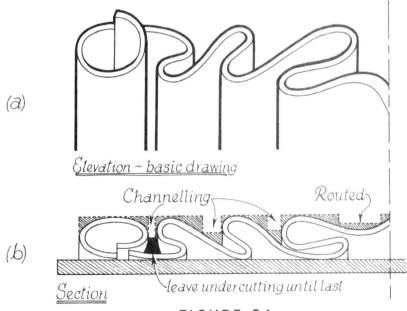

(a)

Elevation ~ basic drawing

Channelling

Routed

(b)

Section ~ leave undercutting until last

FIGURE 34

The two features which characterise the true linenfold are (a) that the "line" of the folds at top and bottom should be continuous, and (b) that the folds of the "linen" should be carved to lap over each other.

To ensure this, one of the first things to do is to draw the design in elevation and also in end view, Fig. 34a and b so that you

to the heavy line shown at (d). Obviously, this is rather difficult to do as you will be marking a line on to an undulating surface. The best way to do it is to mark the principal points of the shape by measuring inwards from the end and joining them up freehand. One thing to bear in mind is that the various channels and curves you have worked will

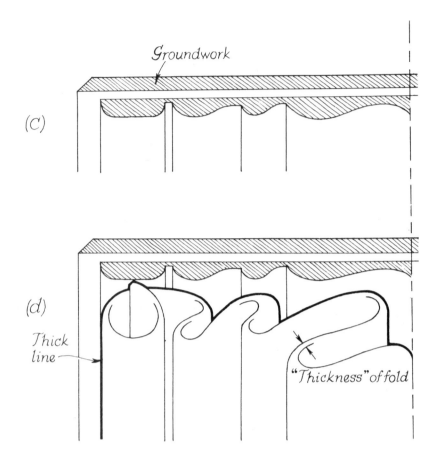

not match up with the back of the marked line, but only with the front.

An important point to note, too, is that when carving out the folds you must allow for their simulated "thickness" and it will help if you draw this in at the same time as you are marking the heavy line referred to above.

Fig. 35*a*, *b*, *c* show the way to tackle the carving of the right-hand half of the central feature, and is typical of the procedure to adopt.

As in all good-class carving, the modelling should be accomplished completely by the use of carving tools to achieve a crisp, clean finish. Finish by taking off the arrises of the folds at an angle of about 45 degrees, as at (*c*).

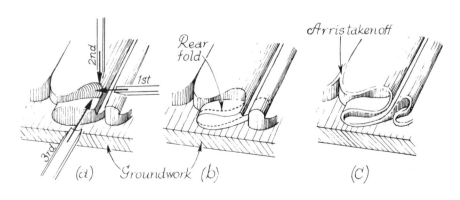

FIGURE 35

CARVED MOULDINGS

When carving any of these mouldings, you must bear in mind that it's impossible to show the complete design in a drawing. As you will appreciate, the detail follows the contour of the moulding and so, to draw the full shape of the acanthus leaves for instance, you would need to be right underneath them.

Both design examples are repeat patterns and obviously the best way to transfer them to the wood is by means of a stencil.

complete egg on a spare piece of moulding and use it as a specimen to work to, both as regards size and depth of cut. Smooth off the surface of the eggs by means of a gouge held hollow side downwards — the curve of this gouge should be slightly flatter than the curvature of the egg so that cutting in is avoided.

A similar type of stencil should be made for the ACANTHUS LEAF moulding, Fig. 37. Treatment is lighter than that used for the egg and tongue and the first task is to define the main leaves from each other where they overlap.

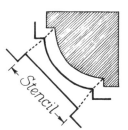

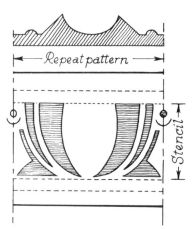

Front elevation

FIGURE 36

A good way to make this is by loosely holding a piece of thin card or stout cartridge paper right round the moulding. You can then crease this to fit snugly into the crevices and contours: when this is done, the pattern can be drawn on to the paper and a stencil cut out. Remember that you will probably have to modify the pattern so that the motif repeats itself an exact number of times in the length to be carved.

Dealing first with the EGG and TONGUE moulding, Fig. 36, cut away the wood at each side of the eggs first, taking care not to obliterate the inner and outer lines — otherwise there is no way of preserving the shape of the egg — and chamfer once you reach the full depth.

Employ a U tool or a small gouge to remove most of the waste, but use it only lightly inside the stencil mark so that you do not spoil the chamfer surface.

Choose a gouge to suit the curve of the egg and chop straight down, following by using a flat gouge to bevel the wood up to the chamfer line.

Depth of cut is purely a matter of choice, depending on the degree of boldness required. A tip to help you here — carve one

At the start, ignore the individual lobes of the leaves, concentrating on making a general cut around the outline and sloping the wood into the cuts on the waste end.

Note that the general lines of the leaves which fold over each other originate from "eyes", and these should be cut in first to act as positive guides. Make them deep as they are supposed to pierce right through the leaf.

The general lines of the modelling need executing with a very keen tool which will allow you to retain the contour of the moulding by raising or lowering the handle.

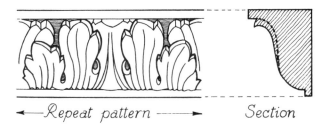

← Repeat pattern →   Section

FIGURE 37

PIE-CRUST EDGINGS

This type of attractive edging was widely used in the eighteenth century for table and tray tops, particularly on circular tops for wine tables and tea poys, and rectangular or oval tops on nests of tables and trays.

In principle, there are two main ways of fashioning these edgings — either they can be worked from the solid, or a "collar" can be glued to the top, and the edge worked on this.

of waste wood can be screwed to it as the screwholes will eventually be covered with baize on the underside. Before doing this you will, of course, have to mark on the limit of the greatest width of the moulded edge so that you do not turn too much away.

If you want to use solid timber for any shape other than a circle (an oval or a rectangle, for instance), the waste wood will have to be removed by means of a portable power router.

The drawing in Fig. 38 will enable you to make a card template which can be re-

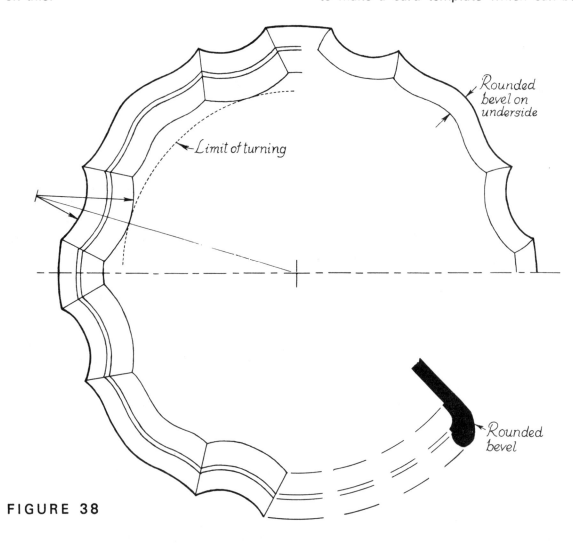

Limit of turning

Rounded bevel on underside

Rounded bevel

FIGURE 38

Dealing with the solid-top method, it is obvious that it is the easiest to work for a circular top as it can be mounted on the face plate of a lathe and turned. This is, though, very wasteful of wood as so much has to be taken away.

However, the wooden blank should be cut full and mounted on the face plate. A piece

peated around the circumference, and the outside shape can then be cut on a bandsaw, or with a jigsaw or coping saw.

The problem now is to ensure that the lines of the carved pattern follow the shapes of the outside edge. The outermost flat bead can be marked with a pencil, using your finger as a gauge (Fig. 39), but you will have

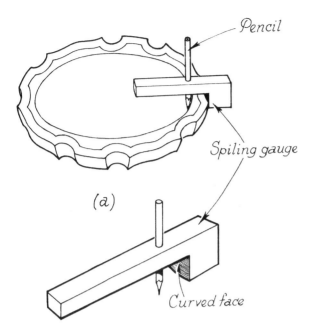

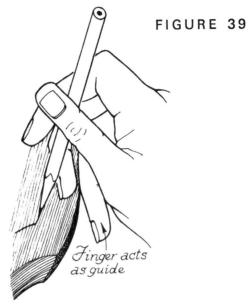

FIGURE 39

to make a "spiling" gauge for the other members.

As shown at (a), this is simply made from scrapwood: important points to note are that the face should be rounded so that the undulations can be followed faithfully while keeping the gauge radial to the curves, and that the pencil should be a snug sliding fit so that it can move up or down.

You will need the gauge, too, for marking the line for the carved bevel on the back of the top, Fig. 38.

CARVING THE ACANTHUS LEAF

Fig. 40 shows a symbolic Acanthus leaf — symbolic because there is, strictly speaking, no set design for this particular ornament. There is, however, a definite style for treating the lobes, the "eyes" and the "pipes".

FIGURE 40

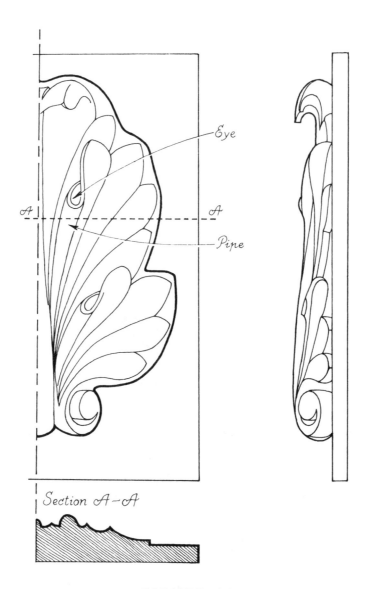

Eye

Pipe

Section A—A

FIGURE 41

In Fig. 41 you can see the outline of the leaf marked in heavily; also shown are the lines indicating the principal components.

The first step is to transfer the drawing to the chosen piece of wood. As the essence of the design is that the edges, eyes, and pipes should all be modelled boldly, the wood needs to be at least $\frac{7}{8}$ inch thick (22 mm) so that a background of about $\frac{1}{4}$ inch full (7 mm) is left. Note from the sectional drawing that the weight of the design is concentrated at the bottom.

Fig. 42 shows the various stages of carving. Before starting to remove the groundwork you will have to gouge a line all round the edges of the block showing the depth to which it has to be cut away.

Next use a medium-sized gouge to cut around the outline as at A about $\frac{1}{16}$ inch (2 mm) away from it. Then remove the waste by gouging in from the edge of the block to meet the first cut; do this until the groundwork is removed to within about $\frac{1}{16}$ inch (2 mm) from the line you have gouged around the block.

Follow on by setting in the outline, B, this is done by using gouges of appropriate curves held vertically and chopping down. When this is completed the groundwork can be finished off by removing the final $\frac{1}{16}$ inch (2 mm).

Before you begin to "bost in", or in other words, to begin to shape the block to the section shown, the main ribs and pipes

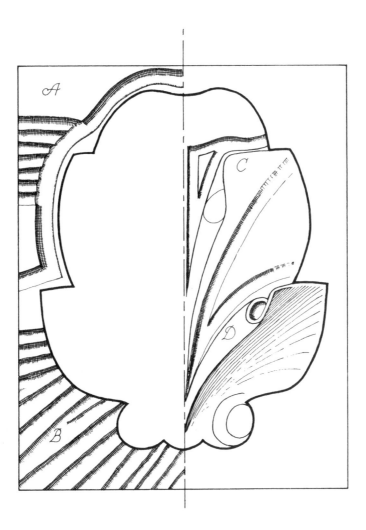

FIGURE 42

should have a channel gouged either side of them so that their location will not be lost when the wood is cut away. This stage is shown at C.

D shows the leaf halfway through the bosting-in. This is really the part which requires you to be able to visualize the final form, bearing in mind that it is best to finish a feature on one side and then finish its counterpart on the other side, so that they appear balanced.

Once the main modelling has been achieved you can mark in (in pencil) the shapes of the lobes and the raised arrises formed by the hollow shapes. Tools must, of course, be razor-sharp, particularly when working the hollows under the tips of the leaves.

MAKING A CABRIOLE LEG

Fashioning a good cabriole leg is practically a work of art in the sense that when it results in a shapely leg it *is* shapely, but if it is even slightly off the mark, it looks appalling!

The first essential is to have a proper shape to work to and Fig. 43 gives this; there are also sections, three types of foot, and details of how to saw out the shape.

Salient points are that the knee should be kept high and that the taper reduces progressively from knee to ankle, then swelling out to the foot. If the leg is to be carved you must, of course, leave enough wood to accommodate it. The earpieces are glued

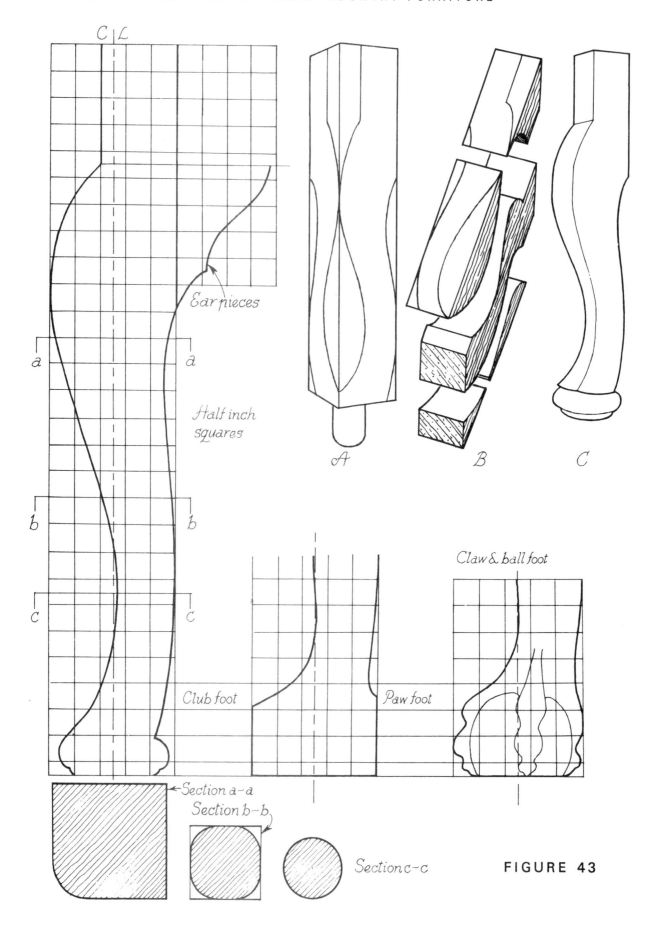

C L

Ear pieces

a   a

Half inch
squares

b   b

c   c

A   B   C

Claw & ball foot

Club foot   Paw foot

Section a-a
Section b-b

Section c-c   FIGURE 43

on separately as to cut them, and the leg, from the solid would be prodigal of timber.

As you can see, the leg (apart from the earpieces) is cut from a 2½ inch (65 mm) square, with a 1½ inch (38 mm) leg block left square at the top. Cut out a template from thick cardboard or hardboard, remembering that any extra wood for carving must be incorporated in it.

The template needs to be marked round in turn on adjacent faces of the square, making sure that you hold it so that the knees face each other and that it is held level on each face as at A.

Next, the foot has to be turned on, as at C: the centres are, of course, in the middle of the square. Obviously, this only refers to the club foot design: in the case of either the paw or claw and ball foot the shape is left roughly cut out.

Use a bandsaw if one is available to cut out the shapes: if not, a bow saw is the best alternative. B shows the offcuts alongside the cut-out leg, the point being that as far as possible you should cut off the pieces in their entirety. Then they can be re-assembled to each side in turn to act as a kind of cradle when the next side is cut.

Final shaping is executed by means of a scraper, a rasp, or a spokeshave. Glue the earpieces on after sawing and before shaping as they have to be blended in with the rest of the leg.

TYPES OF MOULDING

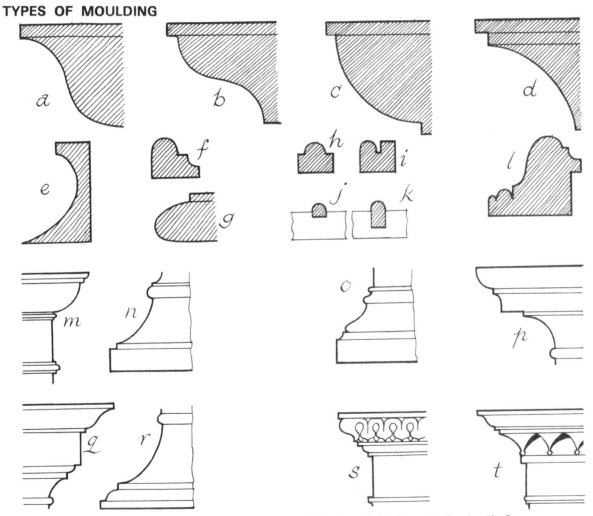

(a) Cyma recta. (b) Cyma reversa. (c) Ovolo. (d) Hollow. (e) Scotia. (f) Ogee. (g) Thumb. (h) Astragal. (i) Astragal and quirk. (j) and (k) Cocked beads. (l) A "Bolection" moulding. (m) Jacobean cornice. (n) Jacobean base moulding. (o) Chippendale base moulding. (p) Chippendale cornice moulding (q) Sheraton cornice moulding. (r) Sheraton surbase moulding. (s) and (t) Hepplewhite cornice mouldings.

CHAPTER 5

Finishes

PLASTIC LACQUERS

The three principal enemies of these lacquers are moisture, oil (or grease), and ballpoint pen marks.

Timber to be lacquered should have no more than 12 to 14 per cent moisture content, and the surrounding atmosphere should be warm and dry — about 20 degrees C (68 to 70 degrees F) is ideal. Any brushes, jars, or other receptacles should be bone-dry, too. A quick and easy way to get rid of small traces of moisture is to twirl the brush around in some methylated spirit, or to rinse the receptacles with the spirit — as it evaporates it will take the moisture as well.

Ideally, the best form of heating the workshop while lacquering (or polishing of any description for that matter) is by means of electricity or a solid fuel stove. Both paraffin and gas heating create a lot of water vapour which may not be noticeable while the temperature remains high but which will condense when the heat decreases.

The problem of oil or grease can come about in different ways. The wood itself can be greasy, like teak, and the treatment here is a light wipe over with a de-greasing liquid. "Teepol" is a good proprietary one, but ordinary white spirit is usually quite adequate.

Another way that oil can get on to the wood is from your using tools which themselves have traces of oil on them. An obvious example is a plane iron which has been sharpened on an oilstone and not wiped clean — or it could be a chisel. Finger marks,

particularly if perspiration is present, can also cause greasy patches.

As for the ball-point pen — the remedy is obvious; use something else for marking out!

Always use the grain-filler that is either supplied or recommended by the lacquer manufacturer. Do not use oil-bound fillers or you may well get poor bonding because of the antipathy between the lacquer and the oil in the filler.

For the same reason it's unwise to use oil stains; water stains or naphtha stains are quite acceptable, however.

It's a good plan to wear some kind of clothing that does not harbour dust while you are doing any kind of polishing, lacquering, varnishing, or painting. And it goes without saying that the bench and workshop should be as free from dust as possible.

I have found that sometimes modern finishes such as plastic lacquers are liable to chip and flake off after several years. The same trouble used to happen with cellulose finishes, too.

After seeking advice about this, I was recommended to apply a priming coat of white French polish before putting on the lacquer. Actually, it does act in very much the same way as a paint primer, as it penetrates the grain and also provides a perfect base for the ensuing lacquer. In this way you will get a good bond and, at the same time, you can seal up any end grain so that it does not absorb more than its fair share of the lacquer.

The difficulty of obtaining a good bond between coat and coat is a similar problem and I have found it best to allow the first coat to dry, or to give the process its technical name, "to cure", for six to eight hours and then de-nib it by very lightly papering it with fine flour glasspaper.

Follow this by flowing on the next coat; never attempt to brush out the lacquer as it should be applied in the same way as a varnish — with a soft brush, well loaded.

The point is that although the first coat is to all intents and purposes cured, it will still retain enough tackiness to bond to the ensuing coat much better than if it were allowed to cure fully.

TEAK OIL

This oil gives a finish similar to that imparted by linseed oil but it has the added advantage that it is more resistant to marking.

Method of application is simple as it is brushed on, working *across* the grain, wiping off surplus oil with a lint-free cloth after allowing half an hour or so for the wood to absorb it.

This is not a finish with which you should try to build up a surface. A second coat should be applied after the first one has dried overnight and it should be a light one brushed out *along* the grain.

Allow at least two days for the oil to dry out thoroughly when, if you want a matt finish, you can rub along the grain with a wad of finest grade steel wool dipped in a good quality wax polish.

This gives a finish which is moderately resistant to everyday hazards but it is not suitable where hot objects (tea pots, coffee pots, and the like) can contact it, nor will it stand up to acids in fruit juices, alcohol, perfumes, etc.

If the surface is damaged, however, it should be capable of being restored. Remove any traces of wax locally with white spirit and paper lightly (or scrape, very gingerly, with an old razor blade) to remove the blemish. Touch in with more teak oil on a pointed brush such as an artist's painting brush, and repeat the process described above for applying the second coat and the wax.

LINSEED OIL

This is a very popular finish but, unless it is done thoroughly, it can be a disappointing one.

Boiled linseed oil is better than the raw oil for this purpose as it is less sticky and dries more quickly — apart from this, however, there is no reason why you should not use the raw oil.

Mix the oil thoroughly with an equal volume of white spirit. The latter simply acts as a vehicle for the oil and helps it to penetrate the grain; having done this it evaporates away without trace. It also helps to add a small quantity of terebine driers (one teaspoonful to 0·3 litre or half a pint) to speed up drying.

Apply the liquid with a stiff brush such as a shoe-polishing brush, working across the grain. It's a good idea to keep the mixture warm by standing its container in hot water — do not use a naked flame as the mixture is highly inflammable.

Wipe off the surplus after allowing the oil two or three hours to be absorbed. Then repeat the process (omitting the white spirit, however) at weekly intervals for 3 or 4 weeks. To work up any kind of a shine, rub along the grain with a soft, lint-free rag wrapped around a weighty object like a brick — the more rubbing, the better the finish!

It is a finish which marks easily but it is resistant to moisture and hot dishes etc; it can be restored easily and does, of course, preserve and enrich the wood as nothing else can.

PETROLEUM JELLY ("VASELINE") FINISH

This has a similar appearance to the linseed oil finish but is, in my view, easier to apply and is a slightly more resistant finish.

Application is just the same as for linseed oil except that you will not need to make so many of them! Again, it helps to keep the "Vaseline" warm by standing the jar in warm water; you will find, too, that it will buff up into a dull shine quite easily and quickly.

WAX POLISH

Although a recipe for a home-made wax polish is given elsewhere in the book, a good proprietary polish will afford just as good a finish if applied properly.

The method is to give the job two coats of white french polish, each coat being lightly glasspapered back. The purpose of this is to impart a sealing coat which will protect the wood from dust and dirt being forced into the grain by continual rubbing over a period of years. It also helps to seal end grain and patches of open grain.

Apply the wax with a stiff-bristled brush of the shoe-polishing type. Put plenty on, working both across and with the grain but finishing with light strokes along the grain. Then let the polish harden for twenty-four hours or so, and buff it up with a clean soft cloth.

The surface will not be resistant to anything but moisture.

BLEACHES

There are several proprietary bleaches on the market and manufacturer's instructions must be followed explicitly. But there are some points which should be borne in mind, as follows:

1. All traces of oil, grease (including finger marks), and adhesive must be removed as they will resist the bleach.

2. Keep bleach in a non-metal container — a glass jar with a cork or wooden stopper is best.

3. When stored, the bleach should be placed in a cool position and out of sunlight, which can weaken it.

4. Do not return unused bleach to the main supply as it will speed up deterioration.

5. Wear rubber gloves and old clothes when applying bleach; wash off any spots on the skin immediately.

6. Subject to what the manufacturer advises, after the bleach has dried, the surface should be neutralized by washing with clean, warm water or methylated spirit.

7. Allow at least two days for the bleach to dry. If you do not, some chemicals may be trapped and cause blistering or wrinkling.

8. Never leave a bleached surface longer than is necessary without a finish on it or it will begin to darken again. A couple of coats of white French polish will both protect the surface and act as a good base for further polishing.

No doubt you will know that oxalic acid is widely used as a bleach. But do you know that its efficiency is much improved by using it in conjunction with "hypo" as used in photographic work? The method is to make up the usual solution of oxalic acid bleach, namely 3 ounces to a quart of hot water; then make up a solution of 3 ounces of hypo to one quart of cold water.

Apply the oxalic acid solution to the work in the usual way, using a piece of cloth wrapped around the end of a stick. Allow this to dry for a few minutes and then apply the hypo solution in the same way, but using a different piece of cloth and stick.

After this second application has dried for a quarter of an hour or so, wash off the surface with a solution of 1 ounce of borax in a quart of water. Leave overnight to dry.

Here is a summary of the staining potentialities of some timbers, which can be taken as a guide:

Bleach easily	May require 2 applications	Difficult or impossible to bleach
Ash	Mahoganies (including most pseudo-mahoganies)	Cherry
Beech		Ebony
Chestnut		Iroko
Elm	Oak	Padauk
Lime	Walnut	Rosewood
		Teak

FUMING WITH AMMONIA

This treatment was popular between the wars, and some really fine effects can be achieved, varying from a warm nut-brown colour down to a very dark brown – almost black, in fact.

You need some kind of cabinet in which you can put the job while the fuming is going on. This can be a box knocked up from hardboard and battens – the important factor is that any cracks or gaps must be sealed to keep in the fumes, and you can use gummed tape or masking tape for this.

Somewhere in the cabinet you will need to bore a hole through which you can insert a test piece, which must be the same species as the timber being fumed.

Two points to note. In any oak job which is to be fumed, the oak should, if possible, be the same type throughout. Thus it would be a mistake to use, say, English oak and Japanese oak in the same job. The reason is that the ammonia reacts with the tannin in the wood and different oaks have different tannin contents. And, of course, the natural variation in colour would also show.

The other point is that as far as is practicable the job should be separated down to its sub-assemblies so that all parts get equal exposure. If there are odd rails etc. that need fuming make sure they do not overlap. It's better to stand them upright on end, pinning or taping them temporarily to the inside of the cabinet.

Length of time involved depends on several factors – colour required, strength of the ammonia (·880 strength is to be recommended), and the reaction of the wood itself. You could need to wait 24 to 48 hours, and obviously the ammonia will need replenishing periodically. When you need to do this, take care that the fumes do not get to your eyes or lungs.

Pyrogallic acid ($\frac{3}{4}$ ounce to a quart of water) can be used to accelerate the process but it tends to give a reddish shade.

A stain made from bichromate of potash crystals dissolved in cold water can be used for matching in any uneven patches. Use it very delicately, however, as you can soon overdo it and make the patch much darker than the rest.

A word about the test piece. If you intend to wax the job after fuming, wet the test piece with water to get the approximate appearance; if it is to be oiled, rub a touch of linseed oil on it for the same purpose.

LIMED OAK

This tends to be rather a novelty finish, but provided it is not overdone it can look most attractive.

Start by staining the job in the usual way; a medium brown colour is best for this finish, and a water stain is the safest one to use.

Then rub across the grain with a rag dipped in a white proprietary filler so that although the open pores are filled, the higher "lands" between them are rubbed clean.

After allowing the filler to set (according to the manufacturer's instructions) give the job a couple of coats of white (clear) French polish, after which it may be waxed.

ANTIQUE FINISH FOR OAK

The rubbed antique finish. This can bring disastrous results if not done with considerable restraint as, in principle, it is supposed to impart the appearance of age by rubbing away the stain from high spots and the centres of panels. The effect can make a good job look cheap if it is not done properly.

The process takes place immediately after staining, which should be applied with a brush. Before it has had a chance to dry, use a clean rag to wipe the stain away from high spots in mouldings, carving, handles and the like and also to remove it from the centre area of the larger panels.

The idea is to simulate the fading of high spots over years of use, while leaving the edges and corners comparatively dark.

Probably a more efficient method, which is the same in principle, is to use an oil stain and lighten the high parts by rubbing gently and delicately with a rag which has been dipped in rottenstone powder.

Fix the oil stain with a couple of coats of clear French polish and then polish with an antique wax. This type of wax is much darker than the ordinary kind, and if you cannot buy it then you can make some up yourself (see the recipe) and darken it to choice by mixing in some black pigment while the wax is molten. The black pigment is most easily obtainable as a tube of artist's oil colour.

Brush the wax on generously with a stiff brush, allow 24 hours or so for the white spirit to evaporate, and then polish as already described. Leave alone the black wax which has settled in crevices and the open pores, and this should give you a good reproduction effect.

STAINING MAHOGANY

Almost certainly, any furniture you make in mahogany will be a mixture of veneer and solid wood, with the consequent variations in colour.

In general, present-day mahoganies tend to be reddish and the best stain to kill the rawness and give a range of pleasant brown shades is bichromate of potash. The crystals are dissolved in water and the amount of dilution governs the depth of colour, of course.

Alternatively, a walnut stain with a touch of mahogany stain could be used, so avoiding any redness.

TREATMENTS FOR PINE

Luckily, pine (particularly yellow pine) answers readily to special treatments. I say "luckily" because with hardwoods being the price they are, it's comforting to know that pine is a very acceptable substitute in its own right.

Bleaching pine is quite straightforward and when the process is over the surface should be given a couple of coats of clear French polish. Allow this to harden over-

night and then rub along the grain with a pad of steel wool.

Then proceed with the normal wax polish procedure.

An alternative finish is "scrubbed pine", which gives a mellow light brown colour reminiscent of the appearance of old pine which has been stripped of the paint or the limewash which was frequently employed to cover it.

Start by applying an oil stain which will impart a medium brown colour — test it on a spare piece of the timber first. Allow it to stand for a minute or two and then wipe off the excess; judge the time it should be allowed to stand by your experience with the test piece as you do not want too dark a colour.

Next, you will need some matt deep cream coloured paint which should be thinned with white spirit to a slightly-thicker-than-water consistency. Brush this on generously and then wipe off almost immediately.

This will leave the surface with a thin film which should approximate to the scrubbed pine finish, particularly when it has been glasspapered and wax polished.

RECIPES

The following are a couple of recipes for "revivers" which will brighten up any French or wax polished surface.

(a) 1 part methylated spirits : 1 part raw linseed oil : 1 part vinegar (preferably white).

(b) 4 parts raw linseed oil : 1 part terebene driers : 12 parts vinegar (again, preferably white).

Apply with a wad of cheese cloth (or mutton cloth) using a large circular motion. Finish by rubbing with the grain with a soft, lint-free cloth.

A general purpose wax polish can be made from 1 lb brown or yellow ("white") beeswax dissolved in $\frac{1}{2}$ pint pure turpentine or, as a substitute, good quality white spirit. To mix it, shred the beeswax into a pan which should be stood in another, larger, pan of boiling water to assist its melting. If you do have to put the pan back over the heat to keep the water hot, be careful to see that the melting wax does not overflow or you'll have a first class fire to deal with! Remove the pan from the heat before adding the turpentine as it is highly inflammable and a few drops spilt can cause an inferno – needless to say, the same remarks apply to white spirit, so move the pan well away from the heat, and give the mixture a good stir.

Another wax polish which will give a high gloss finish with a hard surface can be made from 1 lb carnauba wax, 1 lb paraffin wax, and 1 pint turpentine (or white spirit). Carnauba wax is very hard and you'll need to break it into small pieces: the best way is to put it in a plastic bag and pound it with a mallet. Paraffin wax shreds easily.

You then proceed to make the polish as already described for the general purpose wax polish. If either polish sets too hard, re-heat it, remove it well away from the heat source, and stir in some more turpentine while the wax is molten.

Most woodworkers probably buy their French polish ready-mixed, but for those who would like to make their own, the method is as follows.

Having got your shellac, store it in sawdust which is kept damp. Before use you will have to dry it thoroughly and then dissolve it in the following proportions:

(a) White polish: 7 to 8 oz bleached shellac to 1 pint methylated spirits.
(b) Transparent polish: 7 to 8 oz bleached and de-waxed shellac to 1 pint methylated spirits.
(c) Button polish: 6 oz button shellac to 1 pint methylated spirits.
(d) Garnet polish: 6 oz garnet shellac to 1 pint methylated spirits.
(e) Black polish: $\frac{1}{2}$ oz spirit black aniline dye to 1 pint white polish. Strain before use.

Leave the shellac and methylated spirits in a corked bottle for several days when the shellac should have dissolved. You can help by giving the bottle a shake now and again.

FILLERS AND STOPPERS

One of the oldest and still effective fillers is good quality Plaster of Paris. You need to give the job a couple of coats of clear French polish (after staining as may be necessary, of course) and allow them to dry out for 3 or 4 hours before applying the plaster.

You'll need a flattish dish for the plaster, a bowl of water, several pieces of rag, and a piece of canvas or hessian.

Wet the rag and dip it in the plaster until you have a fairly thick paste. Rub it on the job in a circular motion, exchange the rag for the canvas and rub across the grain with the latter as the plaster begins to set. Don't attempt to do too much at any one application as the plaster sets in a few seconds.

Ordinary deal can be filled with a simple glue-size filler. This is simply common-or-garden glue size mixed with warm water to a thin consistency such that it does not feel sticky to the fingers. Apply with a large brush while it is still warm. Obviously, you can only use this filler on a surface that has been water-stained, not oil-stained.

A paste filler for any wood can be made up from 1 pint boiled linseed oil, $\frac{1}{4}$ pint gold size, and $\frac{1}{4}$ gill turpentine (or white spirit). Mix them together and stir in some china clay until the mixture becomes a stiff paste. Allow it to set for 24 hours and thin it down with turpentine (or white spirit), as required.

Beaumontage is an exceedingly useful stopping which should be coloured to match the stained surface. To make it, mix equal quantities of beeswax, crushed rosin and a few flakes of shellac and melt them in a tin – needless to say, the tin should stand in a pan of boiling water. When it is molten, pour it into the edge of a square tin lid – keep the tin lid tilted so that it forms a rough kind of stick.

A similar stopping can be made by melting the beeswax on its own, as described, and adding a small amount of the appropriate oil colour – this can be from a tube of artist's oil colour.

A cheap and easy stopping results from mixing plaster of paris with Scotch glue, or a PVA adhesive – it will absorb water stain quite readily.

CHAPTER 6

Selected List of Timbers

The following list of timbers comprises those which are most likely to be useful to the woodworker. Emphasis has been placed on working characteristics rather than botanical details and weights, and both hardwoods and softwoods have been included.

ABURA Hardwood from equatorial Africa. Uniform light brown colour with a pinkish tinge, the heartwood and sapwood being practically indistinguishable. Works easily, but you will need keen edges on tools to avoid a slightly fibrous finish. Stains and polishes excellently. Has the unique quality of being highly resistant to acids and is therefore ideal for bar and counter tops, or laboratory benches.

AFARA African hardwood which resembles light oak in colour. Grain is sometimes irregular, and it is advisable to pre-bore the nails and screws. Stains and polishes well — look out for discoloured patches due to faulty seasoning.

AFRORMOSIA African hardwood. It is heavier than abura or afara and is darker in colour — a yellowish brown ground colour with a figuring of darker streaks. The grain is occasionally variable which may cause some trouble when planing or glasspapering. No problems with staining or polishing.

AGBA One of the lighter African timbers which has a straight, consistent grain and a fine even texture. Colour varies from yellowish pink to a light reddish brown. Works easily although sometimes gummy. Stains and polishes well.

ASH This is one of the most unappreciated of British timbers. It is well known for its toughness and elasticity of grain — in former days these qualities made it ideal for carriage and wagon building and for tool handles. Today, they cause the timber to be sought after for its bending properties. It is a yellowish-white wood with a very open grain and hard texture. When straight-grained, the timber works sweetly, but sometimes the grain is interlocked and irregular, depending on how the timber was grown. Stains and polishes reasonably well.

American ash is similar to our own but is not quite so tough, and is slightly coarser in grain.

BASSWOOD As a matter of historical interest (the timber itself is almost impossible to obtain in Great Britain now), this wood is almost identical to English lime although it originates in the U.S.A. and Canada.

BAYWOOD An alternative name for Honduras mahogany, and not a timber in its own right.

BEECH Widely distributed throughout Europe, beech is one of the most popular framing timbers. Because of its tendency to twist when used in the flat, its use is more usually confined to chair frames and carcase construction. As a bending timber it ranks as one of the best. The grain is close and even, and the texture is fine and hard. Colour is a creamy yellow, although when bought as "steamed beech", it can often have a definite pinkish tinge. The wood stains easily but does not respond well to polishing.

BIRCH Although familiar to all of us as a graceful tree, the British birch is not really a commercial proposition as the sizes obtainable are only suitable for small ware. Canadian yellow birch is, however, available in reasonable sizes but is expensive. One of its outstanding characteristics is the ease with which it aborbs stain. It is a light brown colour with a fine even grain and can be coloured to match in with other timbers. One of the best timbers for upholstery frames.

BOXWOOD This wood, whether home-grown or European, is never available in large sizes and, in fact, a width of 2–3 inches (51 mm–76 mm) is about as big as can be expected. It is creamy yellow in colour, and the grain is so dense and even that the cut timber looks to have its own natural polish.

The reason for mentioning it is, that although not a cabinet timber, it is ideal for small, intricate jobs. Thus, if you wanted some tiny turned balusters for the gallery around a table top, the ideal wood would be box as it would retain every detail crisply. Owing to the closeness of the grain, it is tricky to stain but is, nevertheless, capable of taking a fine finish.

CHESTNUT There are, of course, two kinds of chestnut – the Horse Chestnut and the Spanish (sweet) chestnut, and it is only the latter which is of interest to us. The timber often closely resembles oak although it does not contain the silver "flash". Strengthwise it is almost the equal of oak, its main drawback being its liability to ring shakes.

EBONY Like boxwood, this cannot be classed as a cabinet timber, because it is so scarce in any dimensions larger than 4 to 6 inches (102 to 152 mm).

Although it is extremely hard it is not too difficult to work although the grain can sometimes be brittle. It polishes well; there is, of course, no question of staining.

Ideally its use is for decorative purposes either as inlay or small objets d'art.

ELM This is the common English elm, although the equally well-known Wych elm has similar properties. Both are light brown in colour, but the English elm has a more irregular grain which contributes largely to its toughness. Seasoning both timbers can be a slow process and should never be hurried, particularly if the wood is to be used in cabinet work. Because of the variability of grain and colour it is almost impossible to stain either timber uniformly, but polish is accepted quite readily.

GABOON This is also called *Okoume* and is an African timber. It is rather an undistinguished timber being light reddish brown in colour, with no special features. Most of the wood is used in plywood and blockboard but if you can get hold of any you'll find it ideal as groundwork for veneer, or for interior parts of mahogany furniture – drawer stuff, for instance.

It works easily although sharp tools are needed as the grain tends to be fibrous. Staining and polishing is straightforward.

GEDU NOHOR An African timber which is a close relative of sapele, and a useful cabinet timber. It is a warm reddish-brown; the grain is interlocked and this gives a stripey figure when the wood is quarter-sawn. It needs seasoning slowly and takes a lustrous polish.

GUAREA Another African wood which has become a recognized cabinet timber. It is reddish-brown in colour, with a fine texture, and often has an attractive mottled figure. Although it works well, some pieces may be gummy and need care in polishing.

IDIGBO This timber is sometimes called "black afara", and is another African wood. Good as a carcase timber, although as the grain is rather coarse it does not qualify as a "show" wood. It is yellowish-brown in colour, and stains and polishes well.

IROKO Although often called "African teak", it is no relation to the true teak. Sometimes parts are coarse-grained but, even so, it works well and takes a good polish, although the grain may need filling. It is pale to dark brown in colour and is particularly suitable for frameworks and carcases which need to be strong.

KERUING A heavy-weight timber from the Far East which is used mainly for flooring and structural work. It is a dull reddish brown colour and the texture can vary from open to dense; in addition it has an interlocked grain. This makes it difficult to work, and as it is also not responsive to staining and polishing it is not really a cabinet wood. It is included, however, as large amounts are imported and you are bound to meet it sooner or later.

LAUAN   There are two distinct varieties of this timber – Red Lauan and White Lauan, both from the Far East.

Red lauan closely resembles African mahogany in appearance, being reddish-brown in colour with slightly interlocked grain. This can cause slight problems when planing, but the figure can have a beautiful stripe which makes it worthwhile. It has a close, fine texture and takes stain and polish well.

White lauan is actually a straw colour and has virtually the same characteristics – the grain does tend to be more open, however.

LIME   A well-known British and European tree, the timber of which can well serve as a secondary cabinet wood – for drawer stuff, etc.

It is a yellowish white in colour and its outstanding characteristic is that of cutting and working evenly in all directions, although it is quite close-grained. Naturally, this has made it a great favourite with woodcarvers and it is probably the best carving wood of all.

MAKORE   Another West African timber which is sought after for the beauty of its striped figure. As with all timbers with this kind of figure, the grain tends to pick up and planing can be tricky. Otherwise, however, it works well and is often considered to be as good as true mahogany for cabinet work. The colour varies; it can gradate from a light pinkish brown to a deep brown with tinges of purple. It stains and polishes excellently.

MAHOGANY   There are two principal mahoganies of the Swietenia family which are recognized as superlative cabinet woods, namely Cuban and Honduras mahogany (often called "baywood").

Cuban mahogany is now extremely scarce and expensive. It is a hard, comparatively heavy wood which nevertheless is quite easy to work. It has a dense, close texture which permits fine joints to be cut and it polishes superbly to give an unsurpassably lustrous finish. Although a pale reddish brown when first cut, the colour deepens in time to a rich dark red.

Honduras mahogany is lighter in weight than Cuban, but still possesses the same close texture which makes it a first-class cabinet wood. Working the timber is a delight, and it also polishes magnificently. The main difference between the two mahoganies is that Honduras is lighter in colour and is, in fact, a rich, deep golden brown.

Additionally, there are several other timbers (all of the Khaya species) from the West Coast of Africa which are loosely called the "African" mahoganies. Among them are:

Benin Mahogany   About the same weight as Honduras mahogany and available in large dimensions. It has a firm even texture with a straight grain: the colour is reddish brown with, now and again, a tinge of purple. Polishes well.

Grand Bassam   Perhaps the greatest rival to the true mahoganies. Although lighter in weight, it is strong, with a firm texture; quite often it has a beautifully figured grain. Works and polishes well.

Lagos   Very similar to Honduras mahogany in respect of colour and texture; generally the timber is straight-grained but occasionally a figured log is available.

OAK   The British oak is, of course, well-known to us as being one of the toughest and strongest timbers known. However, a glance at the tree in winter when it is bare of leaves will tell us why it is not reliable as a cabinet wood, as the branches grow tortuously with many twists and bends. When left to its own devices, the bole rarely attains any great height clear of limbs; estate-grown oak where measures are taken to prevent too much branching is a much better proposition. It is a sad fact, however, that such trees are few and far between. The colour can, and does, vary from straw to dark brown; its texture is coarse and the grain often refractory. Your tools will need to be razor sharp to work it, but the wood takes a beautiful finish.

Other oaks are:

American Oak There are two varieties, the white and the red. Both are good cabinet woods from the point of view of working, but neither has the individuality of British oak, being rather featureless as regards colour and figure.

Japanese Oak This is the oak "par excellence" for cabinet work. The grain is straight and the texture clean; working the timber is a delight as it is mild and planes and scrapes superbly. The figure, too, is rich and quite often contains a beautiful flash. Staining and polishing are easy.

OBECHE Sometimes called "white mahogany" or "wawa". It is very light in weight and also in colour, being a pale straw colour – add to this the fact that it takes stain well and you have a timber which can be coloured to match the predominant one. Unfortunately, the wood is soft, bruises easily, and is not strong enough to be a carcassing or framing timber. Another fault is that the grain is very open and needs filling. Also it is often "roey" and difficult to plane without its tearing out.

OPEPE Quite a heavy timber (again from Africa) which is a consistent light yellowish brown in colour. As with so many of these African woods, it has an attractive ribbon-stripe figure which requires sharp tools to work it. One fault is that it tends to split unless holes for nails etc. are pre-bored; however, it stains and polishes well.

PADAUK This is a showy timber from the East Indies, being a rich red colour streaked through with darker colour. It is available in large sizes, but the grain can be irregular, making working difficult. The brilliant colour tends to fade when polished.

PINE There are two varieties of pine in general commercial use – the Scots (or Red) and Parana pine.

The Scots pine (often wrongly called "deal", which is a timber term) is universally used in the building trade and has also recently become popular in the furniture trade. It may come as a surprise to some to know that it was often used for wood carving in mediaeval times; also, eighteenth-century cabinet makers regarded it as a good groundwork for veneering. Of course, the timber had to be selected and seasoned properly for this kind of work, but any wood which can span the gap between flooring joists and ecclesiastical carving is something to be admired! Obviously any pine which is to be used for cabinet work must be free from loose knots and shakes, and it must be thoroughly seasoned.

Parana pine has become very popular over recent years and originates from South America. It is one of the strongest softwoods, is straight-grained and even-textured, thus making it an easy timber to work. The sapwood is a pale brownish-straw colour, while the heartwood is brown and often marked with reddish streaks which mar its appearance.

POPLAR There are three varieties of the European poplar which yield useful timber – the grey poplar, the black poplar, and the silver poplar. None of these is the familiar Lombardy poplar, which is valueless as a timber tree.

It can hardly be called a first grade cabinet wood but certainly comes in useful for secondary work such as light framings, drawer stuff, and the like. The fact that although light in weight it is nevertheless tough makes it a good wood for upholstery frames as it will take screws, nails, and tacks without splitting.

The colour is a nondescript greyish-white with a slight green tinge; the grain is quite uniform and uninteresting. Accordingly, although it absorbs stain readily, it is a dull timber even when polished.

RAMIN This is one of the most popular hardwoods from the East Indies and is stocked in one form or another by most D.I.Y. shops – usually as strips and mouldings. It is pale yellow in colour with little difference between sapwood and heartwood. The grain is straight and consistent although the texture tends to be coarse. These attributes have caused it to be used as a companion for oak in much furniture sold today – the more so as ramin accepts stain readily. It is a good cabinet timber in its own right as it works satisfactorily and easily; splinters from it can, however, cause a painful irritation.

ROSEWOOD The three rosewoods originate in Brazil, East Indies, and Honduras.

The Brazilian rosewood (also known as "Rio") is the archetypal rosewood, being strikingly marked. It is heavy and dense with a rather coarse and open grain — this can give rise to one of its main disadvantages when used in the solid, namely a tendency to develop minute cracks in the pores regardless of the amount of polish applied. The colour is purple-brown to black and these colours are often banded or in stripes. Alternating hard and soft grain can call for very sharp tools and care when working.

Indian rosewood is almost identical to the Brazilian in all respects: it is, however, slightly easier to work.

The third example, Honduras, is lighter in colour than the other two but is, otherwise, very similar.

SAPELE Sometimes known as "West African Cedar" — a family to which it is not related. However, the timber is hard and close-grained, like a cedar, and in addition has a roey grain which gives a very regular striped figure. As you would expect, this means that the interlocked grain makes planing and glasspapering difficult, but otherwise the timber works well and polishes excellently.

SPRUCE The "Whitewood" spruce grows in the British Isles, USA, and Canada. From its name you can deduce that the timber is a creamy white colour and, when finished with a clear polish, it presents a very clean and attractive appearance. It is, of course, a softwood and keen tools are necessary to work it to avoid a fibrous finish. As it is not strong it is not really suitable for carcase work but it is often used for light joinery.

The Sitka (silver) spruce grows in Western Canada and the USA and yields timber of gigantic dimensions. When aeroplanes were constructed of wood, this is the timber which was used on account of its toughness, elasticity, and straight grain. It works well and is a light straw colour.

SYCAMORE The timber from this tree is a clear white colour when young, darkening to yellowish brown as the tree grows older. The grain is fine and even, and the texture is close and smooth — all combining to give a lustrous surface. It works excellently and accepts stain and polish well: as a matter of interest, when sycamore is dyed grey it is known as "harewood".

TEAK Tectona grandis is the only true teak, originating in India and Burma. When freshly felled the timber is a consistent yellowish brown which changes to a dark brown with black streaks as the timber ages. The grain is coarse and open, and one of the main characteristics is its greasiness — this makes it necessary to de-grease the timber before applying adhesive. It is well known for its strength and resistance to strains but with all its qualities it is more suited to heavy constructional work (indoors or outdoors) than to cabinet work.

WALNUT The well-known English walnut (which is almost unobtainable now) is part of the large family of French, Italian, and European walnuts.

Young trees yield a light brown timber which lacks the beautiful figuring of older wood. However, at any age, walnut is tough, fairly hard, and resilient — hence its use for gun stocks. Although difficult to season, it is a delight to work and can be polished to a superb finish.

American Walnut (also called American black walnut). Although it does not possess the rich figure of the European woods, it has a handsome appearance of its own, much of it being a uniform brownish purple. This, combined with straight grain and a fine, even texture, has made it a favoured cabinet wood.

CHAPTER 7

Twenty-eight Period Furniture Designs

With complete constructional notes,
measured drawings & cutting lists

1. PEMBROKE TABLE WITH CABRIOLE LEGS

This kind of small flap-table became popular in the second half of the eighteenth century, after Thomas Sheraton had designed one for Lady Pembroke — hence the name. Although our design has cabriole legs, such tables were often made with tapered splay legs, spade-toe legs, or turned column legs. Whatever the style, these tables prove invaluable for a multiplicity of uses.

The actual construction is perfectly straightforward, and is what one would expect and Fig. 3 shows details. The legs are cut from $2\frac{3}{4}$ inch (70 mm) square stuff and Fig. 5 gives the template; the drawing is divided into a one-inch square grid so that you can easily draw it out full-size.

Chapter 4 describes the method for fashioning cabriole legs; the ear-pieces are

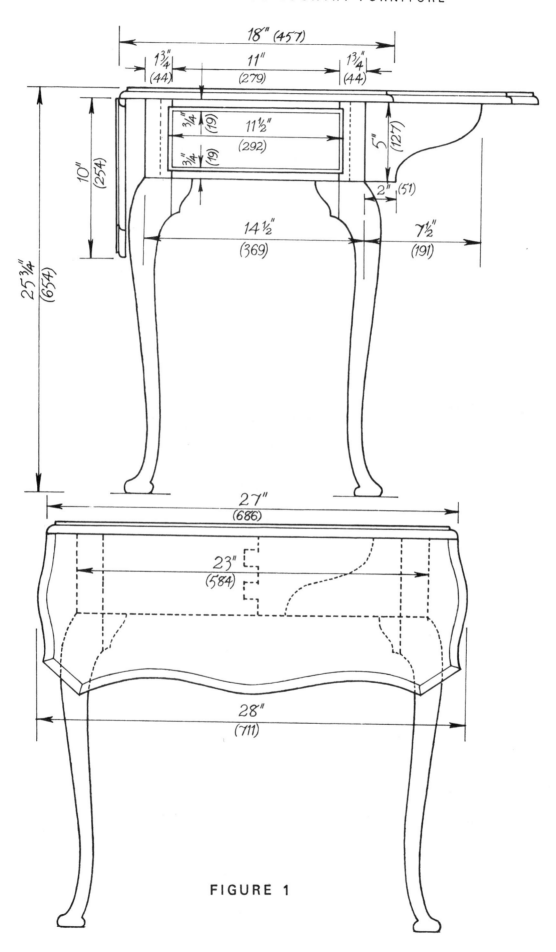

FIGURE 1

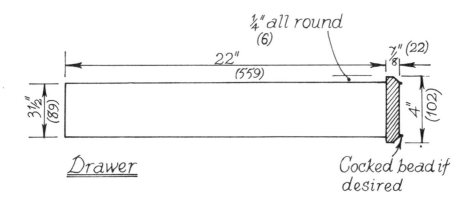

Drawer

Cocked bead if desired

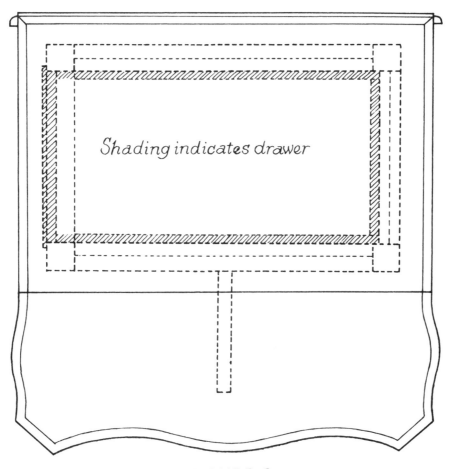

Shading indicates drawer

FIGURE 2

glued on afterwards. At the opening end of the centre bed, the upper drawer rails are dovetailed into the leg squares while the sides are mortise and tenoned. Other drawer rails are glued and screwed in place.

One complication that does arise is the need for the fillets or pads shown in Fig. 3. They are required for two reasons — on the one hand so that the knuckle joint can be made, and on the other as pads to which the ear-pieces of the legs can be glued and dowelled. They can be fixed to the centre bed sides by gluing and screwing from inside.

A small point to note here. When the flap supports are closed against the sides it will be difficult to prise them away from the pad. It's a good idea, therefore, to fashion a small scallop (Fig. 3) which will act as a finger hole.

FIGURE 3

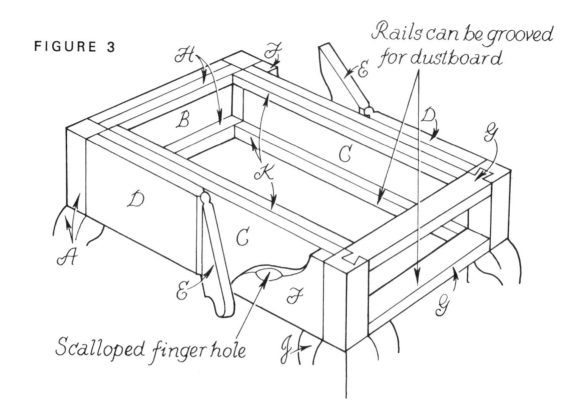

Rails can be grooved for dustboard

Scalloped finger hole

Fixing the top can be done in the usual way, by means of buttoning on the short sides, and pocket-screwing on the longer. A refined touch would be to groove the lower drawer rails as shown in Fig. 3 and insert a dustboard. Not only does this keep out dust from the contents of the drawer but also it gives a neat, professional finish to the job.

The drawer is the conventional type described fully in Chapter 1, and runs almost the whole depth of the bed. Note, however, that the drawer front is rabbeted on the inside face so that it laps over the drawer end by $\frac{1}{4}$ inch (6 mm) all round, and the arrises are bevelled off at 45 degrees. This gives an

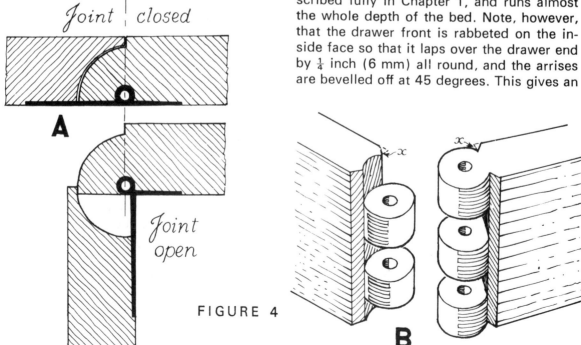

Joint closed

A

Joint open

FIGURE 4

B

opportunity for a cocked bead to be inserted (mitring the corners, of course) and this would be an authentic and elegant feature.

Although solid timber is really needed for the shaped top and flaps, it would be possible to utilize a man-made board with a solid lipping which need not be more than 2 inches (51 mm) wide.

The most difficult job will probably be making the rule joint, and this is shown at Fig. 4A. It is essential that the centre of the hinge pin is on the dotted centre line otherwise you will get unsightly gaps or binding — equally, the leaves of the hinge must be accurately recessed so that the tops of the bed and of the flap are all in one plane.

Another tricky joint to make is the knuckle joint (Fig. 4B), and you can see from the plan that neat, accurate workmanship is required. Once you have marked out the joint saw in the two cuts marked "x", stopping them just short of the circle. The circle (or the cylindrical shape) can be formed by sawing off a series of "flats", and the final shape is best rasped off. Use $\frac{3}{16}$ inch (5 mm) steel or brass rod as a pivot, burring over the ends so that the metal pin does not drop out.

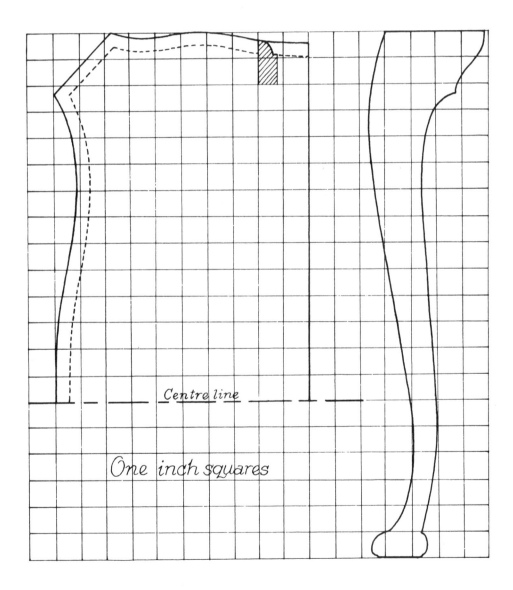

Centre line

One inch squares

FIGURE 5

PARTS LIST *See over*

Parts List

No. req'd.	Description	Long	Wide	Thick
1	Top	28 (711)	19 (482)	$\frac{3}{4}$ (19)
2	Flaps	29 (736)	11 (280)	$\frac{3}{4}$ (19)
4	Legs (A)	26 (660)	$3\frac{1}{4}$ (83)	$2\frac{3}{4}$ (70)
2	Centre bed sides (C)	22 (559)	$5\frac{1}{2}$ (140)	$\frac{3}{4}$ (19)
1	Centre bed end (B)	$13\frac{1}{2}$ (343)	$5\frac{1}{2}$ (140)	$\frac{3}{4}$ (19)
4	Side drawer rails (K)	20 (509)	1 (25)	$\frac{3}{4}$ (19)
3	Lower drawer rails (H)	13 (330)	2 (51)	$\frac{3}{4}$ (19)
1	Upper front drawer rail (G)	13 (330)	2 (51)	$\frac{3}{4}$ (19)
2	Fillets (D)	$12\frac{1}{2}$ (318)	$5\frac{1}{2}$ (140)	1 (25)
2	Shaped fillets/pads (F)	8 (203)	$5\frac{1}{2}$ (140)	1 (25)
2	Flap supports (E)	9 (229)	$5\frac{1}{2}$ (140)	1 (25)
4	Earpieces (J)	$2\frac{1}{2}$ (64)	2 (51)	$1\frac{3}{4}$ (45)
1	Drawer front	12 (305)	$5\frac{1}{2}$ (140)	$\frac{7}{8}$ (23)
2	Drawer sides	24 (610)	4 (102)	$\frac{3}{8}$ (10)
1	Drawer back	12 (305)	4 (102)	$\frac{3}{8}$ (10)
1	Drawer bottom	23 (584)	12 (305)	$\frac{3}{16}$ (5)

Allowances have been made to lengths and widths; thicknesses are net.
Millimetre equivalents in brackets.

2. REGENCY-STYLE SOFA TABLE

FIGURE 1

This is another classical design which has enjoyed continuous popularity since its origins in the eighteenth century. It is, of course, a piece which demands to be made up in mahogany, although walnut would be a good alternative.

A 3 feet (914 mm) bed with two flaps of 10 inches (254 mm) each are more or less standard sizes for this design and you will see that the meeting edges of the top and the flaps are rule-jointed. This joint is very much in keeping with the period, but you could substitute a plain butt-hinged joint if a rule joint is too difficult.

The fact that the flaps have a fairly large radius on their corners means that solid wood should be used if at all possible, otherwise any lipping fitted to a man-made board would have to be a wide one to accommodate the corner curves. Fastening

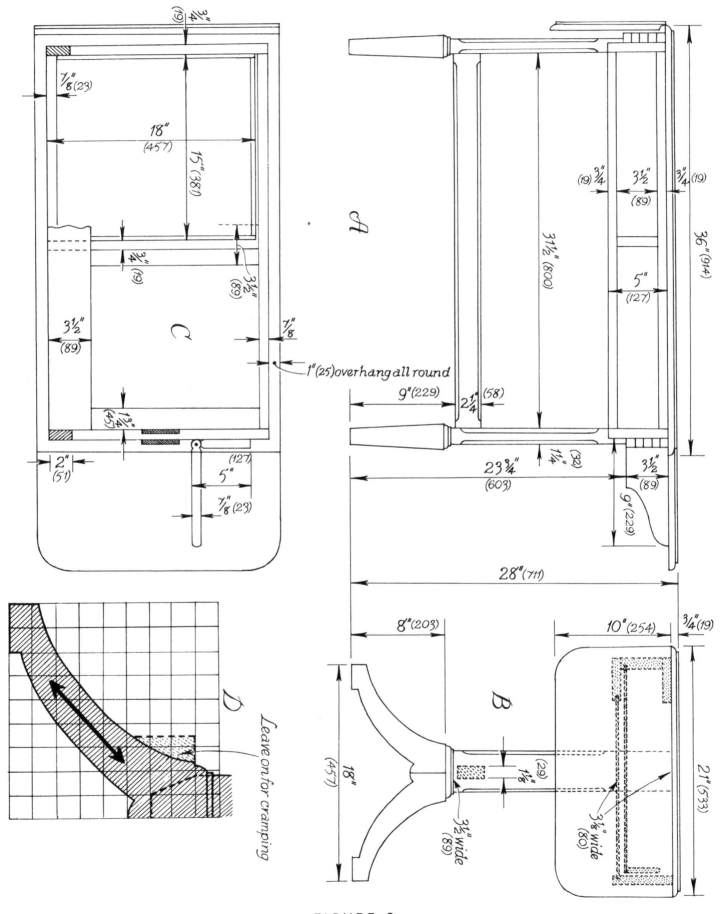

FIGURE 2

down the top is accomplished by means of buttons across the width and pocket-screwing along the length.

Making up the carcase should present no undue problems as it is quite a straightforward construction.

The back is lap-dovetailed into the ends, and a point to note here is that if you wish to incorporate dust-boards, then a groove or a rabbet will need to be cut along the inside bottom edges and you will have to space out your dovetails accordingly. Fitting a dust-board will also entail cutting matching grooves or rabbets on the edges of the drawer runners and the lower drawer rail.

It is always unsightly to see end grain

The centre drawer partition is through-tenoned into the upper and lower drawer rails, while the drawer runners are dovetailed into the back and tenoned into the lower drawer rail respectively. If you do intend to fit dustboards, then you could make these tenons of a size to fit the grooves, and so save yourself some labour.

Perhaps the trickiest part of the job is fitting the pillars. From Fig. 2B you will see that each pillar tapers from $3\frac{1}{2}$ inches (89 mm) to $3\frac{1}{8}$ inches (80 mm) wide at the level of the bottom of the carcase, and this is done to counteract any appearances of heaviness.

From this level upwards the width remains

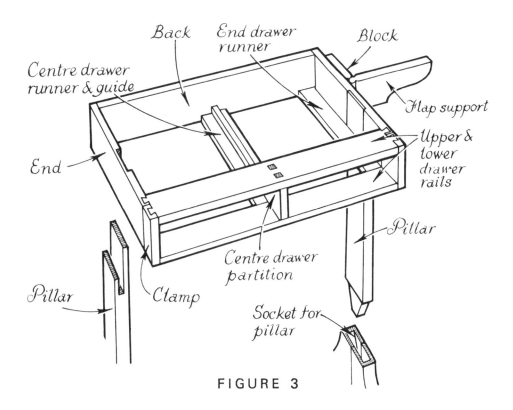

FIGURE 3

showing and, of course, it also poses a problem when polishing as the grain absorbs so much stain and polish as to appear markedly darker than the surrounding timber.

For this reason, a clamp is fastened to the front of the ends, and the most effective way to do this is by means of a plain butted and glued joint reinforced by letting in two dowels.

This joint is further strengthened by the fact that the upper and lower drawer rails are both dovetailed into the end and into the clamp, thus effectively "locking" the joint.

constant at $3\frac{1}{8}$ inches (80 mm), and you have to cut a housing in the centre of each end to this width, across the full depth of the end, and $\frac{3}{8}$ inch (10 mm) deep.

If you look now at Fig. 3 you will see that the top of the pillar is formed into a double tenon, rather like a two-pronged fork with one prong longer than the other. The longer tenon fits into the housing you have just taken out of the end, while the shorter tenon laps over the outside of the end and finishes immediately below the flap support. This makes an extremely strong joint and it can be further reinforced by screws inserted from the inside.

The feet can pose quite a problem unless they are tackled methodically. Size and shape can be obtained from D, Fig. 2, which is divided into one inch squares. From Fig. 1 you will appreciate that the grain of the wood for each foot must be chosen with scrupulous care so that the grain direction runs diagonally to be parallel to the length as far as possible. The arrow in D, Fig. 2 shows the best grain direction.

In the same illustration you will see that a square "corner" is left on at the top of each leg so that you will have a flat surface for your cramp when fitting up the joint. The socket for the large wedge-shaped dovetail which is cut on the bottom of the pillar. (Fig. 3) needs to be taken out of each half of the foot before the two are cramped up. The reeded decoration should also be worked before cramping up.

The whole joint — the pillar and the two halves of the foot — is cramped up together. It can be strengthened with a couple of dowels knocked in from the outside, through into the dovetail of the pillar — they should not, however, penetrate through the complete thickness. As you can see from Fig. 1, a turned patera is glued on to mask them.

Fixing the stretcher rail is achieved by means of a tenon at each end, mortised into the pillars.

A knuckle joint is used for hinging the flap support to the block — the latter can be glued and screwed (or dowelled) to the end — and this kind of joint has been described elsewhere.

Making the drawers calls for no particular comment as they are of conventional construction. Although not shown on our design, a cocked bead all round the drawer fronts would be a nice touch.

A word about the castors. Those illustrated are the plate-type which are simply screwed to the underside of the feet. Alternatively, there are some attractive reproduction lion's paw style socket castors which would be quite suitable for this period piece. The sockets of these fit over the ends of the feet and consequently tend to make the overall height of the table less, and, if used, you may wish to adjust the length of the pillar accordingly.

Parts List

No. req'd.	Description	Long	Wide	Thick
1	Top (Bed)	37 (940)	$21\frac{1}{2}$ (546)	$\frac{3}{4}$ (19)
2	Flaps	11 (280)	$21\frac{1}{2}$ (546)	$\frac{3}{4}$ (19)
2	Pillars	22 (558)	4 (102)	$1\frac{1}{4}$ (32)
4	Feet	13 (330)	5 (127)	2 (51)
1	Stretcher rail	$32\frac{1}{2}$ (825)	$2\frac{1}{2}$ (64)	$1\frac{1}{8}$ (29)
1	Carcase back	$33\frac{1}{2}$ (851)	$5\frac{1}{4}$ (134)	$\frac{7}{8}$ (23)
2	Carcase ends	$17\frac{1}{2}$ (445)	$5\frac{1}{4}$ (134)	$\frac{3}{4}$ (19)
2	Clamps	2 (51)	$5\frac{1}{4}$ (134)	$\frac{3}{4}$ (19)
2	Drawer rails (upper & lower)	$33\frac{1}{4}$ (845)	$3\frac{3}{4}$ (95)	$\frac{3}{4}$ (19)
1	Centre drawer partition	$5\frac{1}{2}$ (140)	$3\frac{3}{4}$ (95)	$\frac{3}{4}$ (19)
2	End drawer runners	15 (381)	2 (51)	$\frac{3}{4}$ (19)
1	Centre drawer runner	15 (381)	$3\frac{3}{4}$ (95)	$\frac{3}{4}$ (19)
1	Guide	15 (381)	1 (25)	$\frac{3}{4}$ (19)
2	Flap supports	$9\frac{1}{2}$ (241)	$3\frac{3}{4}$ (95)	$\frac{7}{8}$ (23)
2	Blocks	$5\frac{1}{2}$ (140)	$3\frac{3}{4}$ (95)	$\frac{7}{8}$ (23)
2	Drawer fronts	$15\frac{1}{2}$ (394)	$3\frac{3}{4}$ (95)	$\frac{7}{8}$ (23)
2	Drawer backs	$15\frac{1}{2}$ (394)	$3\frac{1}{2}$ (89)	$\frac{3}{8}$ (10)
4	Drawer sides	$17\frac{1}{2}$ (445)	$3\frac{3}{4}$ (95)	$\frac{3}{8}$ (10)
2	Drawer bottoms	$18\frac{1}{2}$ (470)	$15\frac{1}{2}$ (394)	$\frac{3}{16}$ (5)

Allowances have been made to lengths and widths; thicknesses are net.
Millimetre equivalents in brackets.

3. QUEEN ANNE-STYLE CORNER CUPBOARD AND DISPLAY CABINET

FIGURE 1

As you can see from Fig. 1, this is a most imposing piece when made up and could well rank as an "heirloom of the future". But the design is not just elegant but useful as well as corners are frequently wasted space and, as you can imagine, a piece of furniture like this has a lot of accommodation.

In principle, the upper showcase is made separate from the lower cupboard and simply rests on it. If required, the two can be linked at the back by screwed-on glass plates; in any event, it is highly desirable that the piece can be split so that it can be moved easily.

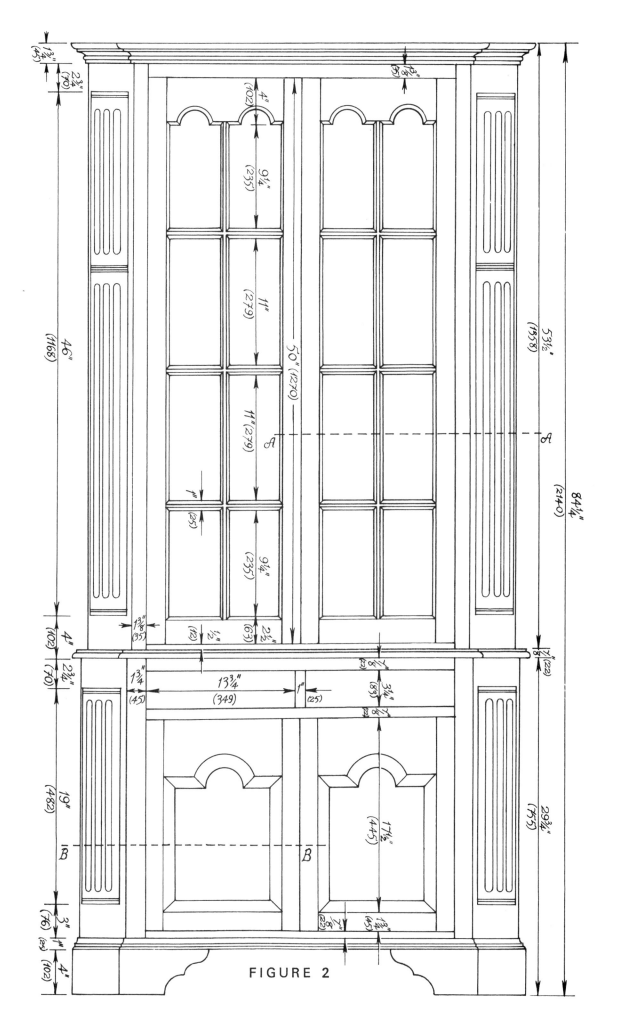

FIGURE 2

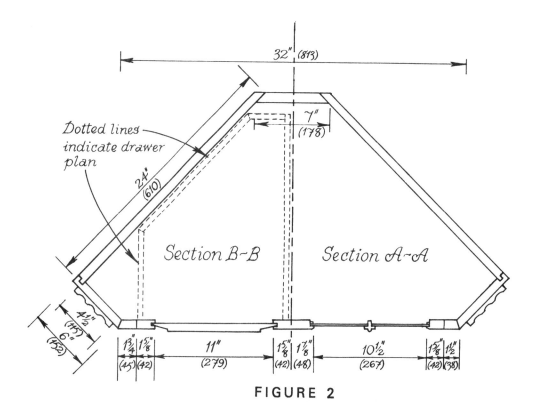

FIGURE 2

With the exception of the return panels (B and R, Fig. 3), the floors of the upper and lower cabinets, and the top, W, all of which can be veneered plywood, the remainder of the parts need to be cut from solid stuff. Obviously, mahogany or walnut are the classical timbers for this kind of work and to keep the cost down, any wood that is not show-wood could be a suitable hardwood stained to match.

The main carcases should be made first, and some care is needed as the angled joints could be tricky.

Dealing with the joints between parts A and C, and P and Q, both are similar and are mitred. Bear in mind that whatever the angle, the mitre angle should be exactly half of it and is not necessarily 45 degrees. Once the faces have been planed you will have to make your mind up whether to dowel the joint, or to insert a hardwood tongue. If you feel dowelling is the answer you will have to be extremely careful to see that the holes match exactly. Tonguing will, of course, call for grooves to be cut on each of the meeting faces. In either case it would be a good idea to strengthen the joint further by rubbing in a series of glue blocks.

As you can see from the sections A–A and B–B in Fig. 2, the return panels B and

R are rabbeted in on their front edges, while the back edges are butted against the back pieces D and T. Gluing and screwing could well be used to reinforce the joint, or a hardwood tongue.

Next, the sub-frame comprising parts F and G. These three pieces are mitred end to end, having loose tenons glued in at each joint. Once assembled, it can be glued and screwed to the plinth assembly, this in turn being similarly joined to the underside of the cupboard.

Now for the floor of this cupboard. It can be veneered plywood supported on fillets glued and screwed on to the bottom edges of the panels as shown in Fig. 4, while its front edge lies in a rabbet cut for it on the inner edge of rail L.

The drawer rails L and M, and also rail X in the upper cabinet, are notched around the stiles C and P respectively – gluing and screwing will ensure strong joints. Before rails L and M are assembled, the central drawer division rail N must be inserted; it can be through-tenoned at top and bottom.

Fig. 2 (section B–B) and Fig. 3 show you the arrangement of the drawer rails and runners and also a plan view (in dotted lines) of the drawer. In the best work, all five

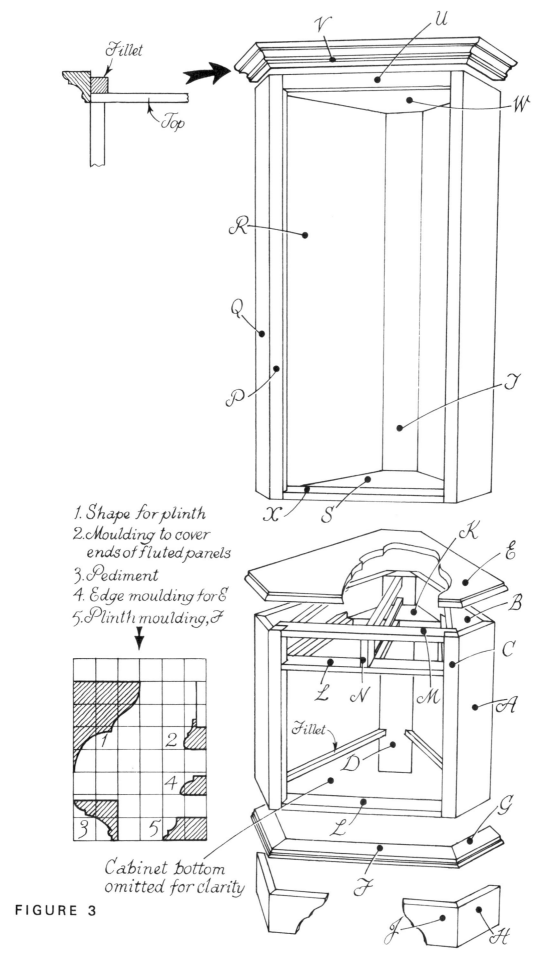

Fillet

Top

1. Shape for plinth
2. Moulding to cover ends of fluted panels
3. Pediment
4. Edge moulding for E
5. Plinth moulding, F

Cabinet bottom omitted for clarity

Fillet

FIGURE 3

joints would be dovetailed, and it would be desirable to do this if at all possible. Otherwise on the two corners where the sides meet at an obtuse angle, you could have a mitred joint which is simply butted, glued,

These would fit around a centre guide rail fitted to the framing so that the drawer is held centrally as it is opened.

Fitting the top, E, is straightforward enough. Its grain should run transversely

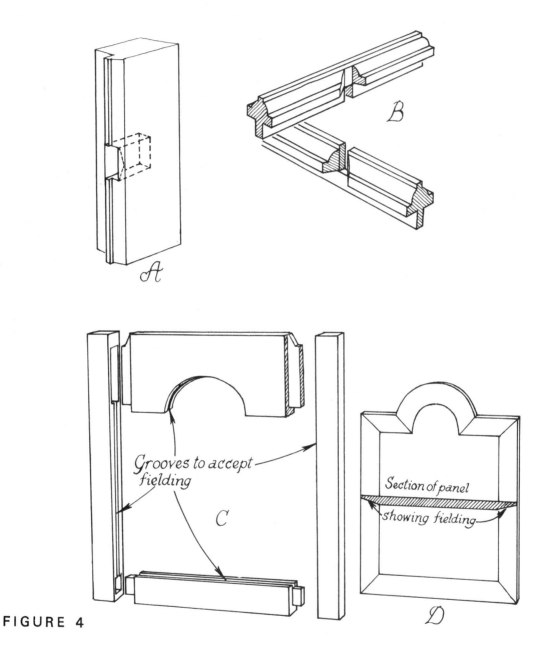

FIGURE 4

and then keyed with thin hardwood keys — e.g. sawcut veneer. Another alternative method is to use dovetails for the two front joints and angled comb joints for the three remaining. Figure 5 shows the method of working the angled comb joint. If desired, each drawer could be fitted with 2 runners glued and pinned to the drawer bottom.

across, parallel to the front of the cabinet and not from front to back. This means that it should, ideally, be held down by buttons fitting into grooves made in the return panels, B, while on the other edges it can be pocket-screwed down.

The bottom, S, for the upper carcase is fixed in a similar fashion as that for the lower carcase. However, the top W lies on the top edges of parts R and T and is screwed down into them; it also laps over on to the top edges of the rail U and the two canted return panels, Q. As you can see from the section, Fig. 3, the pediment moulding butts against the edge of the top and is glued in place. The whole assembly can be strengthened by gluing in fillets which can be screwed to both the top and the moulding. Note that as no provision has been made for shrinkage the top must be veneered plywood or blockboard.

Although they are quite a test of cabinet making to make, the cupboard doors look very elegant when completed. A glance at C, Fig. 4 shows you that, while there is nothing unorthodox in their construction, great care is needed in the grooving so that all the parts will go together sweetly. Probably the most difficult job will be to work the groove around the curve in the top rail; either a French spindle or a powered router will cut the groove accurately and quickly.

Those who have only hand tools will almost certainly need to make a "scratch" for this particular task. The scratch will need to be a steel cutter ground to the requisite width and depth which is held in a wooden stock or handle, which should be fitted with a fence that can be pressed against the wood to guide the cut. A groove $\frac{1}{4}$ inch (6 mm) wide by $\frac{3}{8}$ inch (10 mm) deep would be suitable.

The framing of the doors for the upper cabinet are made similarly, except that the grooving is omitted and the edges of the stiles and rails are bevelled instead. Fig. 4A shows the type of scribed tongue to give a mitred effect.

Fig. 4B illustrates the mitred joint used at each intersection of the glazing bars and this, plus the method of glazing, is the same as that described for the small corner cabinet.

It goes without saying that shelves should be fitted before the doors are hinged on. The method of fitting is shown in the Queen Anne Style corner cabinet.

The fluted decorative panels which are pinned and glued to the corner ends must, of course, be solid wood. A carving gouge of suitable curvature can be utilized to rough out the flutes and to shape the stopped ends, but a scratch-stock with an appropriately shaped cutter is the best tool for making sure that the flutes are uniform in width and depth. Moulding No. 2 in Fig. 3 shows the moulding which is used to cap the ends of these panels.

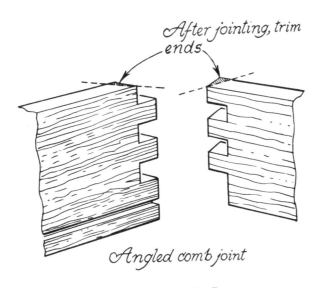

After jointing, trim ends

Angled comb joint

FIGURE 5

PARTS LIST *See over*

Parts List

No. req'd.	Description	Long	Wide	Thick
2	End corner panels (A)	26 (660)	6½ (165)	¾ (19)
2	Return panels (B)	27 (686)	24½ (622)	¾ (19)
2	Bottom cupboard stiles (C)	26 (660)	2¼ (57)	⅞ (22)
1	Bottom back panel (D)	30½ (775)	7½ (191)	¾ (19)
1	Top (E)	43 (1092)	22½ (572)	⅞ (22)
1	Plinth rail (F)	33 (838)	2½ (64)	1 (25)
2	Plinth return rails (G)	8½ (211)	2½ (64)	1 (25)
2	Plinth returns (H)	8½ (211)	4½ (115)	1 (25)
1	Plinth front (J)	33 (838)	4½ (115)	1 (25)
1	Drawer rail support (K)	15 (381)	4½ (115)	1 (25)
3	Drawer rails (L, M)	33 (838)	2 (51)	⅞ (22)
1	Drawer division (N)	5½ (140)	2 (51)	1 (25)
2	Upper cabinet stiles (P)	52½ (1330)	1½ (38)	⅞ (22)
2	End corner panels (Q)	52½ (1330)	6½ (165)	¾ (19)
2	Return panels (R)	52½ (1330)	24½ (622)	¾ (19)
2	Upper (S) and lower cabinet bottoms	41½ (1053)	20 (508)	¾ (19)
1	Upper back panel (T)	52½ (1330)	7½ (191)	¾ (19)
1	Top cabinet rail (U)	30½ (775)	1⅜ (35)	⅞ (22)
1	Pediment moulding (V)	35½ (902)	2¼ (57)	1¾ (45)
2	Pediment moulding returns	8½ (216)	2¼ (57)	1¾ (45)
1	Top (W)	41½ (1053)	20 (508)	¾ (19)
1	Bottom rail (X)	32 (812)	1⅞ (48)	⅞ (22)
2	Bottom decorative panels	20 (508)	5 (127)	½ (13)
2	Top decorative panels	47 (1193)	5 (127)	½ (13)
4	Cupboard door stiles	19½ (495)	1⅞ (48)	⅞ (22)

No. req'd.	Description	Long	Wide	Thick
2	Cupboard upper rails	13½ (343)	5½ (140)	7/8 (22)
2	Cupboard lower rails	13½ (343)	2¼ (57)	7/8 (22)
2	Cupboard panels	15½ (394)	12½ (318)	¾ (19)
4	Upper cabinet door stiles	51 (1295)	2⅛ (54)	7/8 (22)
2	Upper cabinet upper rails	13¼ (337)	4½ (115)	7/8 (22)
2	Upper cabinet lower rails	13¼ (337)	2¾ (70)	7/8 (22)
2	Long glazing bars	45½ (1155)	1⅛ (29)	7/8 (22)
6	Short glazing bars	12¼ (311)	1⅛ (29)	7/8 (22)
1	Central drawer bearer	17 (432)	2 (51)	¾ (19)
1	Central drawer guide	20 (508)	1 (25)	¾ (19)
1	Central drawer kicker	20 (508)	1 (25)	¾ (19)
2	Side drawer bearers	19½ (495)	1 (51)	¾ (19)
2	Side drawer guides	19½ (495)	1 (25)	¾ (19)
2	Side drawer kickers	19½ (495)	2 (25)	¾ (19)
2	Drawer fronts	15 (381)	3¾ (95)	7/8 (22)
2	Drawer long sides	20 (508)	3¾ (95)	¾ (19)
2	Drawer short sides	9 (229)	3¾ (95)	¾ (19)
2	Drawer splay sides	15½ (394)	3¾ (95)	¾ (19)
2	Drawer backs	5 (127)	3¾ (95)	¾ (19)
2	Drawer bottoms	15 (381)	19½ (495)	¼ (6)

Allowances have been made to lengths and widths; thicknesses are net.
Millimetre equivalents in brackets.

4. LONG CASE CLOCK

FIGURE 1

This imposing Long Case (Grandfather) Clock has been designed to harmonise with Chippendale-style furniture and consequently needs to be made up in mahogany, either solid or veneered.

Although the hood has ample dimensions to accommodate most clock movements it would be advisable to check that this is so —

it may well be that you will have to alter the sizes of the door to suit the measurements of your clock face.

Assembly details of the base and case up to waist height are shown in Fig. 3. Note that the base sides and front extend right to the floor, having a plinth glued and screwed (from the back) to them. At the rear there

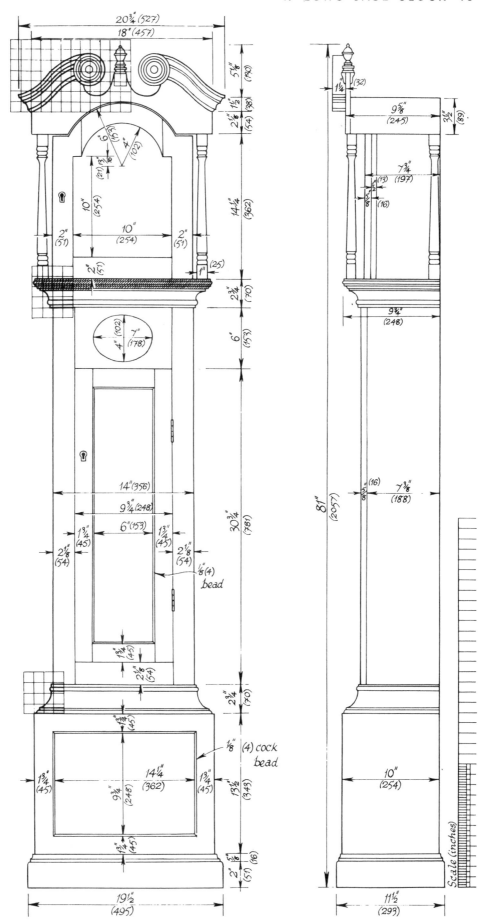

FIGURE 2

is a back plinth rail which is rabbeted to accept the back, while the bottom is inserted into grooves cut in the base sides and front.

Although the base front is one solid piece, a cock bead is grooved in and mitred at the corners to break up what would otherwise be an uninteresting panel.

The case sides are extended by 3 inches (76 mm) at the bottom to lap over the upper ends of the base sides and, as you can see, the two are screwed and glued together through a fillet. By this means, the top of the fillet and the upper edge of the base side form a platform to which the moulding is pinned and glued.

From Fig. 2 it is apparent that the front framing of the case section laps over the front edges of the case sides, and the two can be glued together by means of a long tongued and grooved joint. This method will, of course, combat any tendency to shrink-

age on the part of the case side. A series of triangular glue blocks can also be rubbed into the angle to strengthen the joint still further.

Mortise and tenon joints are used for both the case front framing and for the door; it would be best to use twin tenons on the top panel. The central panel of the door is rebated into the frame, and a bead inserted and mitred at the corners. Traditionally, "acorn" type hinges should be used, but any good quality brass hinges would be suitable.

The waist moulding is pinned and glued around the front and sides of the case at the top. It is important to realise that the complete moulding is a composite one, one part being fixed to the hood section (shaded in the front elevation, Fig. 2) and the other part, as we have seen, is fixed to the case sides and front.

Reverting to Fig. 3, note that the back projects upwards beyond the waist and is shaped to fit under the back of the hood. The size and height of the support for the movement depends entirely on the requirements of the particular movement you are using; adjustment is easy as it is merely screwed at each end to the inside of the case ends. It is better not to glue the support in place as the prime requisite is that it should be dead-level (use a spirit level to check this), and if the clock is moved at any time it is not too difficult a job to withdraw the screws and re-position the whole thing.

You will also need to cut slots in the platform of the support to take the pendulum shaft and the weight chains. Here, again, the size and position of the slots depend upon the movement used.

From Fig. 4 it will be seen that the hood is an open-ended "box" with a domed top. The sides in our design are plain panels, but a small glazed window could be incorporated in each side if desired. At the front, the "box" is enclosed by the hood front, which follows the clock door for size and shape, while at the opposite end the projecting back of the case assembly fits into the aperture.

The hood "box" is planted on rails which form a three-sided rectangular frame, and the waist mouldings are pinned and glued to their outer edges. Thus, the whole assembly will fit on to the top of the mouldings of the case assembly and can be slid forward and lifted off. Don't forget to unhook the pendulum and weight chains before doing this!

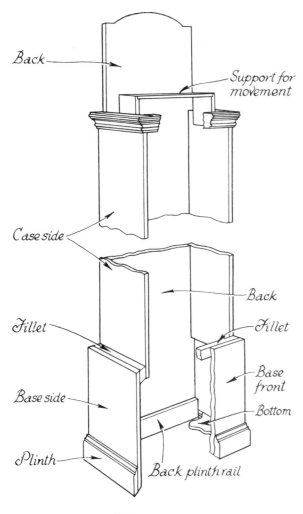

FIGURE 3

Four turned columns support the fascia and scroll pediment, and the assembly is also shown in Fig. 4. The dustboard is optional but very desirable as it helps to strengthen the assembly considerably.

The clock-face door is framed-up as shown in the elevation, Fig. 2, and the appearance is enhanced if a small thumb moulding is worked around the inside edges on the solid wood with a scratch-stock. It is hinged to the front of the hood with a pair of longcase clock hinges (available from clock-parts suppliers) which are flat brass plates.

Drill two fixing holes in each plate, and one hole that accepts a pivot pin driven in the door—the pin can be made from a suitable nail cut to length. A small lock may then be fitted.

Unfortunately there is no easy way to fashion the pediment scrolled mouldings and it is a matter of using carving tools. How-ever, the two circular paterae could be turned on the lathe face-plate and then pinned and glued in place.

The two decorative items – the finial and the oval panel of marquetry – can either be made in the workshop or bought in. Suppliers of clock movements usually also supply brass turned finials of varying designs, while ready-made marquetry inserts can be bought from some suppliers of woodworking accessories.

Details of the mouldings are shown in Fig. 2 and are squared-off into one inch (25 mm) squares for easy enlargement to full size. It is unlikely that mouldings with the exact profiles will be immediately available, in which case two or three mouldings can be glued together to give the desired shape.

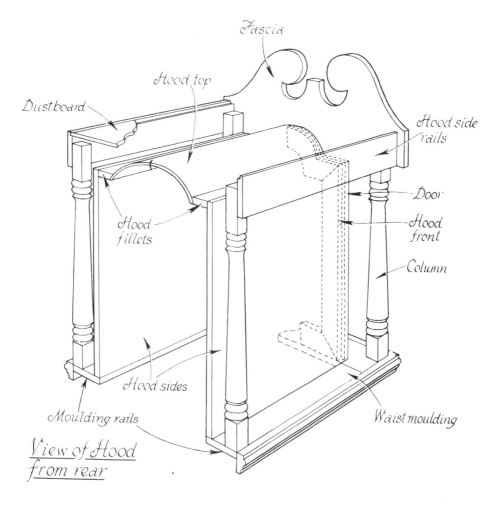

FIGURE 4   PARTS LIST *See over*

Parts List

No. req'd.	Description	Long	Wide	Thick
1	Plinth front	20 (508)	$2\frac{5}{8}$ (67)	$\frac{3}{4}$ (19)
2	Plinth sides	12 (305)	$2\frac{5}{8}$ (67)	$\frac{3}{4}$ (19)
1	Back plinth rail	18 (457)	$2\frac{5}{8}$ (67)	$\frac{3}{4}$ (19)
1	Base front panel	$18\frac{1}{2}$ (470)	$17\frac{1}{4}$ (438)	$\frac{5}{8}$ (16)
2	Base side panels	$17\frac{1}{4}$ (438)	10 (254)	$\frac{5}{8}$ (16)
1	Back	74 (1879)	17 (432)	$\frac{3}{16}$ (5)
1	Bottom	$18\frac{1}{2}$ (470)	10 (254)	$\frac{3}{16}$ (5)
1	Front fillet	$18\frac{1}{2}$ (470)	3 (76)	$1\frac{3}{8}$ (35)
2	Side fillets	12 (305)	3 (76)	$1\frac{3}{8}$ (16)
2	Case sides	$45\frac{1}{2}$ (1155)	8 (204)	$\frac{5}{8}$ (16)
2	Case stiles	$37\frac{1}{2}$ (953)	$2\frac{1}{4}$ (58)	$\frac{5}{8}$ (16)
1	Case bottom rail	12 (305)	$2\frac{1}{4}$ (58)	$\frac{5}{8}$ (16)
1	Case top panel	12 (305)	$6\frac{1}{4}$ (159)	$\frac{5}{8}$ (16)
2	Door stiles	$29\frac{1}{2}$ (749)	2 (51)	$\frac{5}{8}$ (16)
2	Door rails	$8\frac{1}{4}$ (210)	2 (51)	$\frac{5}{8}$ (16)
1	Door panel	$27\frac{1}{2}$ (698)	7 (178)	$\frac{3}{16}$ (5)
4	Columns	$14\frac{3}{4}$ (375)	$1\frac{1}{8}$ (29)	1 (25)
2	Clock door stiles	16 (407)	$3\frac{1}{4}$ (83)	$\frac{5}{8}$ (16)
1	Clock door rail (lower)	12 (305)	$2\frac{1}{4}$ (58)	$\frac{5}{8}$ (16)
1	Clock door rail (upper)	$10\frac{1}{4}$ (261)	6 (153)	$\frac{5}{8}$ (16)
2	Hood door stiles	16 (407)	$3\frac{1}{4}$ (83)	$\frac{1}{2}$ (13)
1	Hood door rail (lower)	12 (305)	$2\frac{1}{4}$ (58)	$\frac{1}{2}$ (13)
1	Hood door rail (upper)	$10\frac{1}{4}$ (261)	6 (153)	$\frac{1}{2}$ (13)
2	Hood sides	$14\frac{1}{2}$ (368)	7 (178)	$\frac{1}{2}$ (13)

2	Hood fillets	6¾ (172)	2 (51)	½ (13)
1	Movement support board	13 (330)	4 (102)	⅝ (16)
2	Movement support sides	6 (153)	4 (102)	⅝ (16)
1	Hood top	13 (330)	6¾ (172)	$\frac{3}{16}$ (5)
2	Hood side rails	9½ (242)	3¾ (95)	⅝ (16)
1	Dustboard	18 (457)	9½ (242)	$\frac{3}{16}$ (5)
1	Fascia	18½ (470)	6 (153)	½ (13)
2	Pediment mouldings	9½ (242)	3¾ (95)	1¼ (32)
	Waist moulding	38 (965)		
	Base moulding	38 (965)		

Allowances have been made to lengths and widths; thicknesses are net.
Millimetre equivalents in brackets.

5. QUEEN ANNE SIDE TABLE

FIGURE 1

This kind of furniture is always acceptable as it not only has a timeless quality which enables it to fit into almost any surroundings but also is a useful and functional piece in itself.

The cabriole legs and the apron call for solid timber, and well-matched veneers are essential for the top and the drawer fronts.

Beginning with the top, this would ideally be from the solid, however, you could get a stable and highly satisfactory result from using veneered blockboard. Such a material would need solid lippings all round but this need not be difficult as the profile of the moulding (Fig. 4A) only extends for an inch and so the lipping need only be, say, $1\frac{3}{4}$ inch (45 mm) wide by $1\frac{1}{4}$ inch (32 mm) thick.

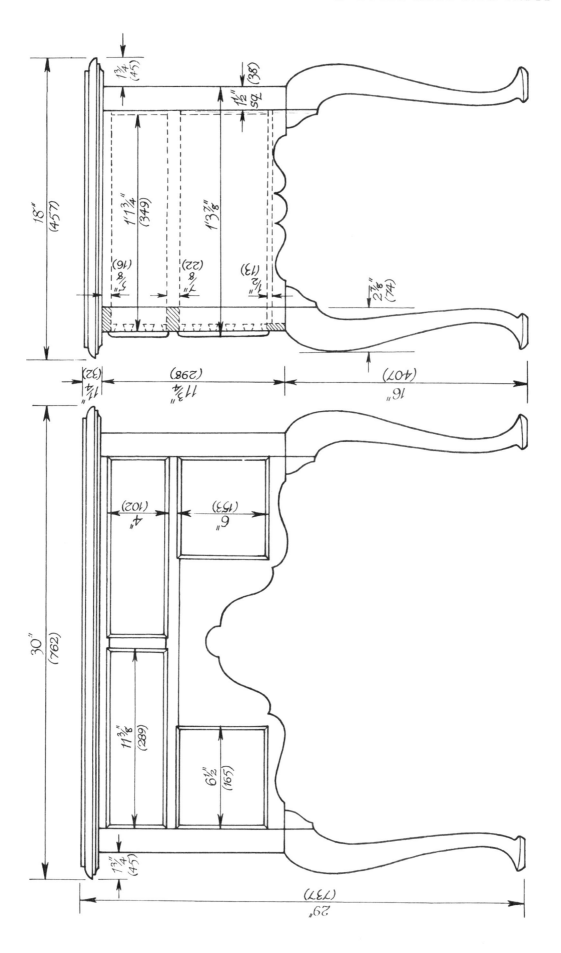

If you do do this, you must remember to add the requisite amount to the lengths of the corner posts, this being the difference in thickness between the blockboard and the lipping.

Fig. 3 shows an "exploded" view of the joints and the construction. The ends (C) should, if at all possible, come out of solid stuff: you could use veneered blockboard if you are prepared to veneer the shaped bottom edge. It would be advisable to lay the veneer all over before cutting the tongues, so you will have to allow for the extra thickness of the veneer when forming the mortises.

At first glance, it might be thought that the apron (B) could be dealt with in the same way, and so it could. But it would be better to go to some pains to use solid timber — the trouble is that the constant opening and shutting of the drawers may sooner or later cause the veneer to lift and splinter around the openings. A $\frac{1}{16}$ inch (2 mm) chamfer on the opening edges will prevent this. As you can see from Fig. 5, the drawer front has a $\frac{1}{4}$ inch (6 mm) overlap

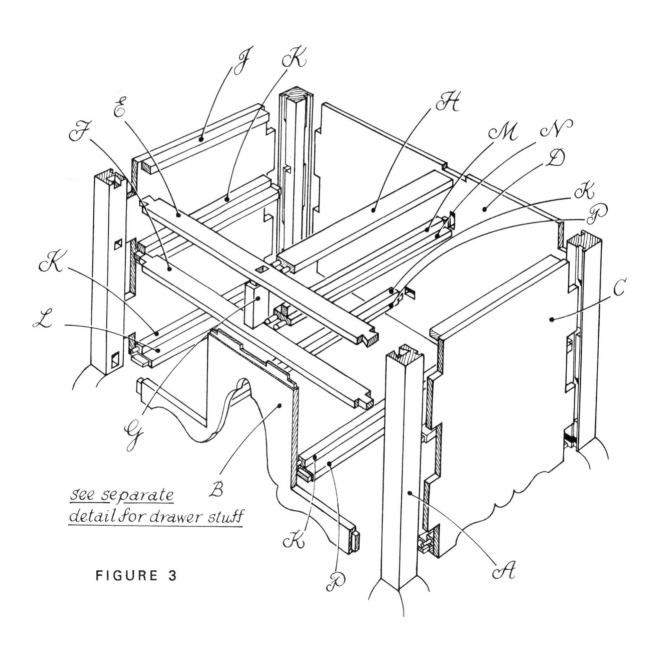

see separate detail for drawer stuff

FIGURE 3

all round.

Drawer construction and fitting are shown in Figs 3 and 5, and both are quite standard procedures. The method of making and shaping cabriole legs has also been dealt with in chapter 4.

Fig. 4A shows the profile of the top edge; (B) a half-shape for the front apron; (C) the shaping of the bottom edge of the end panel, and (D) the shape for the cabriole leg.

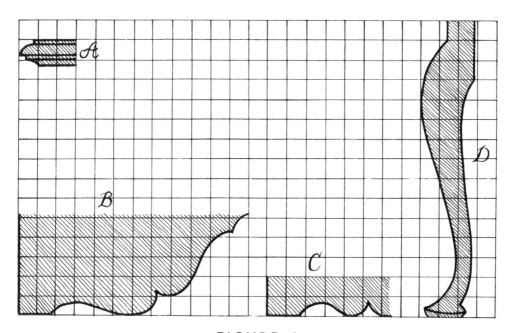

FIGURE 4

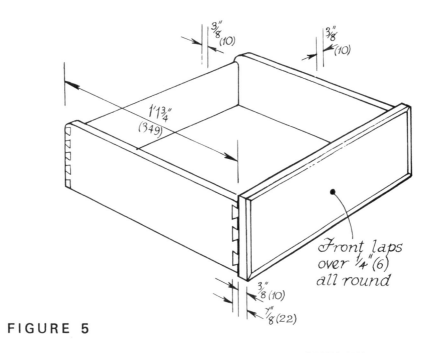

FIGURE 5

PARTS LIST *See over*

Parts List

No. req'd.	Description	Long	Wide	Thick
1	Top	31 (787)	19 (482)	1¼ (32)
4	Legs (A)	29 (736)	3 (76)	2⅞ (73)
1	Apron piece (B)	25½ (648)	8 (203)	¾ (19)
2	Ends (C)	15 (381)	12½ (318)	⅝ (14)
1	Back (D)	25½ (648)	12½ (318)	½ (12)
1	Front top rail (E)	25½ (648)	1¾ (45)	⅝ (14)
1	Front drawer rail (F)	25½ (648)	1¾ (45)	⅞ (23)
1	Drawer division (G)	5 (127)	1¾ (45)	1⅛ (29)
1	Centre rail (H)	13½ (343)	1¾ (45)	⅝ (14)
2	Kickers (J)	13 (330)	1 (25)	⅝ (14)
6	Drawer guides (K)	13 (330)	1 (25)	⅝ (14)
4	Drawer runners (L)	13 (330)	2 (51)	⅝ (14)
1	Centre guide (M)	.13½ (343)	1 (25)	1⅛ (29)
1	Centre runner (N)	13 (330)	2½ (64)	⅝ (14)
2	Drawer runners (P)	13½ (343)	2 (51)	⅝ (14)
2	Drawer fronts	12 (305)	4½ (115)	1¼ (32)
2	Drawer fronts	7½ (191)	6½ (165)	1¼ (32)
4	Drawer sides	14½ (369)	4 (102)	⅜ (10)
4	Drawer sides	14½ (369)	6½ (165)	⅜ (10)
2	Drawer backs	11½ (293)	4 (102)	⅜ (10)
2	Drawer backs	7 (178)	6½ (165)	⅜ (10)
2	Drawer bottoms	14½ (369)	12 (305)	¼ (7)
2	Drawer bottoms	14½ (369)	7 (178)	¼ (7)

Allowances have been made to lengths and widths; thicknesses are net.
Millimetre equivalents in brackets.

6. SEVENTEENTH CENTURY BOOK PRESS

FIGURE 1

The original of this design is one of a pair which flank a doorway in the Great Hall at Dyrham Park, near Bath, and we are indebted to the National Trust for permission to give details.

Although one press is an original, the other is a replica supplied by the Victoria and Albert Museum to replace one which they bought. They are of the same type as those designed by Samuel Pepys, the diarist, several of which are now housed in Magdalene College, Cambridge.

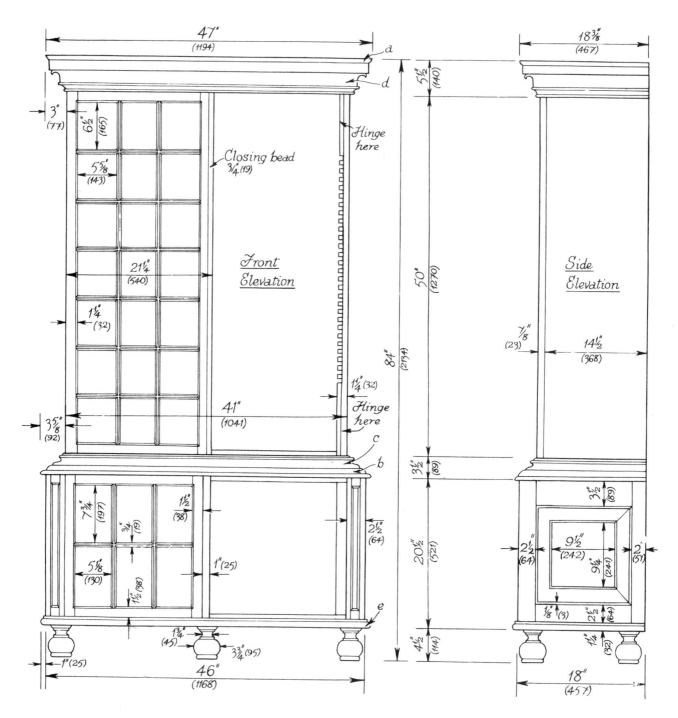

FIGURE 2

All of them (except the replica, of course) are reputed to have been made by Christopher Sympson, a Deptford ship's joiner, in 1666 and subsequent years.

The originals stand over 8 feet (2438 mm) tall, and 4 ft 8 in (1422 mm) wide, and as these sizes would be overpowering in most modern rooms, our design has been scaled down.

The whole job is made throughout in solid oak — not surprising, really, as oak was the staple timber of shipyards in those times.

The two ends (A) are the main part of the structure and are notable in that they run almost the whole height, and rest on the base rails, (C). Obviously, they carry an enormous weight when the press is full of books and this is probably the best way to carry the load without failure.

Another point to note with regard to the ends is that they are trenched out to form stopped housings for the shelves; Figs. 2 and 3. Each housing is about $\frac{5}{8}$ inch (16 mm) wide and $\frac{5}{16}$ inch (8 mm) deep, and the distance between them, centre to centre, is $1\frac{1}{4}$ inches (32 mm).

You may feel that you do not need so many divisions for shelf height, and it is, of course, your choice as to the final number decided on. However, it is essential that a non-trenched portion is left at top and bottom

to allow the hinges to be recessed in (Fig. 5), and each portion should be about 12 inches or so (305 mm).

In order to lighten the appearance of the edges of the ends when viewed from the front, they are rabbeted on the front edge $\frac{5}{16}$ in (8 mm) deep.

From Fig. 3 you will see that the base portion is built out by means of the two pieces (F) at each end, which enclose a narrow panel (J); fillets (H) are also used to give the appropriate width and to provide a groundwork for the waist moulding.

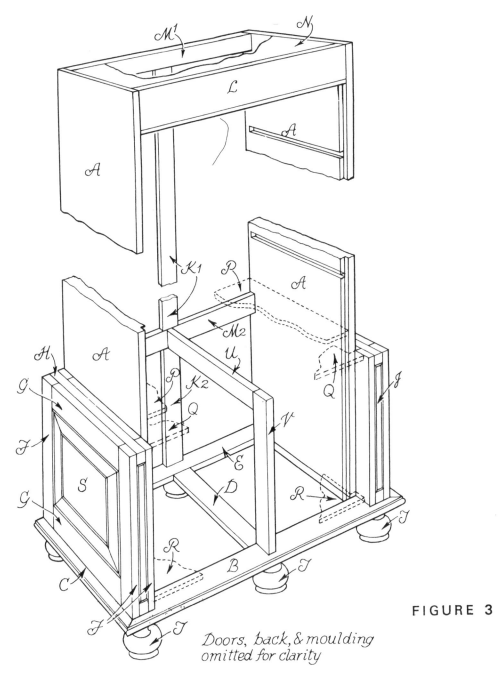

FIGURE 3

Doors, back, & moulding omitted for clarity

FIGURE 4

The panel (S) is a fielded panel with a bolection moulding applied around the centre. All joints on this framing, and indeed, on the remainder of the carcase are mortise and tenon, and in all cases the tenons are pegged.

Construction of the framework generally is straightforward as can be seen from Fig. 3. (P), (Q), and (R) are three linings which comprise the bottom of the main case, and the top and bottom of the base cupboard respectively. Both (Q) and (R) are notched round the case end on its front edge.

The shelves are of solid timber, spanning the entire width and were almost certainly made up from random widths jointed together. It was impracticable to move the press in order to examine the back, but in all probability the back panels would have been rabbeted in.

Now we come to the mouldings, and details of these are given in Fig. 4 — the letters (a), (b), (c) and (d) cross-refer to those in the front elevation in Fig. 2. There is, however, an additional moulding (e) shown on the base rail, and this is the traditional acanthus moulding shown in Fig. 37, page 35.

The drawings are meant to give you an indication of the style of each moulding and they will need to be elongated to match the actual curves.

The turned feet are straightforward, and should have a peg turned on the top for wedging through the base rails.

Although the cupboard doors are hinged in the conventional way, and lock into the centre muntin (V), the doors of the main case are the lay-on type and demanded a special kind of hinge.

This is shown in Fig. 5 and will have to be wrought by hand from iron about $\frac{1}{8}$ inch full (3 mm) thick. As you can see, it is a simple lift-off type of hinge with a loose pin. Fixing is achieved by means of dome-headed rivets, the heads of which are allowed to show.

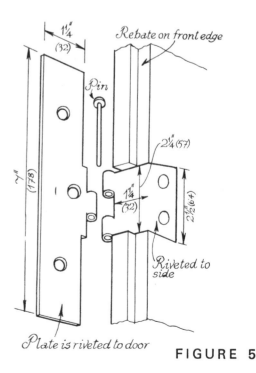

FIGURE 5

Parts List

No. req'd	Description	Long	Wide	Thick
2	Ends (A)	79 (2006)	15½ (394)	1¼ (32)
1	Base rail (B)	48 (1219)	5½ (140)	1¼ (32)
2	Base rail (C)	19½ (495)	5½ (140)	1¼ (32)
1	Middle rail (D)	12 (305)	4½ (115)	1¼ (32)
1	Back rail (E)	38½ (978)	4½ (115)	1¼ (32)
8	Stiles (F)	20 (508)	3¼ (83)	¾ (19)
8	Rails (G)	16 (407)	2½ (64)	¾ (19)
4	Fillets (H)	19 (483)	1½ (38)	1 (25)
4	Panels (J)	17½ (445)	1½ (38)	½ (13)
1	Back muntin (K1)	57½ (1460)	3¼ (83)	⅞ (23)
1	Back muntin (K2)	20½ (521)	3¼ (83)	⅞ (23)
1	Top frieze rail (L)	40 (1016)	5¼ (133)	¾ (19)
1	Top back rail (M1)	40 (1016)	3¼ (83)	⅞ (23)
1	Middle back rail (M2)	40 (1016)	3 (76)	⅞ (23)
1	Top (N)	40 (1016)	14¼ (362)	½ (13)
1	Lining (P)	38½ (978)	14½ (368)	½ (13)
1	Lining (Q)	41½ (1054)	17 (432)	½ (13)
1	Lining (R)	41½ (1054)	17 (432)	½ (13)
2	Panels (S)	15 (381)	14½ (368)	⅜ (10)
6	Feet (T)	6 (153)	4¼ (108)	3¾ (96)
1	Base middle rail (U)	14 (356)	3¼ (83)	⅞ (23)
1	Front muntin (V)	20 (508)	3¼ (83)	1 (25)
4	Case door stiles	51 (1295)	1½ (38)	⅞ (23)
4	Case door rails	20 (508)	1½ (38)	⅞ (23)

4	Long glazing bars	50 (1270)	1 (25)	$\frac{3}{4}$ (19)
6	Short glazing bars	19½ (495)	1 (25)	$\frac{3}{4}$ (19)
1	Closing bead	51 (1295)	1 (25)	$\frac{3}{8}$ (10)
4	Cupboard door stiles	20 (508)	1¾ (45)	$\frac{7}{8}$ (23)
4	Cupboard door rails	19 (483)	1¾ (45)	$\frac{7}{8}$ (23)
4	Vertical glazing bars	19 (483)	1 (25)	$\frac{3}{4}$ (19)
2	Horizontal glazing bars	18½ (470)	1 (25)	$\frac{3}{4}$ (19)
2	Upper back panels	51 (1295)	19 (483)	$\frac{3}{8}$ (10)
2	Lower back panels	19½ (495)	18 (457)	$\frac{3}{8}$ (10)
	Number of shelves to choice			$\frac{5}{8}$ (14)

Allowances have been made to lengths and widths; thicknesses are net.
Millimetre equivalents in brackets.

7. EARLY GEORGIAN-STYLE CORNER CHAIR

FIGURE 1

This elegant chair obviously demands a high standard of workmanship — even so, it has been considerably simplified when compared with the original, which was very heavily carved.

A design such as this calls for a good quality mahogany, although it would be acceptable to make it up in beech with a white painted finish and gilded decoration.

The methods of shaping cabriole legs and carving claw and ball feet have already been dealt with, and in the side elevation, Fig. 2, a one-inch (25 mm) grid has been drawn over the shape of one of the legs to enable you to plot the shape full-size.

Mortise and tenon joints are employed for

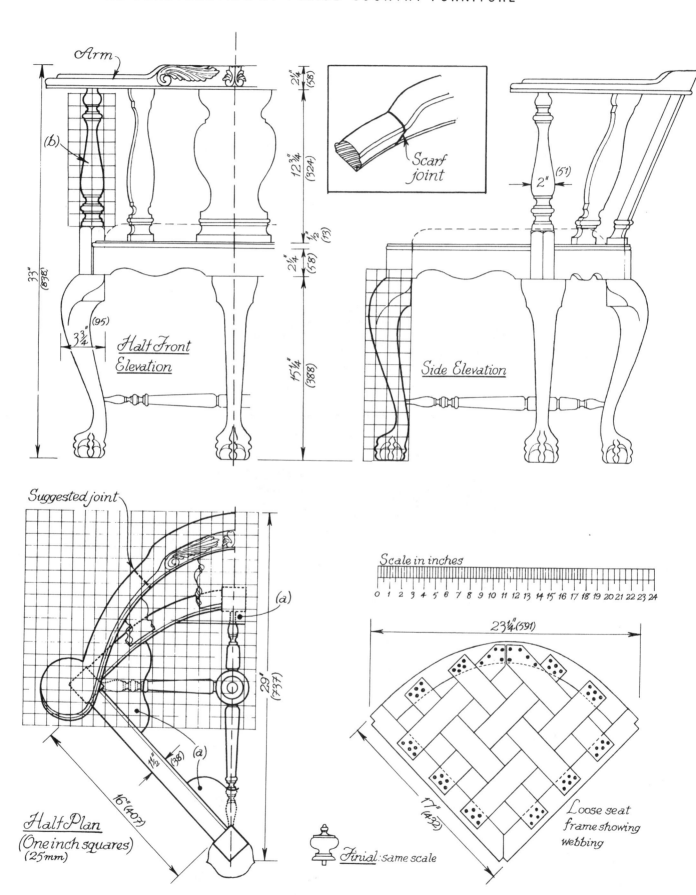

Arm

(b)

33"
(838)

3¾" (95)

Half Front Elevation

2¼" (58)

12¾" (324)

½" (13)

2¼" (58)

15¼" (388)

Scarf joint

2" (51)

Side Elevation

Suggested joint

(a)

29' (737)

1½" (38)

(a)

16" (407)

Half Plan
(One inch squares)
(25mm)

Scale in inches

0 1 2 3 4 5 6 7 8 9 10 11 12 13 14 15 16 17 18 19 20 21 22 23 24

23¼" (591)

17" (432)

Loose seat frame showing webbing

Finial: same scale

FIGURE 2

joining the seat rails to the top squares of the legs; note that the curved back seat rail is divided into two halves, each half being tenoned into the top square of the back leg. A further point to note is that these two rails are deep-cut from the solid, although it would be possible to steam-bend them. Also, on the two legs without turned columns, the moulding on the rail edge is worked through on the edge of the top square.

Before the seat rails are assembled, a rabbet $\frac{1}{4}$ inch (6 mm) wide by $\frac{3}{8}$ inch (10 mm) deep needs to be worked on the upper, inner edge to accept the loose seat. Although the rabbet does afford support for the loose seat, its other function is to prevent a gap being formed between the seat frame and the loose seat through which daylight could be seen.

Further supports for the loose seat are the seat brackets shown at (a) in the half-plan, Fig. 2, and these are screwed and glued in position; they also serve to strengthen the leg and rail joints.

When assembling the underframing, the ends of the stretchers can have a small saw-cut made longitudinally in each of them with a tiny wedge inserted; as the stretcher is glued up and driven home there will be a wedging effect which will hold it firmly; the method is illustrated in Fig. 4. The hole will need to be of such a size as to allow for the expansion of the joint.

As you can see, the cabriole legs are fashioned from 3$\frac{3}{4}$ inch (95 mm) squares, and it would be both difficult and wasteful to turn down the columns marked (b) in the half front elevation, Fig. 2. Accordingly, these two columns are turned as separate pieces with a pin at each end; the lower pin is glued into a hole bored in the top of the leg square, while the upper pin engages in a similar hole bored in the underside of the curved arm.

The central and side banisters are fixed in the same way by means of mortises slotted in the curved back seat rail — the central banister (A), Fig. 3, has twin tenons, while the side banister (B) has a single tenon.

On the original chair, the bottom member at the foot of the banisters is perpendicular to the seat rail and the slope starts immediately above it. This was cut from the solid, as was the ovolo moulding above it, and in order to avoid wasting timber, it is

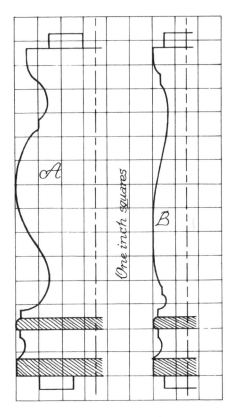

One inch squares

FIGURE 3

suggested that the effect is simulated by pinning and gluing planted mouldings on to the face of the banister, as shown by the shaded portions in Fig. 3.

The arm should, ideally, be sawn from one piece, but if this is impracticable because of the large size needed, it could be made in three pieces. In the half-plan, Fig. 2, you will see the position of the suggested joint which should be a scarfed joint as shown in the inset, also the shape of the arm can be marked out from the squared-off drawing.

FIGURE 4

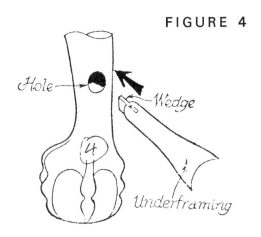

Hole

Wedge

Underframing

The joint could be further strengthened by recessing and screwing on a metal plate to the underside.

A suitable acanthus leaf carving can be adapted from that shown in Chapter 4, while the central motif is a simple anthenion-style design.

Details of the loose seat frame are shown in Fig. 2, and it is webbed with three 2 inch (51 mm) webs each way. Stuffing could well be in the form of a curled hair pad with a canvas backing which should be stitched to the webbing in several places to prevent it moving about during use. An under-cover of linen or similar close-woven material should be tacked over the hair pad, followed by the final cover which, in the original, was leather. A piece of black canvas can be tacked over the underside to impart a neat finish.

When making the loose seat, do try to ensure that the curved rail is one piece and not jointed, as it is subjected to great strain. It is also worth making the loose seat frame slightly oversize so that there is enough surplus to allow it to be trimmed to size by hand.

Parts List

No. req'd	Description	Long	Wide	Thick
2	Legs	18½ (470)	4 (102)	3¾ (95)
2	Legs	19¾ (502)	4 (102)	3¾ (95)
2	Straight seat rails	18 (457)	2½ (64)	1½ (38)
2	Curved back seat rails	15 (381)	2½ (64)	3 (76)
2	Arm pieces (side)	14½ (368)	6 (152)	1¼ (32)
1	Arm piece (centre)	18 (457)	7 (178)	2¼ (58)
3	Stretchers	11¼ (286)	1½ (38)	1¼ (32)
1	Stretcher	6¼ (159)	1½ (38)	1¼ (32)
1	Centre boss	3 (76)	3 (76)	1¼ (32)
1	Centre banister	16 (407)	7½ (89)	¾ (19)
2	Side banisters	16 (407)	3½ (191)	¾ (19)
2	Loose seat rails: straight	17½ (445)	2 (51)	1 (25)
1	Loose seat rail: curved	24 (609)	7 (178)	1 (25)
2	Columns	13 (330)	2½ (64)	2½ (64)

Seat brackets and finial from scrap

Allowances have been made to lengths and widths: thicknesses are net.
Millimetre equivalents in brackets.

8. TRIPOD TABLE

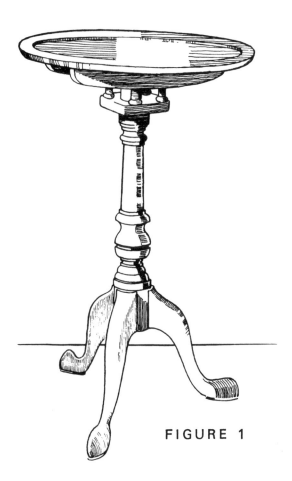

FIGURE 1

This elegant little table is in the style of many similar eighteenth century pieces and could be used either as an afternoon tea table or a wine table.

One of the most interesting points about it is that it embodies a "birdcage" movement under the top. This acts rather like a simple "universal" joint, in that the top is capable of being tilted to a vertical plane and also being rotated while in that position, thus allowing the table to stand near to a wall when not in use.

Although our design has a circular top with a simple moulding around the edge, it would also be eminently suitable as a table with a piecrust top (described in chapter 4), or it could be fitted up with a small, pierced gallery.

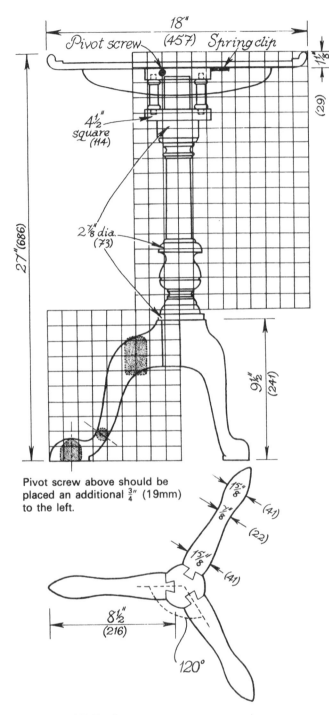

Pivot screw above should be placed an additional ¾" (19mm) to the left.

FIGURE 2

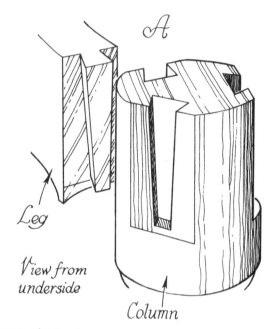

FIGURE 3

here is that there should be a smooth, snug fit — no tightness but no sloppiness.

Probably the trickiest stage of the job is the cutting of the dovetails on the legs and the corresponding sockets on the base of the column. As you can see from Fig. 3 (A),

and from the plan view in Fig. 2, you will have first to chisel "flats" before marking out the sockets. Both the dovetails and the sockets are slightly tapered and there is a good reason for this. If they were left parallel, then the parts would be held together tightly as soon as one entered the other; any tiny surplus or extra tightness could split the wood without warning. On the other hand, the tapered dovetail will not start to tighten until it is right home in its socket and should there be any need to ease any "high spots" then you will at least know about them before any damage is done.

If possible, the top should be turned to its finished appearance entirely on the lathe as this will guarantee accuracy and uniformity — further, the awkward problem of working end grain is greatly reduced.

The top could, however, be shaped by means of a power router: it is an ideal job for a portable router as all such models have a jig of one kind or another for routing circles.

Turning the column is the main job, and there should be no difficulties here. Note that the upper end is reduced to form a shank (B, Fig. 3) which is 1¾ inch (45 mm) diameter, and corresponding holes to accept it have to be cut in the top and bottom pieces of the birdcage. The point to watch

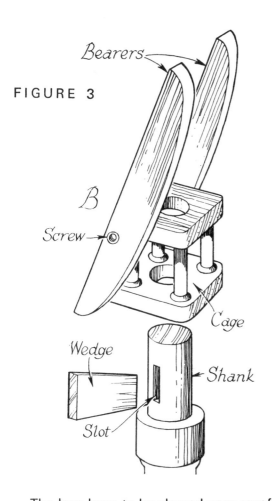

FIGURE 3

The legs have to be shaped very carefully as the slightest deviation from the traditional style can spoil the appearance of the whole job. So the first step is to transfer the shape from Fig. 2 to a piece of card, and the drawing has been divided into 1 inch (25 mm) squares for this purpose.

Next, before you start the shaping, cut and plane the sole of the foot and the face of the dovetail at right angles to each other. It is difficult to explain the precise method of shaping in words and you would undoubtedly find it helpful to study good examples of similar tables in museums or at a reputable antique dealer.

However, some dimensions and sections are shown in the plan in Fig. 2; at the ankle the leg is $\frac{7}{8}$ inch (22 mm) thick and is almost circular. The shape then flows away from this until it approximates to a rectangle with its top slightly rounded and the bottom corners slightly rounded off.

The birdcage is made up from a top and bottom piece joined together with four small pillars (Fig. 3B); these have small pins turned top and bottom which are glued into place. A slot is cut right through the shank to accept the wedge and this slot is positioned so that it lies wholly in the space between the top and bottom of the birdcage. Also, the wedge must not be so long as to foul any of the pillars when it turns.

The two curved bearers are each pivoted on a brass screw which is fitted with a screw-cup for easy movement. They are then screwed to the underside of the top by slot-screwing to accommodate any movement. If you align the bearers at right angles to the direction of the grain of the top, this should further minimize this trouble. A suitable spring-catch will need to be fitted (Fig. 2) to prevent the top tilting when in the horizontal position.

PARTS LIST *See over*

Parts List

No. req'd	Description	Long	Wide	Thick
1	Top	19 (482)	$18\frac{1}{2}$ (470)	$1\frac{1}{8}$ (29)
1	Column	21 (533)	$3\frac{1}{4}$ (83)	$2\frac{7}{8}$ (73)
3	Legs, each	$10\frac{1}{2}$ (267)	9 (229)	$1\frac{5}{8}$ (42)
2	Bearers	$14\frac{1}{4}$ (362)	$2\frac{1}{4}$ (57)	$\frac{3}{4}$ (19)
2	Birdcage top and bottom	5 (127)	$4\frac{3}{4}$ (121)	$\frac{3}{4}$ (19)
4	Pillars	$3\frac{1}{2}$ (89)	1 (25)	$\frac{7}{8}$ (22)
1	Wedge from scrap			

Allowances have been made to lengths and widths; thicknesses are net.
Millimetre equivalents in brackets.

9. NINETEENTH CENTURY-STYLE ÉTAGÈRE (WHATNOT)

FIGURE 1

This type of display stand for bric-a-brac and trinkets was popular in the late eighteenth century, and even more so throughout the nineteenth. Basically it is quite a simple design and does not use much timber; making one up will reward you with an attractive and useful piece of occasional furniture.

The design is reminiscent of Chippendale and, strictly speaking, should be constructed of mahogany. However, walnut would be equally acceptable, particularly if the panels were covered with a showy veneer – a burr walnut, for instance, or amboyna.

Essentially the piece comprises four legs

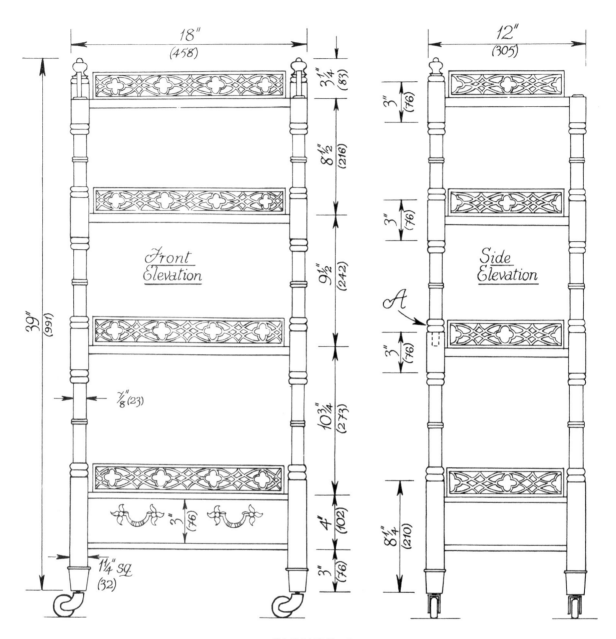

FIGURE 2

joined by five frames; the lower two of the latter are boxed in to contain a small drawer, while the remaining three are infilled with veneered panels.

If the leg is too long to fit between the centres of your lathe for turning, then it could be made up in two parts. Point A in the side elevation, Fig. 2, shows where the two pieces can be joined — either by a peg turned on one part being glued into a mating hole on the other, or by means of a loose pin.

Fig. 3 shows how the frame rails are tenoned into the legs by means of off-set tenons. This arrangement ensures that the tenons do not foul each other inside the leg. Of course, the joint could also be made with tenons arranged normally provided that each tenon is mitred.

Note that the inner edges of the frame rails are rabbeted $\frac{3}{8}$ in by $\frac{3}{8}$ in (10 mm × 10 mm) to accept the veneered panels, and that the corners of the rabbet are mitred.

The patterns for the small gallery rails are shown in Fig. 4, pattern A being for the ends, and B for the backs. The front of each tier is, of course, left open. Fig. 4 is divided into one inch (25 mm) squares so that the patterns can easily be transcribed — one half of each is shown, and when this has been drawn it can be turned over and traced through to complete the design.

A machine fretsaw would be ideal for cutting out the patterns as it could cope with 3 or 4 at one pass. Failing this, the bolder parts could be cut away with a coping saw while using a hand fretsaw for the more delicate cuts; this would mean cutting one piece at a time. When finished, each could

FIGURE 3

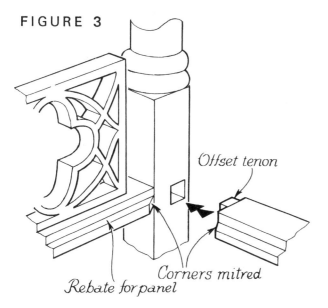

Offset tenon

Corners mitred

Rebate for panel

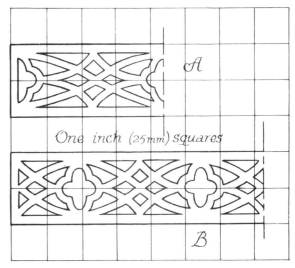

A

One inch (25mm) squares

B

FIGURE 4

be fixed by gluing and screws driven through from under the rail.

The drawer is a conventional one, and the construction of similar ones has been given elsewhere in the book. The front is veneered, while the side panels and back can be of solid wood, tongued into the frame rails and legs. Typical Chippendale-style handles are shown but these could be replaced by turned wooden knobs if desired.

PARTS LIST *See over*

Parts List

No. req'd	Description	Long	Wide	Thick
2	Legs	40 (1016)	$1\frac{1}{2}$ (39)	$1\frac{1}{4}$ (32)
2	Legs	37 (940)	$1\frac{1}{2}$ (39)	$1\frac{1}{4}$ (32)
10	Frame rails, long	17 (432)	$1\frac{1}{2}$ (39)	$\frac{3}{4}$ (19)
10	Frame rails, short	11 (279)	$1\frac{3}{8}$ (35)	$\frac{3}{4}$ (19)
4	Panels	16 (407)	10 (254)	$\frac{1}{4}$ (6)
1	Bottom	16 (407)	10 (254)	$\frac{3}{16}$ (5)
4	Gallery rails, long	15 (381)	$2\frac{1}{4}$ (58)	$\frac{3}{8}$ (10)
4	Gallery rails, short	9 (228)	$2\frac{1}{4}$ (58)	$\frac{3}{8}$ (10)
1	Drawer front	$15\frac{1}{2}$ (394)	$3\frac{1}{4}$ (83)	$\frac{1}{2}$ (13)
2	End panels	$10\frac{1}{4}$ (261)	4 (102)	$\frac{1}{4}$ (6)
1	Back panel	$16\frac{1}{4}$ (413)	4 (102)	$\frac{1}{4}$ (6)
2	Drawer sides	$9\frac{1}{2}$ (241)	$3\frac{1}{4}$ (83)	$\frac{1}{4}$ (6)
1	Drawer bottom	$15\frac{1}{2}$ (394)	10 (254)	$\frac{3}{16}$ (5)
1	Drawer back	$15\frac{1}{2}$ (394)	3 (76)	$\frac{3}{16}$ (5)
2	Drawer rails	$9\frac{1}{2}$ (242)	$1\frac{1}{2}$ (39)	$\frac{3}{4}$ (19)
2	Drawer guides	$9\frac{1}{2}$ (242)	$\frac{3}{4}$ (19)	$\frac{1}{2}$ (13)

Allowances have been made to lengths and widths; thicknesses are net.
Millimetre equivalents in brackets.

10. FARTHINGALE CHAIR

FIGURE 1

This design of chair was introduced in the time of James I specifically to accommodate the huge "farthingale" dresses of the period. The main feature of such dresses was the enormous hooped skirt which made it impossible for the lady to sit in any kind of armchair without crushing her apparel.

Construction follows standard procedure, but note that the seat rails are set flush with the outside faces of the front legs, and do not stand back, as is usual. This is so that the fringe and gimp can be nailed on to present a trim appearance.

It would be advisable to use mortise and

tenon joints throughout, except for the back seat rail. Here, the problem arises that the tenons on the side seat rail and the back seat rail could easily foul each other, and in any event, cutting two mortises would inevitably weaken the leg.

Accordingly, it would be a worthwhile plan to retain tenons on the side seat rails, and to use dowels on the back seat rail, arranging them to penetrate the tenons and "pin" them.

Quite a variety of materials was used to stuff early upholstery, amongst them dried seaweed, dried moss, wood shavings, wool, and animal hair — usually hogshair or horsehair.

For our purposes, hair would probably be best for the back upholstery. It can be bought ready-fixed to a canvas base; the latter can then be stitched to the webs to prevent it sliding about.

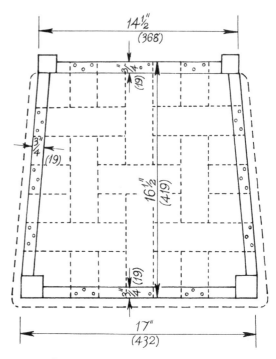

Seat Plan at A-A

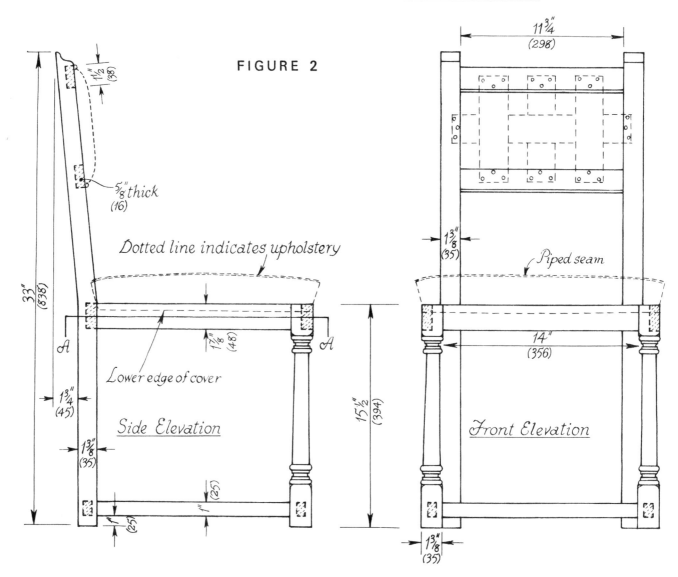

FIGURE 2

Dotted line indicates upholstery

Lower edge of cover

Side Elevation

Piped seam

Front Elevation

It's worth noting that hair should always be covered with a closely-woven material such as cotton duck before being upholstered with the final cover, otherwise odd strands of prickly hair will insinuate themselves through the material, to the discomfort of the occupant!

The seat is rather more complicated, and you will need to use a piped seam in order to achieve the "wedge" effect. This means sewing a length of piping cord into the seams between the edge-panel and the top.

Again, use a hair pad for the base of the seat filling and sew it to the seat webs. The main filling could be a form of wadding such as cotton linters, making sure it is well rammed home to create the desired shape.

The bottom edges of the cover can be tacked to the outside of the side and front rails and to the inside of the back seat rail. Either a length of gimp or braid can be pinned on to mask the tacks and, finally, a fringe can also be close-nailed in place.

Parts List

No. req'd.	Description	Long	Wide	Thick
2	Back legs	34 (863)	$3\frac{3}{4}$ (95)	$1\frac{3}{8}$ (35)
2	Front legs	$16\frac{1}{2}$ (419)	$1\frac{5}{8}$ (41)	$1\frac{3}{8}$ (35)
1	Front seat rail	16 (406)	$2\frac{1}{4}$ (58)	$\frac{3}{4}$ (19)
2	Side seat rails	$16\frac{1}{2}$ (419)	$2\frac{1}{4}$ (58)	$\frac{3}{4}$ (19)
1	Back seat rail	13 (330)	$2\frac{1}{4}$ (58)	$\frac{3}{4}$ (19)
1	Front under-rail	15 (381)	$1\frac{1}{4}$ (32)	$\frac{5}{8}$ (13)
2	Side under-rails	16 (406)	$1\frac{1}{4}$ (32)	$\frac{5}{8}$ (13)
1	Back under-rail	13 (330)	$1\frac{1}{4}$ (32)	$\frac{5}{8}$ (13)
2	Back rails	13 (330)	$1\frac{3}{4}$ (45)	$\frac{5}{8}$ (13)

Allowances have been made to lengths and widths; thicknesses are net.
Millimetre equivalents in brackets.

11. QUEEN ANNE-STYLE CORNER CABINET

FIGURE 1

Corner cabinets are always popular designs as they offer display and accommodation for precious things while occupying the minimum of space. This piece is no exception, and it relies largely upon the use of choicely-figured timber for its attractiveness, plus the Queen Anne touches in the capping moulding and the heads of the doors.

The drawings in Fig. 2A, 2B, and 2D show the plan, front elevation, and a section respectively with all the dimensions marked. Fig. 2C is an "exploded" view which shows the method of construction.

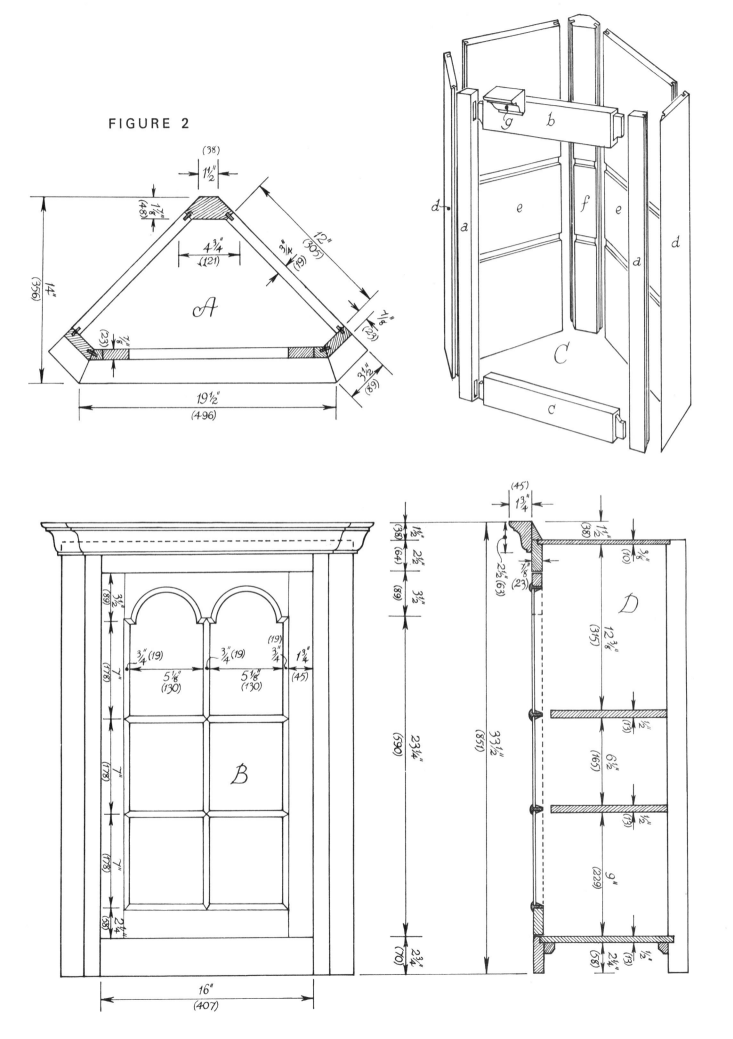

FIGURE 2

A cabinet of this period really calls for the use of walnut, but, of course, mahogany would be an agreeable substitute. From Fig. 2C you will see that all the parts (except for the top and bottom which can be plywood) are assumed to be cut from the solid. The form of jointing is by means of loose tongues glued into grooves on the meeting edges as detailed in the plan, Fig. 2A.

However, this method of jointing would be equally suitable for veneered blockboard or plywood panels, so there is no objection to using them.

As far as the carcase of the cabinet is concerned, construction is perfectly straightforward. You can see from Fig. 2C, that the front framing is made up with mortise and tenon joints, while the capping moulding is glued and screwed to the top of the carcase with the screws inserted from the back. A triangular fillet is then glued behind it as shown in Fig. 2D.

What kind of support you provide for the shelves is your choice, the criterion being whether you want them to be fixed or adjustable.

Fig. 2C shows one way of dealing with fixed shelves which is neat and unobtrusive. It involves cutting housings into the ends (e) and the rear post (f) in which the shelves rest. An alternative method is to glue and screw on shelf bearers.

Details of the door are shown at Fig. 3A, B, and C, and, again, you can see that the construction is simple enough. The barred-door moulding (Fig. 3B) can be in a contrasting wood if desired and in any case it should be a timber which can readily be bent to fit round the curves at the top of the door.

A tricky job is making the two right-angle joints on the centre bead, and this is illustrated at Fig. 3C. Essentially it is a halved joint, the curved section being mitred as shown. The glass can be puttied in in the traditional way, although unless it is done very carefully it can look rather untidy. As an alternative you could use an epoxy such as "Araldite", with a few small veneer pins as additional fastenings.

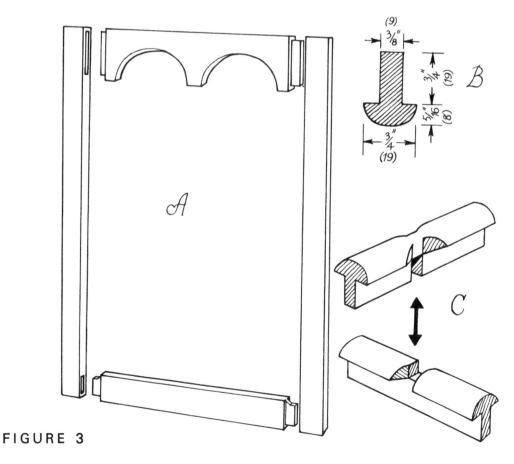

FIGURE 3

Parts List

No. req'd.	Description	Long	Wide	Thick
2	Framing stiles (*a*)	33 (838)	1½ (38)	⅞ (23)
1	Top frame rail (*b*)	18½ (470)	2¾ (70)	⅞ (23)
1	Bottom frame rail (*c*)	18½ (470)	3 (76)	⅞ (23)
2	Corner pieces (*d*)	33 (838)	3¾ (96)	⅞ (23)
2	Ends (*e*)	33 (838)	12½ (318)	¾ (19)
1	Back post (*f*)	33 (838)	5 (127)	1⅞ (48)
1	Top	21½ (546)	10½ (267)	⅜ (10)
1	Bottom	21½ (546)	10½ (267)	½ (13)
2	Shelves	21½ (546)	10½ (267)	½ (13)
2	Door stiles	27½ (698)	2 (51)	⅞ (23)
1	Door top rail	17¼ (438)	3¾ (95)	⅞ (23)
1	Door bottom rail	17¼ (438)	2½ (64)	⅞ (23)
1	Capping moulding	20½ (521)	2¾ (70)	1¾ (45)
2	Capping moulding	3¾ (96)	2¾ (70)	1¾ (45)
	Barred-door moulding	120 (3046)	1¼ (32)	¾ (19)

Allowances have been made to lengths and widths; thicknesses are net.
Millimetre equivalents in brackets.

12. EIGHTEENTH CENTURY-STYLE DINING TABLE

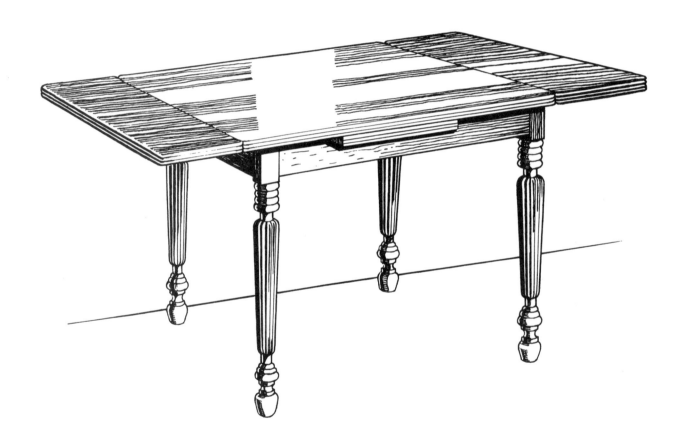

This table shows the influence of Sheraton in the elegantly reeded turned legs and the matching reeding around the edges of the top. Although the method of extending leaves is not strictly in period it is straightforward to make and trouble-free in operation.

The beauty of a table like this lies in the grain and figure of the top, and if possible solid wood should be used. Alternatively, well-matched veneered panels could be framed up, although a solid top is shown in the drawings.

From the plan in Fig. 2, you will see that

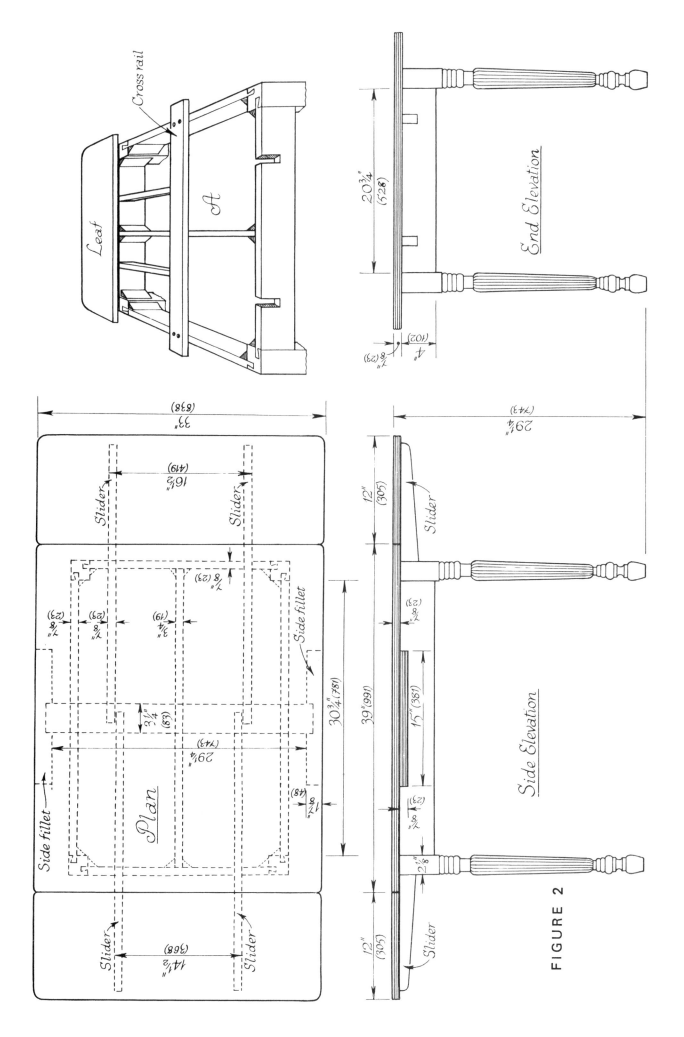

Cross rail

Leaf

A

End Elevation

20¼" (528)

⅞" (23)

4" (102)

33" (838)

Slider

16½" (419)

Slider

⅞" (23)

⅞" (23)

¾" (19)

Side fillet

Side fillet

Plan

29¼" (743)

3¼" (83)

1⅞" (48)

30¾" (781)

Slider

14½" (368)

Slider

Side fillet →

Side Elevation

29¼" (743)

12" (305)

Slider

⅞" (23)

39" (991)

15" (381)

⅞" (23)

2⅛"

12" (305)

Slider

FIGURE 2

the main frame of the table (shown in dotted lines) is conventional in construction. The rails are slot-dovetailed into the legs, each joint being strengthened with glue blocks. An additional rail is screwed in centrally, parallel to the longer sides and, again, glue blocks are used.

Note the cross-rail which is screwed across the top of the table frame (A, Fig. 2). This does, of course, greatly reinforce the frame but its real function is to prevent the inner ends of the sliders rising when any weight is applied to the leaf.

The main part of the top is called the ''bed'', and all four edges are reeded. Two side fillets (Fig. 2, plan) are screwed and glued to the underside of the top with the outer edge of each flush with the top edge, and reeded to match.

The function of these side fillets is two-fold. From the plan, Fig. 2, you will see that a ¾ in deep (19 mm) notch is taken out on the inside edge of each fillet to accommodate the end of the cross-rail, thus enabling the ''bed'' to be located easily on the main frame. Additionally, they serve to fill the gap which would otherwise exist when the leaves are in the closed position.

To open or close the leaves, the ''bed'' is lifted up slightly at the appropriate end and the leaf can then be drawn out from under it. A point to note here is that the underside of the ''bed'' should have baize or felt strips glued to it to prevent the leaf being scratched as it is operated.

The depth of the slots for the sliders is best achieved by trial and error; start with a depth of about 1½ inches (38 mm) and ease it out until the correct depth is obtained.

Fig. 3 shows the shape of a slider — note the position of the dowel peg, which prevents the leaf being accidentally pulled out completely.

The same illustration also shows the pattern for the leg, which has 12 reeds. Turning the leg is straightforward enough, but working the reeds can be tricky. They would best be made entirely by hand by fixing each in the lathe and carving the reeds with a Vee tool and a skew chisel. Finish them off by wrapping a piece of glasspaper around a pointed stick which will fit the grooves. The lathe tool rest will be invaluable as a guide for marking out and for steadying your hand while carving.

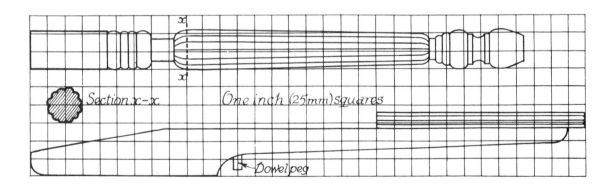

Section x-x.   One inch (25mm) squares

Dowel peg

FIGURE 3

Parts List

No. req'd	Description	Long	Wide	Thick
1	Bed	40 (1016)	34 (864)	$\frac{7}{8}$ (23)
2	Leaves, each	34 (864)	13 (330)	$\frac{7}{8}$ (23)
4	Legs	30 (762)	$2\frac{1}{4}$ (58)	$2\frac{1}{8}$ (54)
2	Table frame rails, long	34 (864)	$4\frac{1}{4}$ (108)	$\frac{7}{8}$ (23)
2	Table frame rails, short	24 (610)	$4\frac{1}{4}$ (108)	$\frac{7}{8}$ (23)
1	Centre frame rail	34 (864)	$4\frac{1}{4}$ (108)	$\frac{3}{4}$ (19)
1	Cross rail	31 (787)	$3\frac{1}{2}$ (89)	$\frac{7}{8}$ (23)
4	Sliders	32 (813)	3 (76)	$\frac{7}{8}$ (23)
2	Side fillets	$15\frac{1}{2}$ (388)	2 (51)	$\frac{7}{8}$ (23)

Glue blocks from scrap.

Allowances have been made to lengths and widths; thicknesses are net.
Millimetre equivalents in brackets.

13. SHERATON-STYLE CHAIR

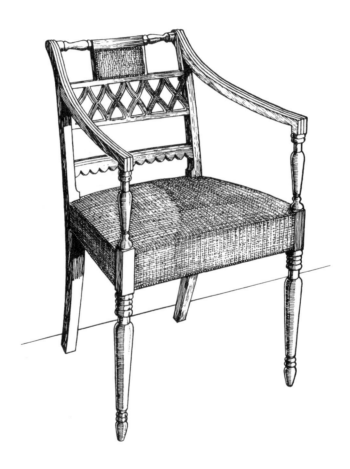

FIGURE 1

The design of this chair is derived from one in the Parker Knoll Chair Museum at Brympton d'Evercy in Somerset.

To combine delicacy with strength such a chair demands the use of best quality timber and for a polished finish the obvious choice would be a good class mahogany.

However, chairs of this type were frequently made up in beech and painted, and this would be a very acceptable substitute.

The seat rails are mortise and tenoned into the front and back legs in the usual manner, but the joint between the top end of the arm and the back leg is rather special. It

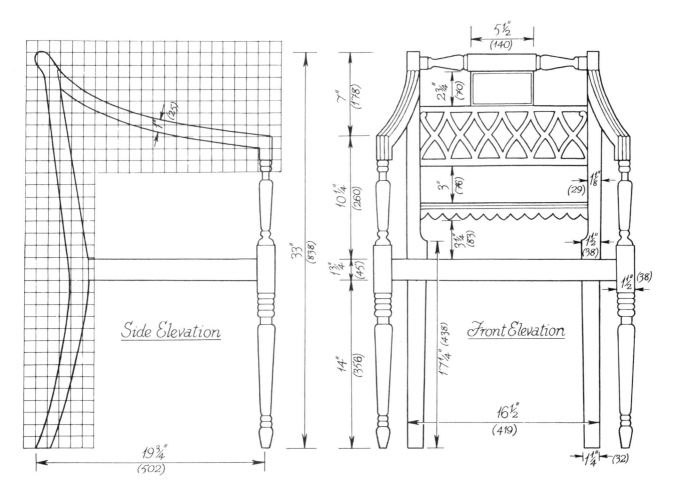

Side Elevation

Front Elevation

FIGURE 2

is illustrated in Fig. 4A and you will see that it is made with loose dowels; a point to note is that the leading edge of the joint on the arm is cut off to fit into a corresponding rabbet in the back leg, thus avoiding a feather edge.

Note, too, that the lower end of the arm terminates in almost a right angle bend which is dowelled into the top of the front leg.

All rails in the back are slightly curved (see plan, Fig. 2). The top back rail consists of three parts — the central square, plus a turned spindle at each side of it; these spindles have pins turned on which fit into the central square and the back legs respectively. The lattice frame would have been deep-cut from solid, and it finishes ½ inch (13 mm) thick. Similarly, the pelmetted rail also needs to be cut from the solid and finishes ¾ inch thick (19 mm). The alternative

Upholstery omitted for clarity

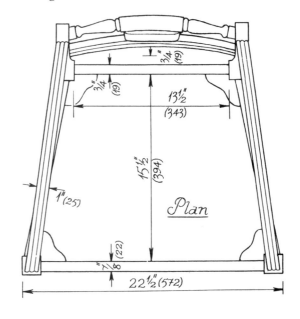

Plan

to deep-cutting the lattice frame is to steam-bend it, and in this case it should be made in beech. If the pattern is cut out before bending, the job will be much easier.

Small dowels can also be used to fix the small upholstered back panel in place, and this need not follow the curve.

Start by tacking on three 2 inch (51 mm) webs each way on the top edges of the seat rails. Next comes the stuffing and the handiest stuff to use is a pad of curled hair which is already mounted on a canvas backing. This enables you to stitch the canvas backing to the webs to anchor it so that it does

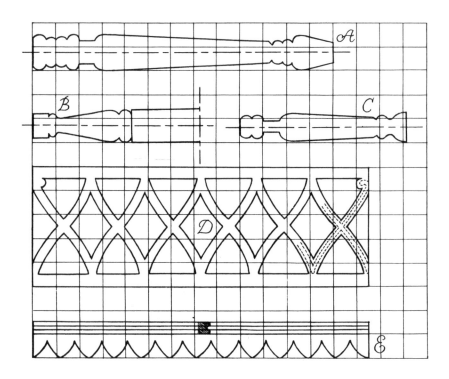

FIGURE 3

Fig. 3 shows at (A), the pattern for the front leg; at (B) the half-elevation of the top back rail; at (C) a pattern for the stump; at (D) the lattice design for the main panel, which is fret-cut from the solid; and at (E) the pattern for the pelmetted rail. If desired, a simple channelling can be worked on (D) as shown by the dotted lines.

The seat brackets shown in the plan, Fig. 2, should be screwed and glued in position towards the lower edges of the seat rails so that the webbing does not foul them when the seat is occupied.

Now to the stuffover upholstery. You will see that all seat rails are set back from the edges of the legs by $\frac{3}{16}$ inch or so (5 mm) to allow for the thickness of the covering materials.

not move about in use. In addition you can distribute a few handfuls of loose hair on top of the pad to achieve a domed effect. Again, this will need a few long criss-cross stitches to keep it in place.

Once a good shape has been obtained, a piece of calico or similarly close-woven cloth should be tacked on over the stuffing — the method of cutting this to fit at the corners is shown at (B), Fig. 4. This will prevent the hair working through but to make absolutely sure (and to get a nicely rounded effect), a layer of thin wadding should be stitched over the work.

The final cover can now be cut to shape, fitting it around the legs as already mentioned. As the cover will almost certainly be expensive, it's a good idea to make a pattern first from some scrap material.

Fixing the cover is easy as it can be held in the first instance by means of gimp pins, followed by close-nailing with roundheaded nails. The small back pad is simply stuffed with wadding, with the cover close-nailed all round.

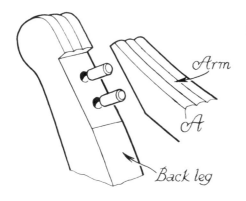

FIGURE 4

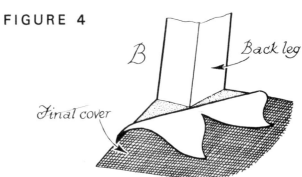

Parts List

No. req'd	Description	Long	Wide	Thick
2	Back legs	34 (864)	6 (152)	1½ (38)
2	Front legs	25 (635)	1¾ (45)	1½ (38)
2	Arms	23 (584)	4 (102)	1⅛ (29)
1	Front seat rail	21½ (546)	2 (51)	⅞ (23)
1	Back seat rail	15 (381)	2 (51)	⅞ (23)
2	Side seat rails	17 (432)	2 (51)	⅞ (23)
1	Top back rail	16 (407)	2¼ (57)	1⅜ (35)
1	Lattice frame*	16 (407)	5½ (141)	1¼ (32)
1	Back pelmet rail	16 (407)	1¾ (44)	1½ (38)
1	Back pad	6 (152)	3 (77)	½ (13)

Seat brackets from scrap

Allowances have been made to lengths and widths; thicknesses are net.
Millimetre equivalents shown in brackets.

* The Lattice Frame can be ½ in (12 mm) thick if it has to be bent.

14. JACOBEAN OVAL GATE-LEG TABLE

FIGURE 1

This sturdy and useful table is typical of the work which would have been turned out by a country carpenter of this period. One could say, in fact, that it is one of the last examples of furniture made before the advent of cabinet-making as a separate trade.

Solid timber is needed throughout and, traditionally, it should be oak; however, ash could be used for the framework of the bed. The top calls for selected stuff which will almost certainly need to be jointed to obtain the requisite width. A ball-faced edge is worked round the top and the hinge-joint is, of course, a rule joint. Details of this type of

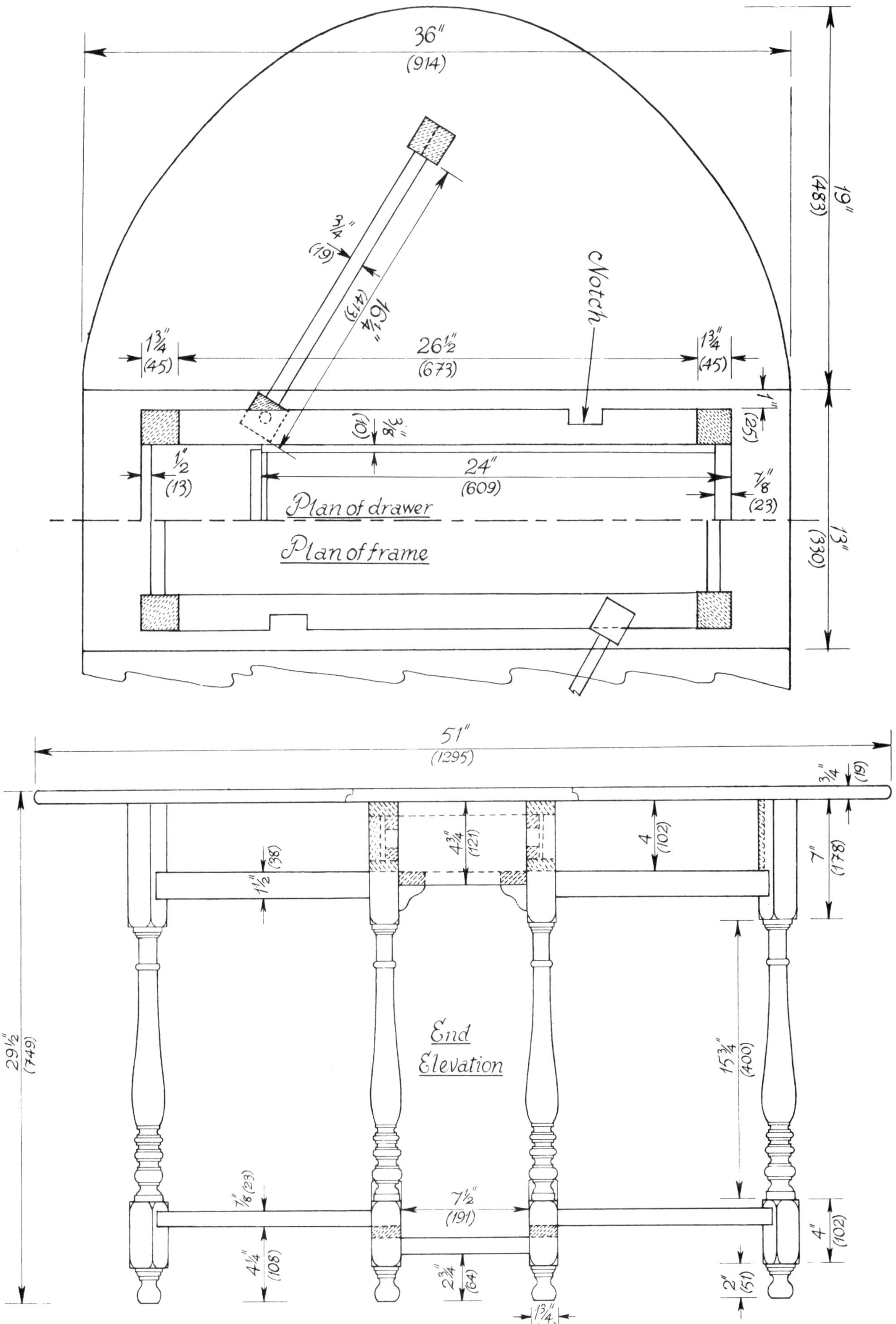
36"
(914)
19"
(483)
3/4"
(19)
16 1/4"
(413)
Notch
1 3/4"
(45)
26 1/2"
(673)
1 3/4"
(45)
1"
(25)
3/8"
(10)
1/2"
(13)
24"
(609)
7/8"
(23)
Plan of drawer
Plan of frame
13"
(330)
51"
(1295)
3/4"
(19)
29 1/2"
(749)
1 1/2"
(38)
4 3/4"
(121)
4
(102)
7"
(178)
End
Elevation
15 3/4"
(400)
7/8"
(23)
7 1/2"
(191)
4"
(102)
4 1/4"
(108)
2 3/4"
(64)
2"
(51)
1 3/4"
(45)

FIGURE 2

hinge and the fixing of such hinges are given elsewhere. The top can be pocket-screwed on along the long sides and buttoned on across the short sides.

Fig. 3A shows the construction of the bed. As you can see, at one end the upper drawer rail is dovetailed into the legs and the rails, while at the opposite end the panel can be rabbeted in. As shown, the panel would be of plywood, and if solid wood is used the grain should be run from side to side. Glue blocks could be used to strengthen the joint. The wide drawer runners (which are made extra wide so that the gate frames can be notched into them) are mortise and tenoned into the legs, as are the upper rails above them. Again, the lower drawer rail at the end uses the same kind of joint, but the drawer guides need only be pinned and glued in place. The lower underframing rails are also mortise and tenoned into the legs, being set horizontally instead of vertically.

Details of the gate-leg frames are shown in the elevation and plan in Fig. 2. Again, mortise and tenon joints are employed throughout. The completed frames are pivoted to the underframe rail at the bottom

and to the lower drawer runner at the top. The pivots are formed by turning ½ inch (12 mm) dia. pins on the top and bottom of the gate hinge post, and the insertion of the gate frame is achieved by a screwed-on (removable) block as shown in Fig. 3.

Once the gate-frames are pivoted on, the notches can be located, marked on and cut out; you will also need to screw small "stops" to the undersides of the flaps to prevent the gate-frames opening too far.

The drawer is only a shallow one but would be quite acceptable as a cutlery drawer or for table linen. As you can see from Fig. 3B, the construction is quite conventional; the front laps over the drawer rails at top and bottom, the sides being flush and lap-dovetailed to the front.

The pattern of the turned legs is typical of the Jacobean style and should present no difficulty; note that the corners of the squares adjacent to the turned parts are rounded off or "pummelled". The small bracket blocks can be glued and dowelled in position.

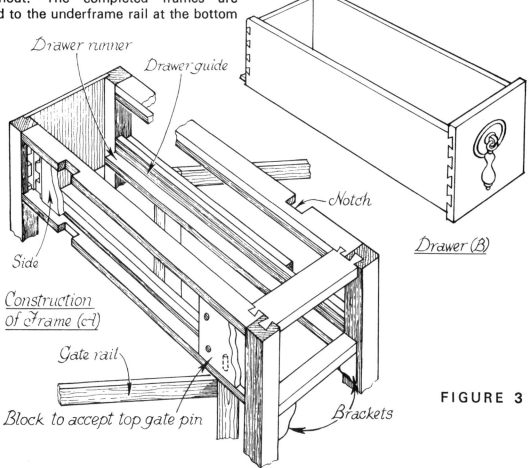

Drawer runner

Drawer guide

Notch

Drawer (B)

Side

Construction
of Frame (A)

Gate rail

Block to accept top gate pin

Brackets

FIGURE 3

Parts List

No. req'd	Description	Long	Wide	Thick
1	Top (bed)	37 (939)	14 (356)	$\frac{3}{4}$ (19)
2	Top (flaps)	37 (939)	20 (508)	$\frac{3}{4}$ (19)
6	Legs	30 (762)	2 (51)	$1\frac{3}{4}$ (45)
2	Gate vertical posts	$22\frac{1}{2}$ (571)	2 (51)	$1\frac{3}{4}$ (45)
2	Upper gate rails	$17\frac{1}{2}$ (445)	$1\frac{3}{8}$ (35)	$\frac{5}{8}$ (16)
2	Lower gate rails	$17\frac{1}{2}$ (445)	$1\frac{3}{8}$ (35)	$\frac{5}{8}$ (16)
2	Long underframe rails	$27\frac{1}{2}$ (698)	2 (51)	$\frac{5}{8}$ (16)
2	Short underframe rails	$8\frac{1}{2}$ (216)	2 (51)	$\frac{5}{8}$ (16)
2	Drawer rails (kickers)	$28\frac{1}{2}$ (724)	2 (51)	$\frac{3}{4}$ (19)
2	Drawer rails (runners)	$28\frac{1}{2}$ (724)	$3\frac{1}{4}$ (83)	$\frac{3}{4}$ (19)
1	Front upper drawer rail	$9\frac{1}{2}$ (242)	2 (51)	$\frac{3}{4}$ (19)
1	Front lower drawer rail	$9\frac{1}{2}$ (242)	2 (51)	$\frac{3}{4}$ (19)
1	End panel	$9\frac{1}{2}$ (242)	$5\frac{1}{4}$ (134)	$\frac{1}{2}$ (13)
1	Drawer front	8 (203)	$5\frac{1}{4}$ (134)	$\frac{7}{8}$ (23)
2	Drawer sides	$24\frac{1}{4}$ (616)	5 (128)	$\frac{3}{8}$ (10)
1	Drawer back	8 (203)	$5\frac{1}{4}$ (134)	$\frac{3}{8}$ (10)
1	Drawer bottom	25 (635)	8 (203)	$\frac{1}{4}$ (6)
4	Bracket blocks	3 (76)	$2\frac{3}{4}$ (70)	$\frac{3}{4}$ (19)

Allowances have been made to lengths and widths; thicknesses are net.
Millimetre equivalents in brackets.

15. FIFTEENTH CENTURY OAK STOOL

FIGURE 1

As you can see from Figs 1 and 2, this pretty little stool is comparatively simple to make as it consists of only four basic pieces. Its appeal depends on the carving and shaping of the various parts, and both operations — the carving and the shaping — would probably give the best results if executed by hand and eye as far as possible, rather than by machine.

Just as a handwritten manuscript has a charm all of its own because of the inevitable irregularities as compared with a printed text, so the decoration of this stool would benefit from the vagaries of the hand-held tool.

Fig. 2A shows the plan, Fig. 2B the side elevation, and Fig. 2C the end elevation; Fig. 2D a squared-off drawing of the carving details.

Construction is simple as all joints depend on a wedging action. Although the tenons of the ends which project through the top are shown wedged, it is unlikely that this would be the case with a genuine design.

The pegs which are used to "anchor" the ends to the under-rail will have to be very slightly tapered on the inside face so that they tighten as they are driven home. For this reason they should be cut over-long to start with and tapered and driven home as a test-fit. You can then mark them so that an equal amount protrudes on each side of the rail and cut them to length accordingly.

A point here to note. These types of wedged or pegged joints would normally have been made "dry", without glue. The

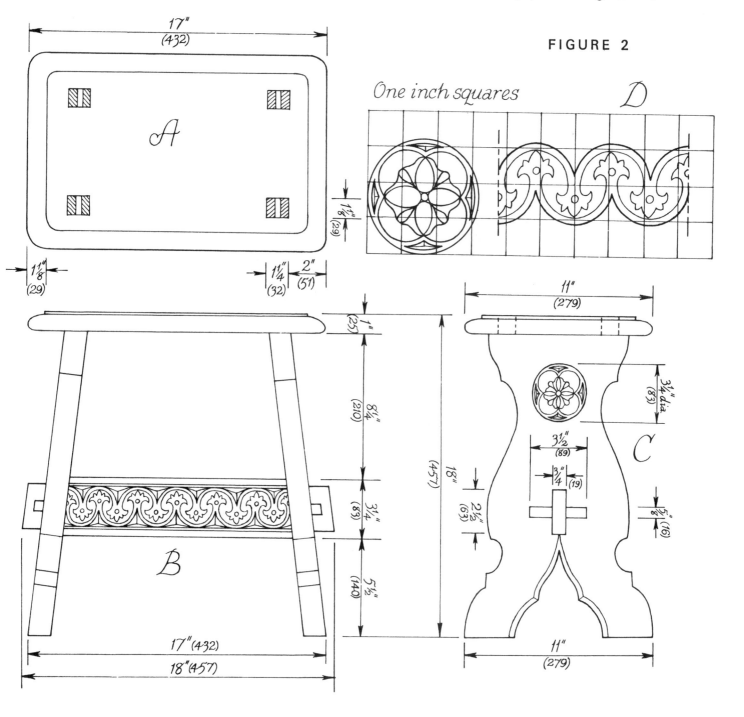

FIGURE 2

One inch squares

parts would have been warmed by a fire until they were bone-dry and with a very low moisture content, and then assembled in this state.

As a high moisture content was pretty well guaranteed all the year round in mediaeval buildings, the timber parts would be bound to swell and lock themselves together as effectively as many of our modern adhesives!

Fig. 3 is, again, a squared-off drawing (one inch — 25 mm — squares) and gives you the shape of the end, the size and positions of the tenons, the centre for the carved circle, and the position for the mortise through which the under-rail projects.

The motifs of both designs of carving are geometric and do not allow the same freedom of expression as may be associated with, for instance, acanthus leafage or swags of flowers and leaves. This means that it is a higher development of "chip" carving and is in comparatively low relief, the greatest amount cut away not exceeding ⅜ inch (10 mm).

Such a design as this stool obviously calls for an unsophisticated, traditional finish, and the linseed oil and wax finish described elsewhere in the book would be ideal.

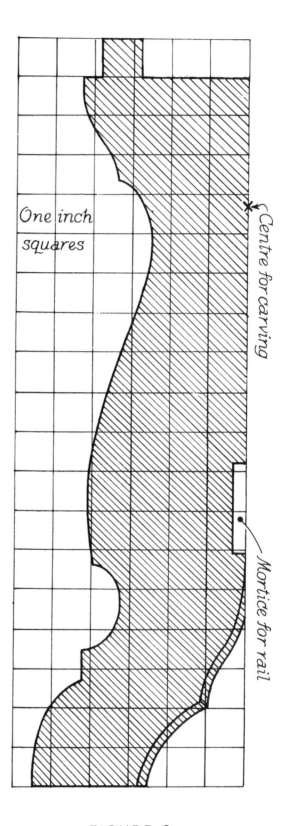

One inch squares

Centre for carving

Mortice for rail

FIGURE 3

Parts List

No. req'd.	Description	Long	Wide	Thick
1	Top	18 (457)	12 (305)	1 (25)
2	Ends	19 (482)	12 (305)	1¼ (32)
1	Under-rail	19 (482)	4 (102)	¾ (19)

Wedges and pegs from offcuts

Allowances have been made to lengths and widths; thicknesses are net.
Millimetre equivalents in brackets.

16. LADDER-BACK CHAIR

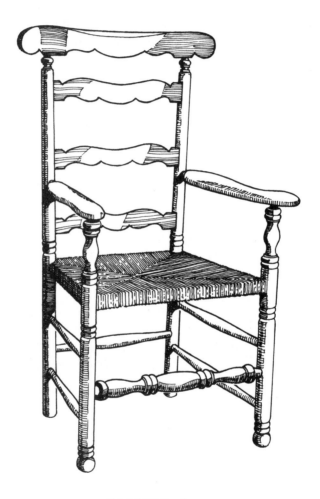

FIGURE 1

This is the typical design of the kind of chair which used to be made up by village carpenters all over the country — with local variations, of course. A rush-covered seat is more or less obligatory and as this is a craft on its own, I would strongly recommend that you have the work done by one of the associations for blind or handicapped persons if you feel that this part of the work is beyond your capabilities. There are however, at least two publications in print (at the time of writing) on this subject which would no doubt be very helpful: "Cane and Rush Seating" by M. Brown (Batsford, London) and "Seat Weaving" by L. Day Perry (Bennett, USA). These may be available from your local library or, if you wish to buy a book, try a specialist bookseller such as Stobart & Son Ltd., 67–73 Worship Street, London EC2A 2EL.

Such pieces were invariably made up from whatever hardwoods were available and could well have resulted in a mixture. As far as we are concerned, pretty well any home-grown hardwood such as oak, ash, or beech will be suitable, but for the curved

splats (or "rungs") and the top rail ash or beech would be best.

The actual construction is so straightforward that little explanation seems necessary. Many of the joints consist of pegs turned on the ends of the members which are glued into holes bored to receive them, and these are shown on the squared-off drawing in Fig. 4.

In such cases, the important point to bear in mind is that a small gap should be left between the end of the peg and the bottom

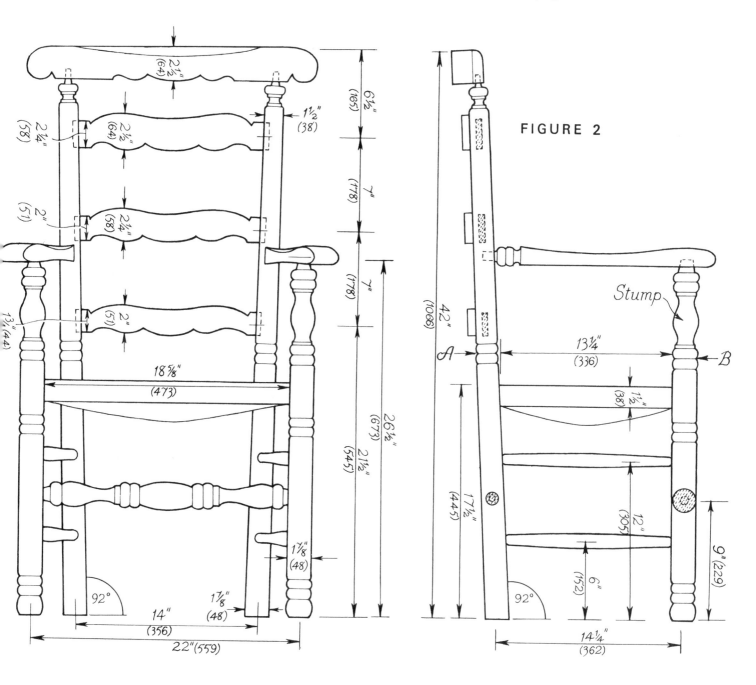

FIGURE 2

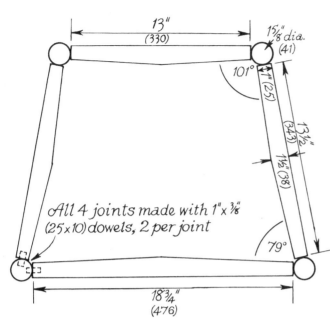

*All 4 joints made with 1″x ⅜″
(25x10) dowels, 2 per joint*

13″ (330)

1⅝″ dia. (41)

101°

1″ (25)

13½″ (343)

1½″ (38)

79°

18¾″ (476)

FIGURE 3

of the hole. This empty space is for the glue to occupy — if you do not leave it the chances are that it will all be squeezed out, leaving you with a dry joint. About $\frac{1}{16}$ inch (2 mm) or so will be adequate. Shallow longitudinal saw-cut grooves along the pins or dowels will allow any surplus glue to escape, thus ensuring that the pins go right home.

The back feet are simply turned and slightly tapered, and no difficulties should be encountered. If you haven't a lathe with enough space between centres to take the full length of the back foot, you could turn

FIGURE 4

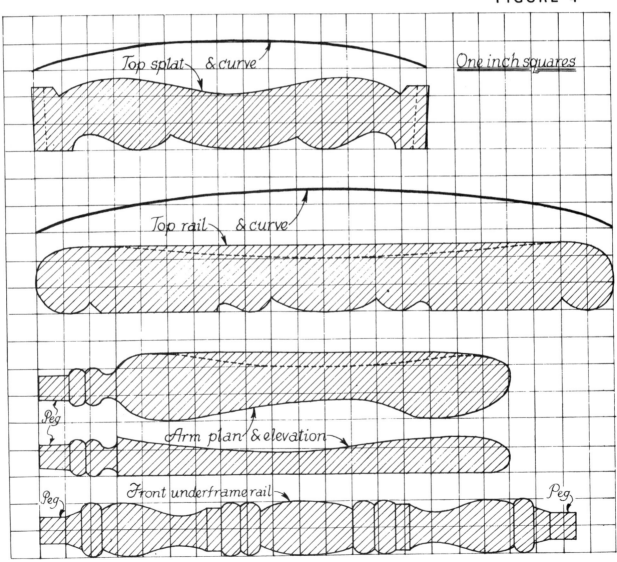

Top splat & curve

One inch squares

Top rail & curve

Peg

Arm plan & elevation

Peg

Front underframe rail

Peg

it in two parts. This would mean that the pieces would join at (A), Fig. 2, and they could be fixed either by a loose dowel glued into a hole bored in each piece, or a pin could be turned on the end of one piece. While we are dealing with this, you could consider using the same expedient for the front leg and stump.

For reasons of space we have been unable to give larger details of the turning patterns for the back feet, front legs, and stumps than appear in Fig. 2. This should not cause you any difficulty, however, as the patterns are purely arbitrary and there is nothing to prevent you altering them as you please. The spars which form the underframing are turned from $1\frac{1}{4}$ inch (32 mm) stuff and reduced gradually down to $\frac{3}{4}$ inch (19 mm).

To return to the back feet. A one-inch (25 mm) pin is turned on the top end of each one, its diameter being reduced to $\frac{1}{2}$ inch (13 mm), and these fit into holes, $\frac{3}{4}$ inch (19 mm) deep, bored into the underside of the top rail.

You will also need to chop out mortises for each of the splats, and lengths for these are shown in Fig. 2. The splats are $\frac{3}{8}$ inch full (11 mm) in thickness, being cut from $\frac{1}{2}$ inch (13 mm) stuff, and their full thickness is housed in the mortises which are $\frac{1}{2}$ inch (13 mm) deep.

Another point to note is that the holes for the pins on the arms, and those for the dowels on the seat rails, plus the holes for the underframing, all need to be bored at an angle slightly greater than a right-angle — 92 degrees, in fact. The corresponding holes on the front legs, however, are all bored at conventional right angles.

The pattern of the arms is, again, a matter of choice, although too flamboyant a design would be out of place. As you can see, the stump has a pin turned on its end which locates into a hole bored on the underside of the arm. An extra inch or so has been allowed on the length in the parts list to allow for centring in the lathe.

Probably the most tricky part of the whole job will be steaming and bending the splats and the top rail. Details of a steaming box and the process itself are included in the section dealing with Windsor chairs. Actually, if you have chosen a good bending timber like beech, the procedure should not be too difficult as the curves are comparatively shallow.

PARTS LIST *See over*

Parts List

No. req'd	Description	Long	Wide	Thick
2	Back feet	41 (1041)	2¼ (58)	1⅞ (48)
2	Front legs	27 (686)	2¼ (58)	1⅞ (48)
2	Side seat rails	14 (356)	1½ (38)	1½ (38)
1	Front seat rail	19¼ (489)	1½ (38)	1½ (38)
1	Back seat rail	13½ (343)	1½ (38)	1½ (38)
1	Top rail	23 (584)	3 (77)	⅞ (23)
1	Top splat	16 (407)	3 (77)	⅜ (10)
1	Middle splat	15½ (394)	2½ (64)	⅜ (10)
1	Bottom splat	15 (381)	2¼ (58)	⅜ (10)
2	Arms	19 (482)	3 (77)	1⅜ (35)
4	Side underframe spars	15 (381)	1¼ (32)	1 (25)
1	Back underframe spar	14½ (368)	1¼ (32)	1 (25)
1	Front underframe rail	21 (533)	2¼ (58)	1⅞ (48)

Allowances have been made to lengths and widths; thicknesses are net.
Millimetre equivalents in brackets.

17. TUDOR-STYLE REFECTORY TABLE

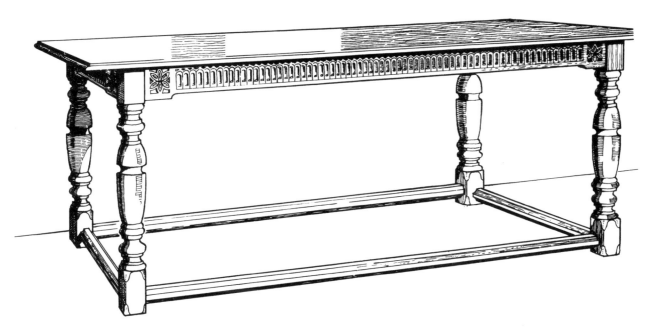

FIGURE 1

Massive tables such as these were used in monasteries and large houses, and exemplify two aspects of the beginnings of fine furniture design. The first is the fact that as the country became peaceful and free from the internal wars which had ravaged the nation for hundreds of years, large landowners were able to concentrate on beautifying their houses rather than fortifying them.

The other is that the design shows the gradual influence of the Renaissance as compared to that of the Church — the strictly Gothic styles began to be superseded by the more naturalistic motifs of the Renaissance.

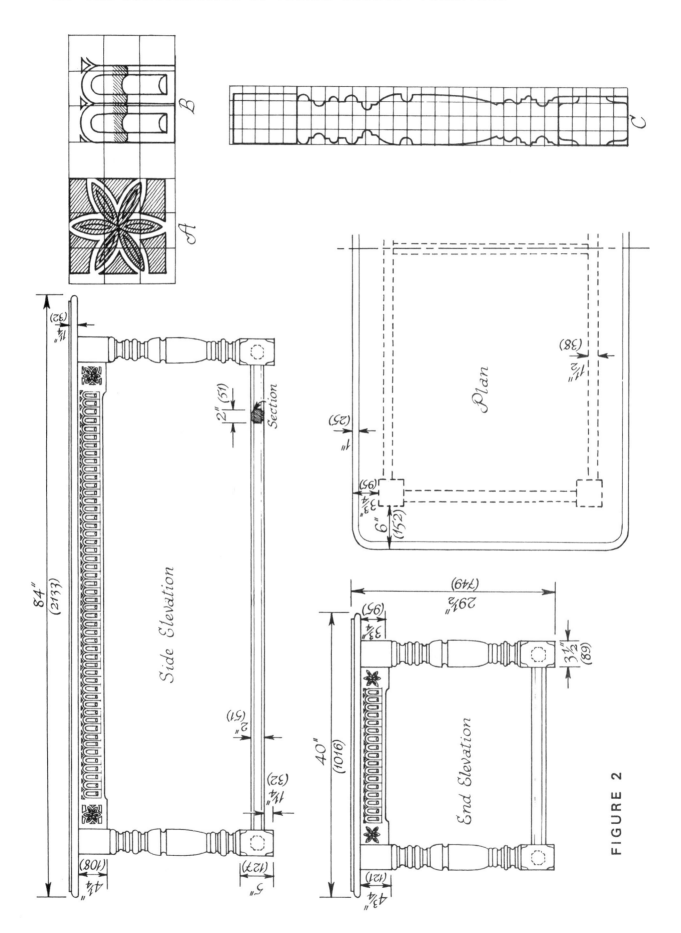

FIGURE 2

Our example does, of course, demand solid timber throughout and that timber must traditionally be oak. The top will have to be jointed and, to reduce the effect of shrinkage to a minimum, it should be held down to the framing by buttons across each end and by pocket-screwing along the length.

All other joints are conventional mortise and tenon and can be "pegged" – that is, having two dowels or pegs driven through pre-bored holes in the tenon from the outside. It does not matter that the ends of these pegs are visible, as this is an accepted characteristic of such joints.

The carved ornamentation is really only a step forward from chip carving in the sense that, once the flutes have been hollowed out by the gouge, the remainder of the cuts can be achieved by a single stroke of the mallet for each cut.

Parts List

No. req'd.	Description	Long	Wide	Thick
1	Top (widths according to pieces available)	85 (2158)		1¼ (32)
4	Legs	30½ (775)	3½ (89)	3¼ (83)
2	Long frame rails	68 (1727)	4½ (115)	1½ (38)
2	Short frame rails	27½ (698)	4½ (115)	1½ (38)
1	Centre frame rail	30 (762)	4¼ (108)	1½ (38)
2	Long underframe rails	68 (1727)	2¼ (58)	2 (51)
2	Short underframe rails	27½ (698)	2¼ (58)	2 (51)

Allowances have been made to lengths and widths; thicknesses are net.
Millimetre equivalents in brackets.

18-19. WINDSOR CHAIRS

FIGURE 1

The Windsor chair is said to have derived its name from the fact that George III admired cne on which he had been sitting. Be that as it may, the design is probably one of the most widely used in the world and its popularity is as strong today as ever it was.

Traditionally, the **bow of the** back, and the legs and underframe spars should be beech, while the seat should be elm. While it would be wise to stick to ash for the bow because of its bending qualities, almost any other hardwood could be used for the other parts.

The seat and the bow are obviously the

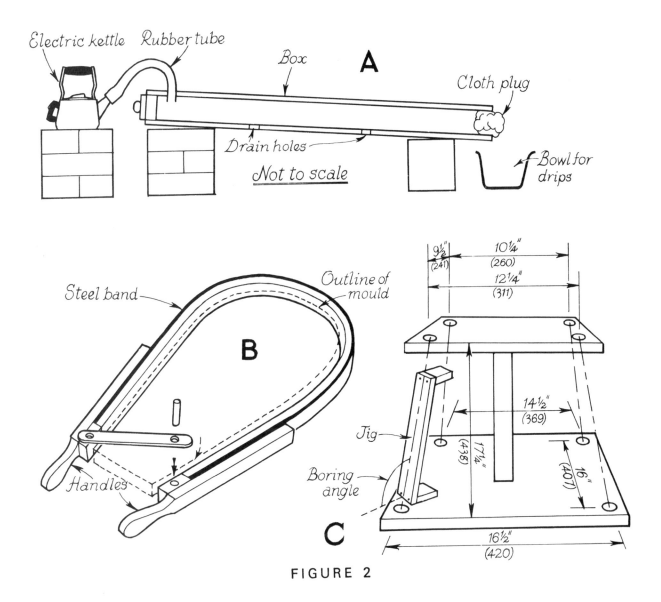

FIGURE 2

most difficult pieces to deal with, so let us describe them first.

As already mentioned, the seat is best made of elm because of its grain structure which is often completely random and almost always cross-grained. Such features make it very suitable for receiving the many holes bored into it without undue weakness resulting.

The shape of the seat is shown in Fig. 3, which is squared-off into one-inch squares to enable you to plot the curves easily.

Traditionally, the "bodgers" who made Windsor chairs in the Chiltern beechwoods cut out the seats with a bowsaw (often called a "Betty" saw). The modern equivalent is, of course, a bandsaw, and it will do

the job easily and quickly. Failing this, you could use a jigsaw or a coping saw.

There is, however, a point to watch here. Elm is notoriously difficult to season and cannot be hurried — we have often seen pieces with over 300 per cent moisture content. In the trade, the seats were first cut as oversize blanks and stacked for several months to finish drying. If you have any doubts about the dryness of your elm it would be advisable to adopt the same procedure. Obviously, if the seat finishes drying after the chair has been assembled, any twisting will mean that it will never stand properly.

Assuming that you now have the seat cut to shape, the next job is to hollow it out to the well-known contours shown in Fig. 1.

The traditional tool used for this operation is the adze and the method is to place the seat on the floor in front of you and to take a stance with the legs open to the width of the seat. Proceed with a gentle forward swinging motion of the adze making contact with the seat part which you wish to cut. The seat, during this dishing work, can be held steady by scrap blocks of wood securely wedged or screwed down if possible to the floor. The very experienced adze worker can stand on the sides of the seat whilst working.

It cannot be stressed too highly that this tool, when used, requires a great deal of care and the inexperienced worker is strongly advised to make use of one of the modern suitably shaped shaper-tools. Stanley Tool Company Ltd. make a small curved one which can be pushed or pulled (by reversing the blade), and this would, I think, be just the tool. It could be used in conjunction with a machine router.

In Figs 3 and 6 the dotted lines on the seat plans indicate the limits of the dishing-out: I must point out, however, that a peak is left centrally at the front, and you can see this in the front elevations in Figs 3 and 5. Bear in mind that the thinnest part of the seat should not be less than $\frac{3}{8}$ inch (10 mm) thick.

Logically, the next step should be boring the holes for the legs, sticks, etc. but as this is bound up with determining the angles for boring holes in general, it will be dealt with a little later on.

Moving on to the bow, you will first of all need a strip of beech (or ash, which would be an acceptable substitute) 50 inches (1270 mm) long, by $1\frac{1}{8}$ inches (29 mm) square. This allows you plenty in the length for cutting off once the bending is done; the finished section is 1 inch square (25 mm), so the extra allowance of $\frac{1}{8}$ inch (3 mm) all round will allow for shaping. The finished section is actually shown in Fig. 4.

You will need to make up a steaming box, plus a bending strap, shown in Fig. 2 as (B) and (C) respectively.

The steaming box can be made up from lengths of softwood and must, of course, be a few inches longer than the bow itself. Steam is provided by means of an electric kettle and a rubber tube; the upper end of the box has a wooden lid with a handle while the lower end has a cloth or rag plug stuffed into it. This acts as a primitive safety valve which will blow out if too much pressure builds up. Any condensed steam drips away either through the ventilation holes or into the rag. I prefer an electric kettle rather than an ordinary kettle on a gas ring, as rubber tubes can catch fire.

As you can see, the bending strap comprises a 1 inch by $\frac{1}{16}$ inch (25 × 2 mm) mild steel strip bolted or screwed to a pair of wooden handles. These handles have blocks screwed to them to form a kind of "step" into which the bow locates at either end. Note, too, the strip which is fixed to one block and swivels so that it can be locked into position on the other.

In addition you will need a mould, the outline of which is shown dotted in Fig. 2 (B). This can be built up from scrapwood to a final thickness of approximately 1 inch (25 mm), and must be shaped to the exact curve required for the inside face of the bow. Once made, it must be firmly screwed or bolted to a substantial baseboard, or to your bench.

The procedure is to insert the beech strip into the steaming box and leave it in there for 30 to 40 minutes. Then withdraw it and quickly position it around the mould; follow by fixing the bending strap round it and locking it in place. Leave the assembly for 24 hours or so to set. Incidentally, it's a good idea to wear some kind of gloves — gardening gloves, for instance — as the strip will be very hot when it comes out of the steaming box.

Now we can get on to boring the holes. This is not quite so simple as it may appear as the holes should be square-ended. This means that twist bits, or any similar bits with a screw-thread tip, are not really suitable as the hole made by the tip will project a $\frac{1}{4}$ inch (6 mm) or so further than the bottom of the hole and may, consequently, break through.

The old chairmakers got over this by using "spoon" bits which formed just the right kind of hole. The best modern equipment is a Forstner bit, or a flat-bit used with a power drill.

Fig. 2C shows the set-up for determining the angles for the legs. It comprises two pieces of scrap board which are held apart by a column of, say, 2 inches square (51 mm) softwood. The height, of course,

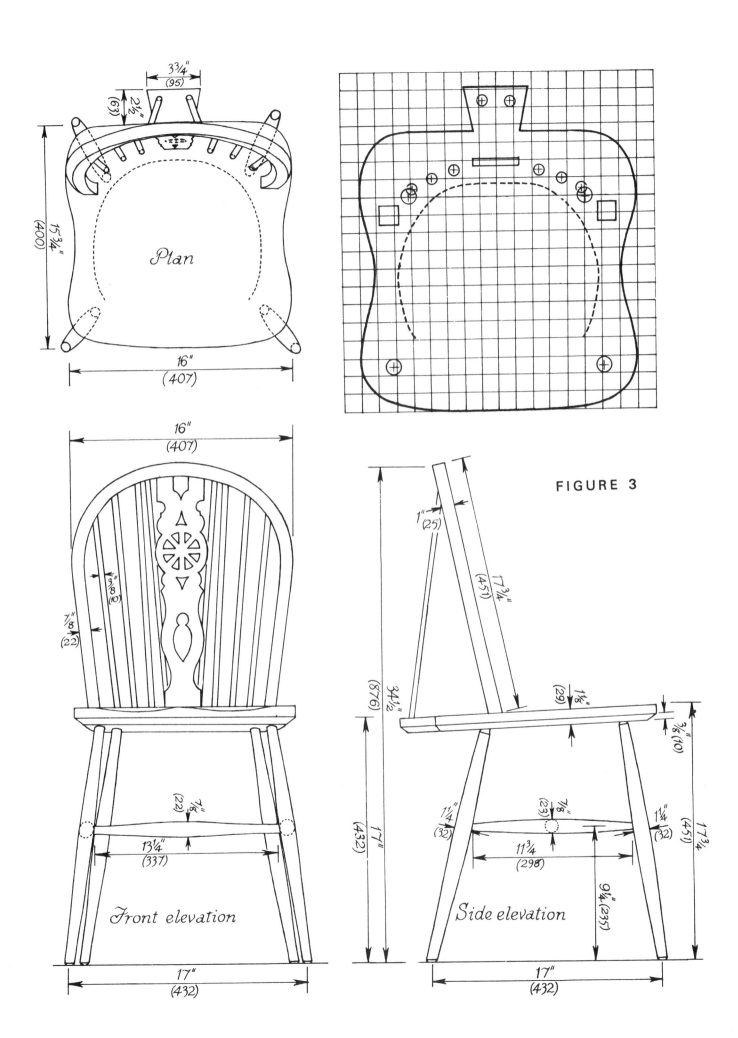

3¾"
(95)

2½"
(63)

15¾"
(400)

Plan

16"
(407)

16"
(407)

FIGURE 3

⅜"
(10)

⅞"
(22)

1"
(25)

17¾"
(451)

1⅛"
(29)

⅜"
(10)

34½"
(876)

17"
(432)

17¾"
(451)

⅞"
(22)

13¼"
(337)

Front elevation

1¼"
(32)

⅞"
(23)

11¾"
(298)

1¼"
(32)

9¼"
(235)

Side elevation

17"
(432)

17"
(432)

corresponds to the height of the chair seat above the ground.

If you bore holes in the two pieces of board at the centres shown, you will have a representation of the angles for the legs and a simple jig can be made up as shown on which your brace and bit can rest as a guide. A piece of dowel can be inserted through the holes and pencil lines marked parallel to it.

Assembly of the back comes next, and you will see from the seat plans in Fig. 3 that, at its apex, the back edge of the bow is immediately above the back edge of the seat.

This means that if you make up a template by nailing two pieces of scrap battens together at right-angles, you can insert one "arm" of the template under the seat on its centre line, and position the bow to rest against the other arm. This will give you the angle at which the mortises have to be chopped out.

To locate the sticks, knock the bow into its position, dry. The holes for the bottom ends of the sticks and the splat are shown in Fig. 3 and, assuming you have bored them, the sticks can be inserted into them. The task then is to arrange them in a pleasing "fan" formation, with the centres equidistant.

We have not mentioned turnery yet, and there is not really a great deal to say. It must be borne in mind that there is really no limit to the variations you can introduce into the turning details.

In general, however, you will get a much better appearance if all the turned members have a graceful "swell" as in Fig. 5. Don't attempt to turn a shoulder on the ends of the legs or underframing — by all means taper them off a trifle, but remember that it is the wedging action that is all-important.

The wheel-back splat is a straighforward, if tricky, piece of jig-sawing. Probably it would be best to use a coping saw for the cut-out internal pieces, confining the jigsaw

FIGURE 4

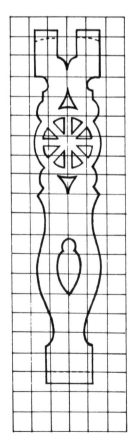
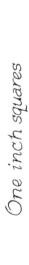
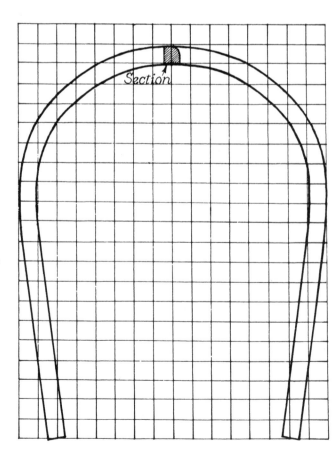

One inch squares

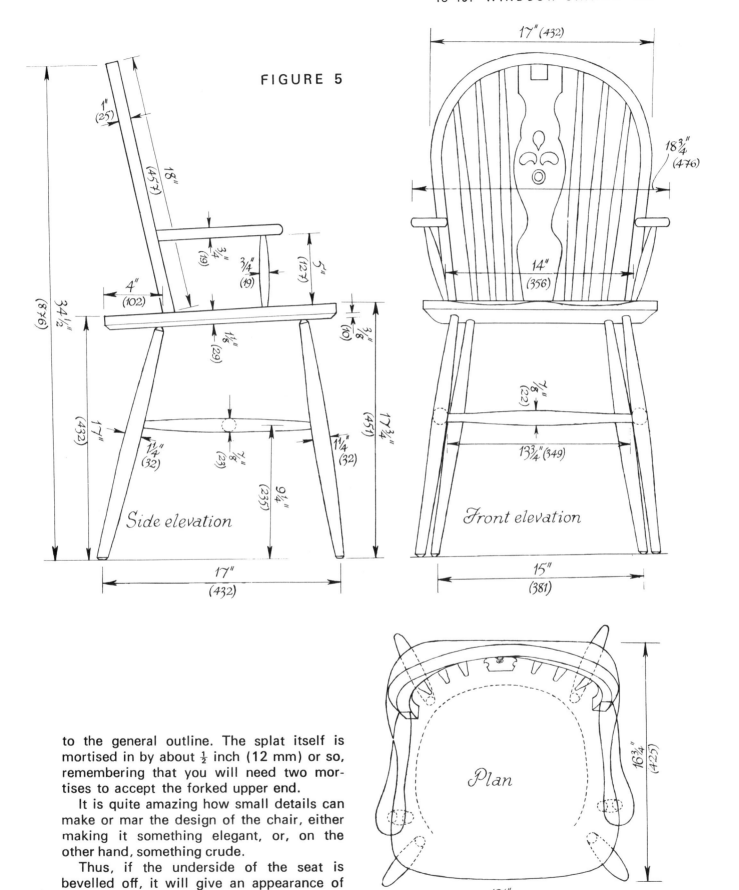

FIGURE 5

Side elevation

Front elevation

Plan

to the general outline. The splat itself is mortised in by about ½ inch (12 mm) or so, remembering that you will need two mortises to accept the forked upper end.

It is quite amazing how small details can make or mar the design of the chair, either making it something elegant, or, on the other hand, something crude.

Thus, if the underside of the seat is bevelled off, it will give an appearance of lightness. Again, the angle at which the bow meets seat is critical; if the bow and• the sticks are all in one straight line across the back of the seat the whole chair looks crude. In our design, the ends of the bow are brought well forward, and the sticks and splat are arranged in a concave pattern.

The "tail" shown on the seat for the wheel-back is optional, though usual; note, too, the two stays which act as supports for the back.

The armchair is slightly larger all round, as you can see from Fig. 5. Instead of a wheelback splat, that shown in Fig. 6 incorporates a cut-out fleur-de-lis pattern which is often used as an alternative.

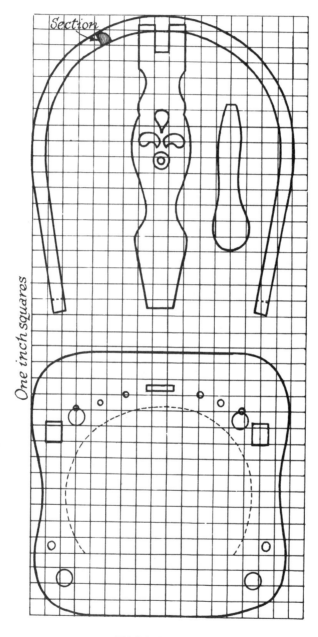

FIGURE 6

Parts List

No. req'd.	Description	Long	Wide	Thick
	Wheelback			
1	Seat	19 (482)	16¾ (425)	1¼ (32)
1	Bow	50 (1270)	1¼ (32)	1⅛ (29)
1	Splat	18 (458)	3½ (89)	⅜ (10)
4	Legs	17¾ (451)	1³⁄₁₆ (30)	1¼ (32)
2	Side underframe spars	13 (330)	1 (25)	⅞ (22)
1	Centre underframe spar	14½ (368)	1 (25)	⅞ (22)
6	Sticks (based on longest)	16¾ (425)	½ (13)	⅜ (10)
2	Stays	18½ (470)	½ (13)	⅜ (10)
	Fleur-de-Lis			
1	Seat	18 (457)	17½ (444)	1¼ (32)
1	Splat	19 (482)	5 (127)	⅜ (10)
2	Arms	10 (254)	2½ (64)	⅝ (16)
2	Arm stumps	7 (178)	1 (25)	¾ (19)

The bow, legs, underframe spars, and sticks are same dimensions as for the wheelback.

Allowances have been made to lengths and widths; thicknesses are net.
Millimetre equivalents in brackets.

20. WELSH DRESSER

FIGURE 1

Strictly speaking, there is no particular design for a Welsh dresser; the term is·used to embrace a whole variety of styles which were, and still are, found in Wales and the Welsh Border counties. They were originally made up by the local village carpenters or joiners, as was so much early furniture, and the timbers used would be a mixture of woods found in the locality.

We could, perhaps, learn something from them in this respect as they had no inhibitions about employing different hardwoods in any one job — indeed, they were not averse to including softwoods, too!

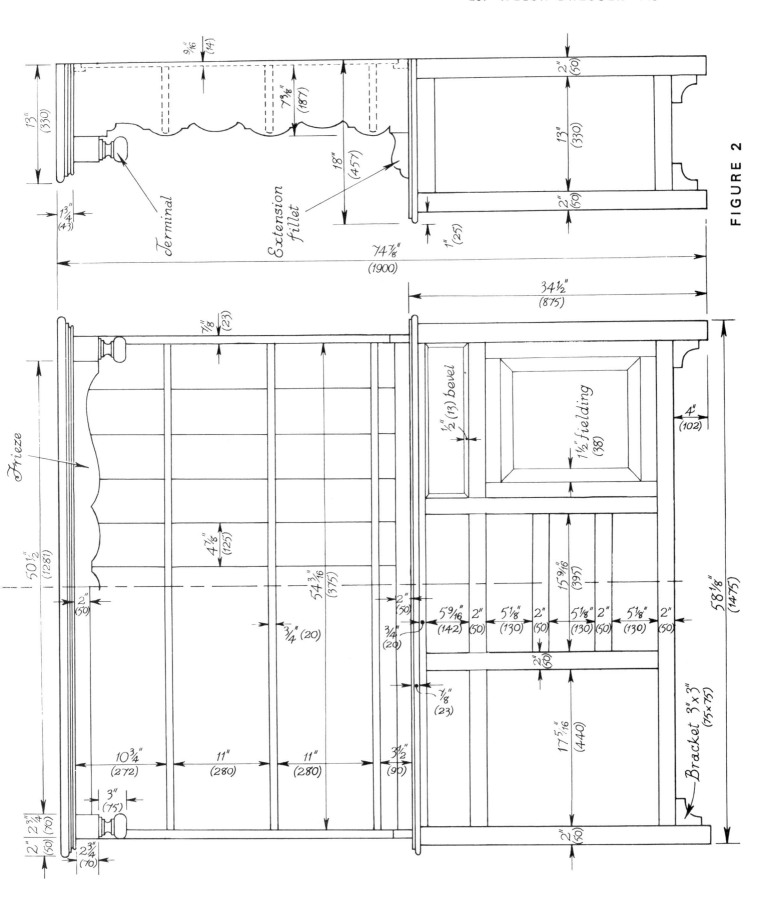

FIGURE 2

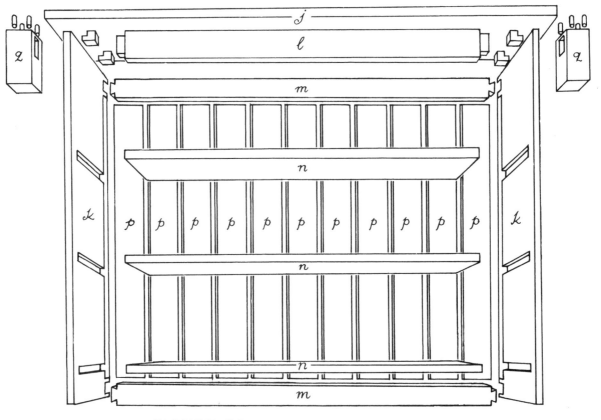

FIGURE 3A

FIGURE 3B

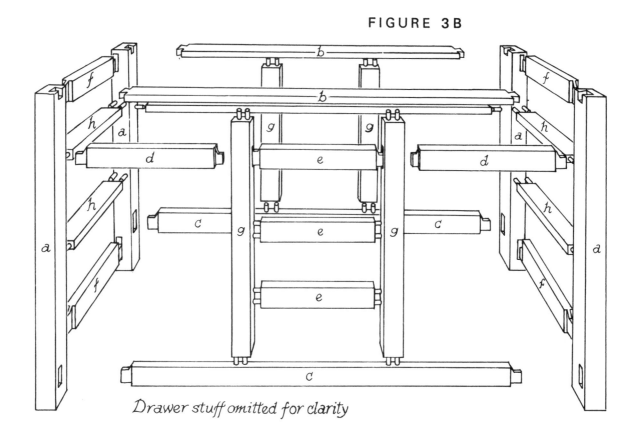

Drawer stuff omitted for clarity

During, and towards the end of, the eighteenth century, the designs became grander in their conception, and mahogany began to be widely used in their construction. By the early eighteen hundreds, some Welsh dressers were being created which could lay just claim to being fine pieces of cabinet work – a far cry from their plain, functional predecessors.

There are two main types of Welsh dresser – the kind which we shall be dealing with here, which comprises a cupboard-bottom with an open-shelved dresser part, and the "pot-board" dresser.

The latter does contain the usual dresser part, but the bottom part usually consists of two or three deep drawers, or shallow cupboards, ranged alongside one another. They are supported on legs which are connected towards the bottom by an underframe, and it is on this underframe that boards or planks are laid so that cooking pots and similar utensils can be stacked on them.

Returning now to our design, the first consideration must be whether to use solid wood for the various panels, or man made boards such as veneered plywood or blockboard. From the illustration you will see that the door and carcase end panels are fielded, and that a bevel is run around the drawer fronts.

These features can only apply if solid timber is used. However, the alternative of using say, veneered plywood need not pose any serious problems – obviously, you will have to dispense with the fielding and groove the panels into the muntins and stiles instead. This could be made to look very attractive by chamfering off the inner edges of the stiles etc. as shown in Fig. 5A – a method often used by old-time craftsmen.

Veneered ply or blockboard could be used for the drawer fronts. The edges would, of course, need to be lipped all round, and this lipping could be bevelled.

As the boards in the dresser back are one of the main show-features it is highly desirable to select them from timber which is as well-matched as possible. If this involves using softwood there is no real reason why you should not do so.

Fig. 2 shows the front and end elevations with dimensions, while Fig. 4 shows the following (all squared off into one-inch grids): A – one half pattern of the dresser-part frieze; B – pattern of dresser-part end; C –

template for terminal; D – template for extension to dresser-part end; E – template for foot bracket.

Exploded views show the construction of the dresser-part in Fig. 3A, and the cupboard part in Fig. 3B. In each case only the principal constructional members are shown to avoid confusion and the idea is to show method rather than detail.

Dealing with the dresser-part first, the top (*j*) is buttoned across the width to the ends (*k*), and pocket-screwed to the frieze (*l*) and the upper rail (*m*). This top can be $\frac{7}{8}$ inch (22 mm) solid, or made from blockboard or ply lipped round with the appropriate moulding, see Fig. 5E. The terminals (*q*) are mortise and tenoned on to the ends of the frieze (*1*) and need to be dowelled to the underside of the top and glued to the face edge of the dresser ends.

The dresser ends themselves need to be rabbeted on the back edge to accept the end tongued and grooved back boards (*p*). Similarly, the upper and lower rails (*m*) need to be rabbeted to house the ends of the boards (*p*).

Before the back can be assembled, however, $\frac{1}{2}$ inch (12 mm) deep stopped housings have to be cut on each end to accept the shelves – don't forget that the shelves will have to be notched as shown at Fig. 5B to give a neat finish.

As you can see, the top and bottom rails are dovetailed into each end to make up the frame which contains the tongue and groove boards. When assembling these boards, do it dry so that some movement can take place – by the same token, do not drive the tongues fully home or buckling could result. It is also a good idea to assemble them with the heart sides alternating (Fig. 5C). Note, too, that the edges are slightly bevelled off to mask any misalignment due to shrinkage, etc.

The extension fillet (shown on Fig. 2, but not in Fig. 3A) serves to oppose any tendency the dresser-part may have to topple forward, and it therefore needs to be well glued and dowelled in place.

Proceeding now to the cupboard (bottom) part, the construction basically follows that shown in Fig. 9, page 16. The legs, or posts (*a*) are mortise and tenoned together by the rails (*f*) to form ends; these ends are then joined by the upper rails (*b*) which are dovetailed into sockets in the legs, and the

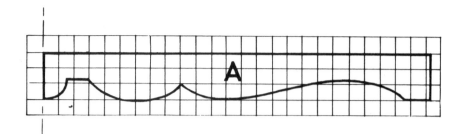

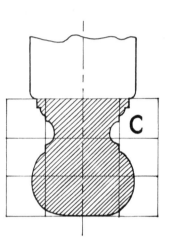

All one inch squares

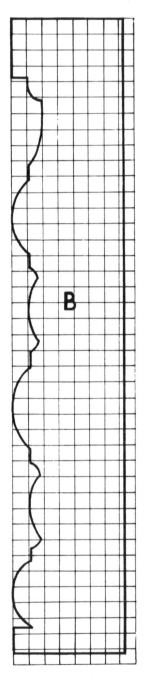

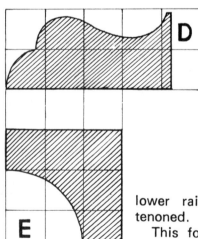

FIGURE 4

lower rails (c) which are mortise and tenoned.

This forms the basic framing which is strengthened by the following intermediary members — (h) shelf-bearers; (d) and (e) drawer rails; and (g) muntins. The muntins are shown as being dowelled into rails (b) and (c); alternatively, they could be fixed by means of foxtail-wedged through tenons.

Drawer rail construction is the same as that shown in Fig. 9, page 16, and the drawers themselves are the conventional type illustrated in Fig. 1, page 9. As they are comparatively narrow there will be no need for a central muntin in the drawer bottom.

The fielding of the door and end panels is shown at Fig. 5D, together with the alternative rebate and groove treatment. In neither case should the panel be glued or in any way fixed in, as the groove will take care of any movement.

The back panels need rabbeting into the back rails and, while the rabbets can be taken out before the rails are assembled, you will probably find it easier to do the job when the frame is made up. Quarter-inch (6 mm) plywood is the best material for this.

Fixing the dresser-part to the bottom can either be done by pocket-screwing down through rail (m) into the top of the cupboard — from the back, of course, or by screwing on glass plates to the back of the cupboard top and the back of rail (m).

Actually, the weight of the dresser-part is usually quite enough to keep it in place, particularly when it is furnished with crockery, etc. In any case, the extension fillet will also help considerably.

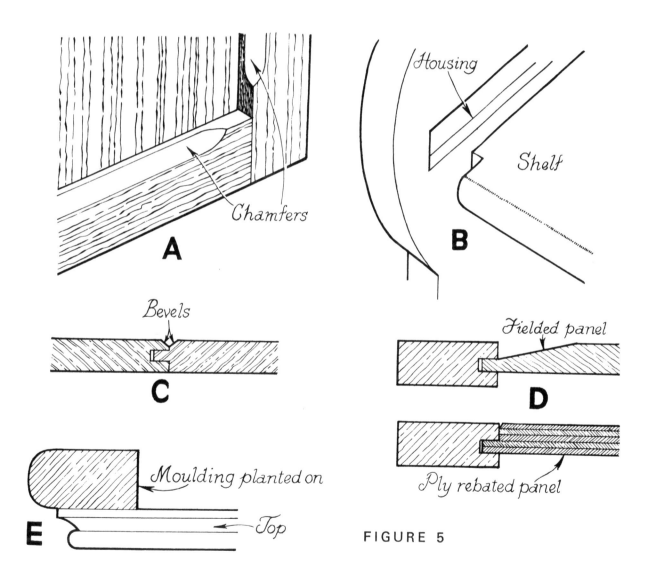

Chamfers

A

Housing

Shelf

B

Bevels

C

Fielded panel

D

Ply rebated panel

Moulding planted on

Top

E

FIGURE 5

PARTS LIST *See over*

Parts List

No. req'd.	Description	Long	Wide	Thick
1	Dresser part top (j)	62 (1575)	12½ (318)	⅞ (23)
1	Front lipping for above	64 (1625)	2 (51)	1¼ (32)
2	End lippings for above	14 (356)	2 (51)	1¼ (32)
2	Dresser part ends (k)	38½ (978)	8 (203)	⅞ (23)
1	Frieze (l)	53 (1346)	3½ (89)	¾ (19)
2	Terminals (q)	6¼ (159)	3 (77)	2¾ (70)
2	Rails (m)	55 (1396)	2¼ (58)	⅞ (23)
3	Shelves (n)	56 (1422)	7½ (190)	⅞ (23)
9	Backboards (p)	36 (915)	5 (127)	9/16 (15)
2	Backboards (1 at each end)	36 (915)	5¼ (134)	9/16 (15)
1	Top (for cupboard part)	61 (1549)	18½ (470)	⅞ (23)
4	Legs (a)	34 (864)	2½ (58)	2 (51)
2	Rails (b)	56½ (1435)	2 (51)	⅞ (23)
2	Rails (c)	56½ (1435)	2¼ (58)	⅞ (23)
2	Drawer rails (d)	19½ (495)	2¼ (58)	¾ (19)
1	Drawer rails (e)	17¾ (451)	2¼ (58)	¾ (19)
2	Drawer rails (e)	16¼ (413)	2¼ (58)	¾ (19)
4	End rails (f)	15½ (394)	2¼ (58)	⅞ (23)
4	Muntins (g)	28 (711)	2¼ (58)	⅞ (23)
4	Rails (h)	16 (407)	2 (51)	¾ (19)
2	End panels	26½ (673)	13½ (343)	⅜ (10)
2	Back panels	28½ (724)	18¼ (463)	¼ (6)
1	Centre back panel	28½ (724)	16¼ (413)	¼ (6)

No. req'd.	Description	Long	Wide	Thick
4	Door stiles	$20\frac{1}{2}$ (521)	$1\frac{7}{8}$ (48)	$\frac{3}{4}$ (19)
4	Door rails	18 (458)	$1\frac{7}{8}$ (48)	$\frac{3}{4}$ (19)
2	Door panels	21 (533)	$18\frac{1}{2}$ (470)	$\frac{3}{8}$ (10)
2	Drawer fronts	$17\frac{3}{4}$ (451)	6 (153)	$\frac{3}{4}$ (19)
4	Centre drawer front	16 (407)	$5\frac{1}{2}$ (140)	$\frac{3}{4}$ (19)
8	Drawer rails	16 (407)	2 (51)	$\frac{3}{4}$ (19)
6	Drawer sides	14 (356)	6 (153)	$\frac{3}{8}$ (10)
3	Drawer back	16 (456)	$5\frac{1}{2}$ (140)	$\frac{3}{8}$ (10)
6	Drawer sides	14 (407)	$5\frac{1}{2}$ (140)	$\frac{3}{8}$ (10)
3	Drawer backs	16 (407)	5 (127)	$\frac{3}{8}$ (10)
4	Drawer bottoms (ply)	16 (407)	14 (356)	$\frac{1}{4}$ (6)
2	Drawer bottoms (ply)	18 (458)	14 (407)	$\frac{1}{4}$ (6)
8	Brackets	$3\frac{1}{2}$ (89)	$3\frac{1}{4}$ (83)	$\frac{7}{8}$ (23)

Additional drawer stuff from oddments
Allowances have been made to lengths and widths; thicknesses are net.
Millimetre equivalents in brackets.

21. ROCKING CHAIR

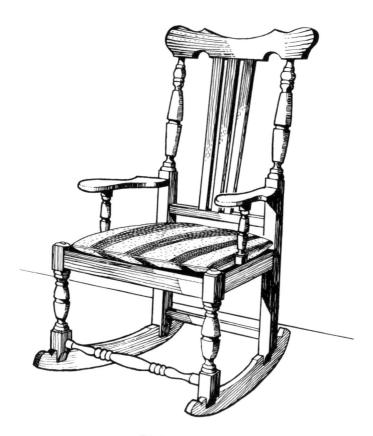

FIGURE 1

Rocking chairs are real favourites, and often the seat would be woven with rushes, or caned. In our design, however, we have incorporated a flat solid seat which can be "softened" by means of a loose squab cushion which is held in place by tapes tied round the back legs and the arm stumps.

Although not shown, a similar cushion for resting the head could hang from the top back rail.

Being very much a "country design, the most suitable wood is oak or ash or a judicious mixture of the two, using oak for the primary members and ash for the rest.

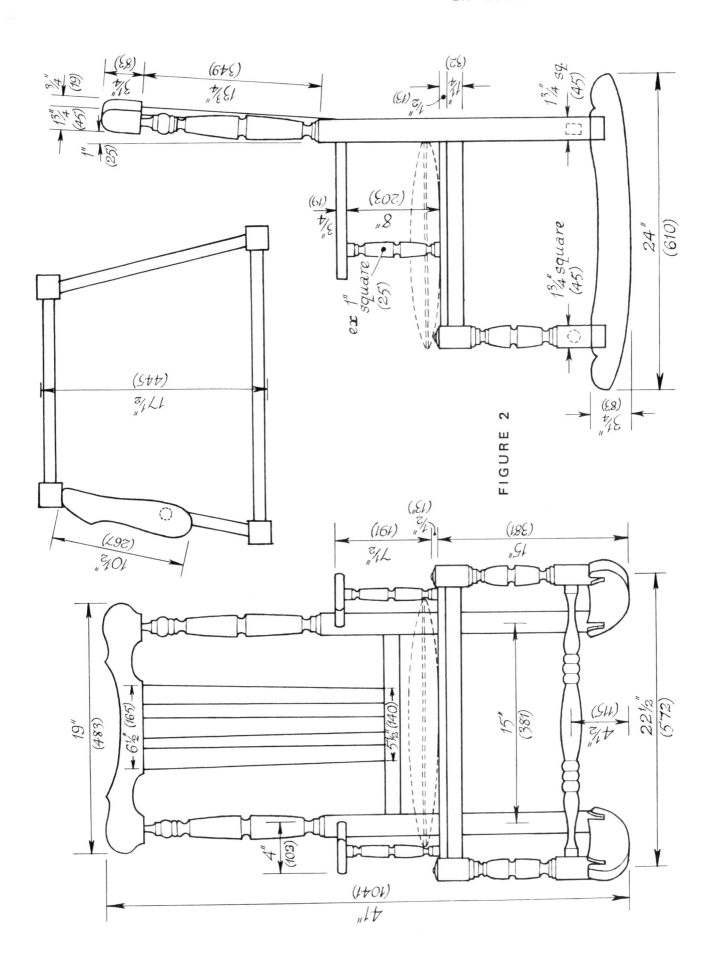

FIGURE 2

Starting with the back legs, the first point to note is that the turned section at the top is set at a slight rake. This means that this part has to be a separate piece, turned to the pattern shown in Fig. 3E with a pin at the lower end. This pin fits into a corresponding socket bored in the upper end of the bottom part of the leg, and this socket has, of course, to be bored at a slight angle to correspond to the rake. Similarly, the bottom member of the turned section has to be eased off to allow it to sit snugly.

Note, also, that the upper end of this turned section has a pin to fit into a socket

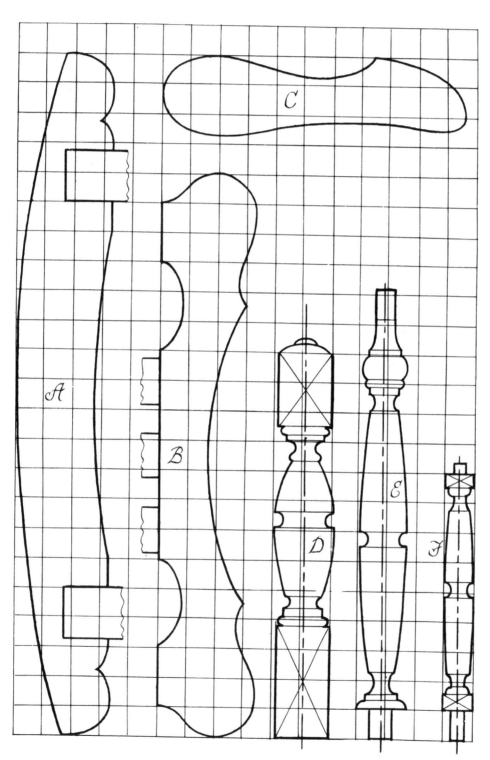

FIGURE 3

on the underside of the top rail.

The arm stumps, Fig. 3F, are also turned with pins on each end which fit into sockets on the underside of the arms and the seat respectively.

Fig. 3D shows the pattern for the front legs which are quite straightforward; the top of each leg is pummelled off and finished with a turned button. A transverse turned front rail spans the width between the legs at the front, and a plain rectangular one does the same job between the back legs.

Mortise and tenon joints are used on the seat framing, and the shoulders on the side seat rail joints need to be trimmed to allow for the fact that they are set at an angle. The solid seat should be pocket-screwed to the rails and will need to be notched round the legs at each corner.

The bottom of each front leg is bridled over its rocker and then shaped off as shown in Fig. 3D, the joint being well glued. For extra strength you can either insert a dowel crosswise through the joint, or screw up from below through the thickness of the rocker and into the bottom of the leg. Or, for that matter, you could do both! The shape of the rockers is shown at Fig. 3A.

In the back, the three stays each taper slightly in width from $1\frac{3}{4}$ inch (44 mm) at the top to one 1 inch (25 mm) at the bottom, and are slotted into the middle back rail and the top back rail.

The top back itself is cut from $3\frac{1}{2}$ inch by $2\frac{1}{2}$ inch (89 mm by 64 mm) stuff and has a regular sweep to a depth of $\frac{3}{4}$ inch (19 mm). It will need to be bandsawn to the shape shown in Fig. 3B.

Lastly, the arms (which are quite flat and not dished) should be sawn to the pattern shown in Fig. 3C. They are fixed to the back legs by means of stub tenons and are, of course, supported at their front ends by the arm stumps.

PARTS LIST *See over*

Parts List

No. req'd.	Description	Long	Wide	Thick
2	Front legs	16 (407)	2 (51)	1¾ (45)
2	Back legs, bottom part	23 (584)	2 (51)	1¾ (45)
2	Back legs, upper part	15½ (394)	2 (51)	1¾ (45)
2	Rockers	24 (610)	3½ (89)	¾ (19)
1	Top back rail (from)	20 (508)	3½ (89)	2½ (64)
1	Front seat rail	23 (584)	1½ (38)	¾ (19)
2	Side seat rail	15¾ (400)	1½ (38)	¾ (19)
1	Back seat rail	15 (381)	1½ (38)	¾ (19)
1	Seat	23½ (597)	18 (457)	½ (13)
2	Arms	12 (305)	3 (76)	¾ (19)
2	Arm stumps	10 (254)	1⅛ (29)	1 (25)
1	Front turned stretcher	22½ (572)	2 (51)	1¾ (45)
1	Back stretcher rail	15 (381)	1¼ (32)	¾ (19)
1	Middle back rail	15 (381)	1¼ (32)	¾ (19)
3	Stays	20½ (521)	2 (51)	1 (25)

Allowances have been made to lengths and widths; thicknesses are net.
Millimetre equivalents in brackets.

22. OAK HIGH-BACKED SETTLE

FIGURE 1

This design is a logical development of the plain benches originally used in the larger manor houses of mediaeval times. In a way it was transitional, as although it did not possess the added comfort of upholstery it was, at least, more comfortable than a bench. No doubt the high back was intended to shield the occupants from that bane of all ancient buildings – draughts!

As it has been drawn, the design will give you a large piece of furniture ideally suited to the spacious hall or the larger country-style kitchen or living room. Should a smaller piece be preferred there is no doubt that the

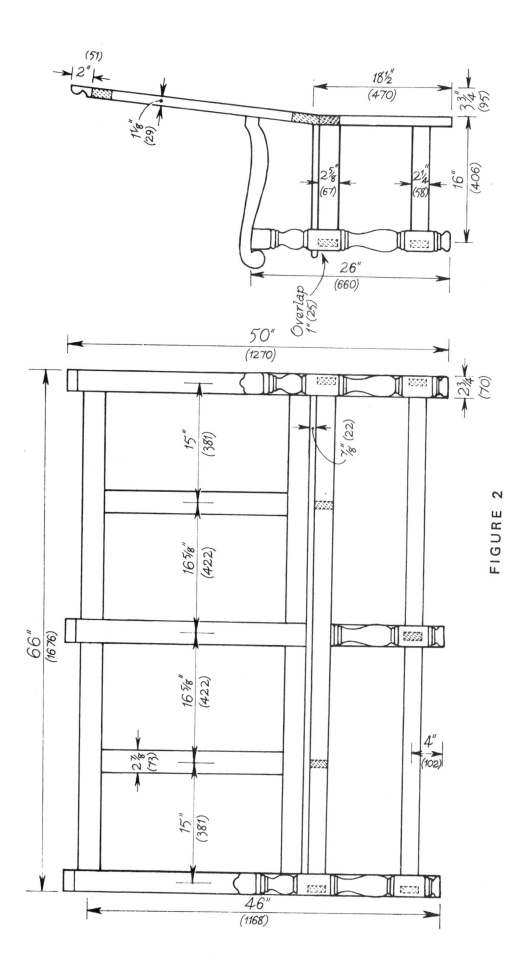

FIGURE 2

dimensions of the principal members could be reduced without any dangerous loss of strength.

Oak is obviously the timber for the job but, of course, it is expensive. To cut down the cost, you could use oak-veneered plywood panels for the back — this would also dispense with shrinkage problems. It might well be possible to find some ash which could be used for the underframe rails, which would constitute another saving. You could also consider using ramin as an alternative for these same rails as it can closely resemble a straight-grained oak.

Starting with the three back feet, the first thing to note is that the rake starts at seat level, and there is no backward splay at the bottom, Fig. 2. For economical cutting out it is advisable to have the grain running with the length of the angled, upper, portion.

Mortises will need to be cut on the two end backfeet for (a) the two longitudinal back rails and the seat rail; (b) the end seat rail and the end underframe rail; and (c) the tongue on the end of the arm; see Fig. 4. Also a groove $\frac{5}{16}$ inch deep by $\frac{1}{4}$ inch wide (18 mm by 6 mm) has to be made for the back panel; you will see in Fig. 4 that it runs between the mortises for the top and bottom back rails.

The centre back foot needs different treatment. First, there is no need for a mortise to receive the arm; second, you will need to cut mortises on the two opposite edges for the back (top and bottom) rails and the back seat rail; third, as there is no central seat rail there will be no need for a mortise — in fact, the back foot can be screwed to the back edge of the seat; fourth, you will need a mortise for the central underframe rail; and lastly, grooves will have to be made to accept the back panels.

Now for the two end legs. Details of the turning are given in Fig. 3 which is squared-off into a one-inch (25 mm) grid. You have the choice of either turning the leg in one piece, or turning a pin on the end of the bottom part as shown, and gluing this into a hole drilled on the bottom end of the arm stump. A pin should also be turned on the upper end of the arm stump and this will fit into a hole bored on the underside of the arm.

Again, these legs have to be mortised to accept tenons on the end and front seat rails, and the end and front underframe rails.

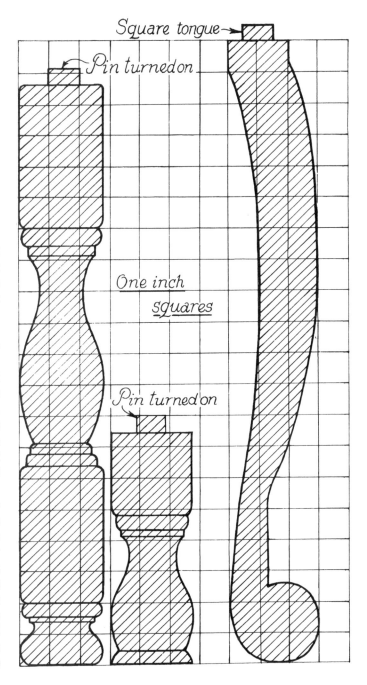

FIGURE 3

These mortises should not be deeper than $1\frac{1}{2}$ inches (38 mm), otherwise the tenons on the adjacent rails could obstruct each other. In any case, it would also take away a lot of wood at a rather critical part.

The centre leg follows the same turning pattern as the bottom parts of the end legs. Note, however, that the top square is notched out to accept the front seat rail as shown in Fig. 4. This notch is the same

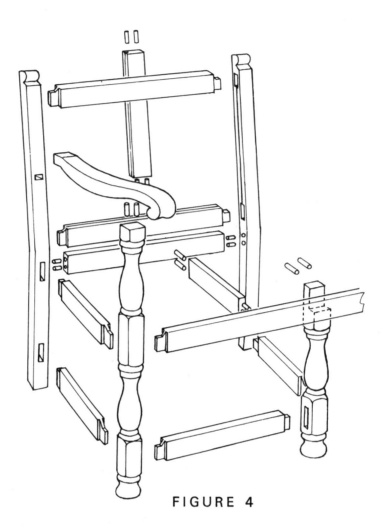

FIGURE 4

dimension as the seat rail, namely $2\frac{5}{8}$ inches by $\frac{7}{8}$ inch (67 mm × 22 mm). You can see, too, that the rail and leg are dowelled together with loose dowels.

All the rails are the same thickness, $\frac{7}{8}$ inch (22 mm), but do vary in width. The seat rails, for instance, are $2\frac{5}{8}$ inches (67 mm) wide: the underframe rails $2\frac{1}{4}$ inches (58 mm), and the back rails $2\frac{7}{8}$ inches (73 mm).

Fig. 4 shows the method of assembling these rails into the frame. In general, it is by means of haunched tenons, although some are dowelled so that they can be framed in more easily.

The shape of the arm is shown in Fig. 3 and is cut from a block 21 inches by 3 inches square (533 mm × 76 mm square). It is shown with the scroll fluted, but this is not essential. Note that there is a "flat" immediately behind the scroll on the under-

side so that it fits over the end of the front leg, to which it is dowelled.

As the seat is such an important feature, every effort should be made to use solid timber if at all possible, and if necessary you could resort to jointing pieces together.

If you do this, the seat should be fixed by means of buttons along the short edges (to accommodate any shrinkage), and pocket-screwing along the long edges. It will, of course, need to be notched round the squares of the front legs.

Alternatively, you could use oak-veneered plywood. However, this will need a wide 4 inch (102 mm) lipping along the front edge, and a narrower 2 inch (51 mm) one at each end. These will mask the edges and allow you to pocket-screw into them for fixing, and in the case of the wide front one it will offer enough solid wood for the notch to be cut out.

Parts List

No. of pcs.	Description	Long	Wide	Thick
3	Back feet	52 (1320)	3 (76)	2¾ (70)
2	Front legs	27½ (698)	3 (76)	2¾ (70)
1	Centre leg	18 (457)	3 (76)	2¾ (70)
2	Back rails, top	32 (812)	3 (76)	1⅛ (29)
2	Back rails, bottom	32 (812)	4 (102)	1⅛ (29)
2	Back seat rails	30 (762)	3 (76)	1⅛ (29)
2	Back muntins	25 (635)	3 (76)	1⅛ (29)
1	Front seat rail	63 (1600)	2¾ (67)	⅞ (23)
2	End seat rails	17 (431)	2¾ (67)	⅞ (23)
2	Seat bearers	14 (356)	2¾ (67)	⅞ (23)
3	Underframe rails, short	17 (431)	2¾ (64)	⅞ (23)
2	Underframe rails, long	32 (812)	2½ (64)	⅞ (23)
2	Arms	21½ (546)	3½ (89)	3 (76)
2	Back panels (ply)	26 (660)	15 (381)	¼ (7)
2	Back panels (ply)	26 (660)	16½ (419)	¼ (7)
1	Seat	78 (1676)	17½ (445)	⅞ (23)

Allowances have been made to lengths and widths; thicknesses are net.
Millimetre equivalents in brackets.

23. UPRIGHT SPINNING WHEEL

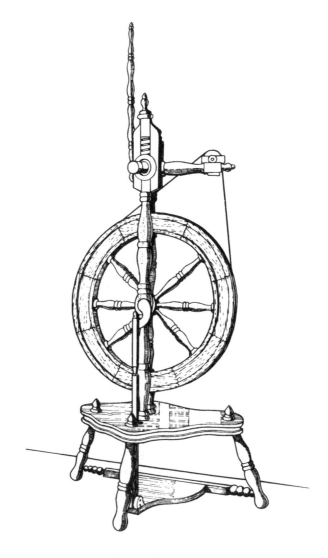

FIGURE 1

Apart from their purely functional role, spinning wheels make very decorative pieces of occasional furniture in a period setting. There are, of course, several designs but this one, which is a Welsh-style spinning wheel, is perhaps the most compact and attractive of all.

The piece needs to be made up in hardwood, and looks extremely well in mahogany or walnut, although selected beech is an ideal alternative. The shape of the stand is shown in Fig. 3, while Fig. 2 shows the splay of the legs, each of which is set at an angle of 70 degrees. To achieve this, work on the under-

FIGURE 2

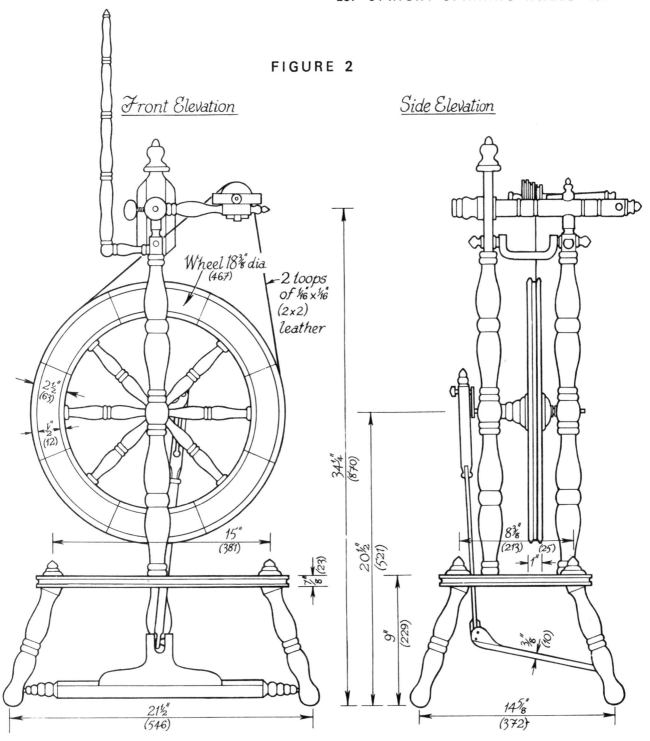

Front Elevation

Side Elevation

Wheel 18⅜" dia. (467)

2 loops of ¹⁄₁₆" × ¹⁄₁₆" (2×2) leather

2½" (63)

½" (12)

15" (381)

34¼" (870)

20½" (521)

9" (229)

7⁄₈" (23)

21½" (546)

8⅜" (213)

1" (25)

⅜" (10)

14⅝" (372)

side of the stand: cut one face of a piece of scrap-wood at 70 degrees and cramp it to the stand so that it will act as a guide for the bit. You will probably find it best to bore a small hole first and then enlarge it.

Boring holes for the spokes in the hub is shown in Fig. 4B, illustrating a simple jig

for drawing the guide lines. Before inserting the hub into the hole you will need to mark the centre line first, with a further line ¹⁄₁₆ inch (4 mm) away from it. With the centre line uppermost push the hub into the hole so that the second line is level with the face of the jig all round. The jig can, of course, be made

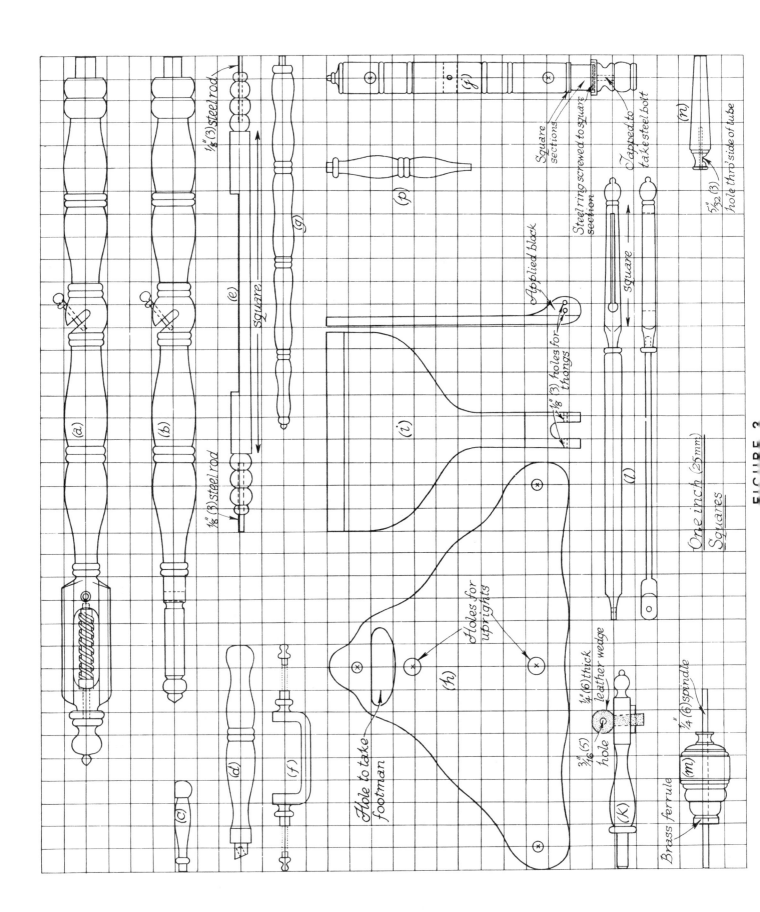

FIGURE 2

One inch (25mm)
Squares

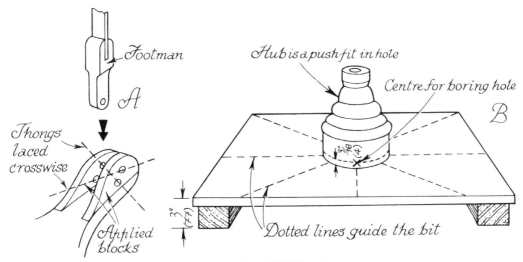

Footman

A

Hub is a push-fit in hole

Centre for boring hole

B

Thongs laced crosswise

Applied blocks

$3''$ (77)

Dotted lines guide the bit

FIGURE 4

from scrap timber; the hole should accept the hub as a push-fit.

When boring the holes in the felloes (which are the segments of the wheel) and the hub make sure they are all exactly the same depth, otherwise the wheel will not be true.

The spokes must be inserted dry without glue, as a tight fit, and so must the dowels which join the felloes. Do not use more than two dowels at any of the joints between the felloes — one is best — nor should a loose tenon be used as damage could result if the wheel should go into winding. If you do not have a band cramp, the wheel can be cramped up with a loop of stout string around it into which a short piece of dowel rod is inserted and twisted to tighten it (in fact, a "Spanish Windlass"). The wheel must be laid on a perfectly flat surface and well weighted down while this is done to keep it true. The only glue used should be on the meeting edges of the felloes.

The screw-thread in the upright (*a*), Fig. 3, should traditionally be wooden and would normally be worked with a screwbox and tap. However, a metal thread is just as effective and a suitable one might be obtained from an old vice or G-cramp.

The square section of the mother-of-all (*j*), Fig. 3, should be slightly less than $1\frac{1}{8}$ inches (30 mm) square. A female thread has to be tapped through the square section to receive the screw-thread and it is highly advisable to cramp scrap pieces around it while the operation is being done. A hole has also

to be bored through the mother-of-all which will slide over the top of the upright (*b*) ensuring that it is lined up exactly with the female thread. Also, bore a hole at 90 degrees for the clamp screw — $\frac{5}{16}$ inch Whitworth — the thread can be tapped directly into the wood with a No. 2 tap.

A steel plate $1\frac{1}{8}$ inches (30 mm) square is screwed to the end of the square section of the mother-of-all with a $\frac{5}{16}$ inch (8 mm) Whitworth steel bolt brazed or welded to the centre of it, and a brass ferrule is fitted to the driving end of the hub to reduce wear.

The driving quadrant (B, Fig. 5) is made from $\frac{1}{8}$ inch (3 mm) brass plate which is brazed to the $\frac{1}{4}$ inch (6 mm) spindle. A hole is bored through the centre of the hub to accept the spindle; also drill a $\frac{3}{32}$ inch (2 mm) hole through the ferrule, hub, and spindle; a small steel pin is inserted in this to lock the assembly.

Shape the spindle slots by drilling a $\frac{1}{4}$ inch (6 mm) dia. hole through both uprights and saw slots to meet each other at an angle of 45 degrees — these slots must be identical and lined up very carefully. Leather pads should be cut to fit into the slots so that the spindle is held in place, free to rotate but not to wobble.

The spool and smaller pulley should be turned as one piece, the other two pulleys separately. The outer end should be turned on the flyer (A, Fig. 5) first before it is shaped; throughout this assembly the lathe centres should be used as centres for drilling the holes to accept the steel tube.

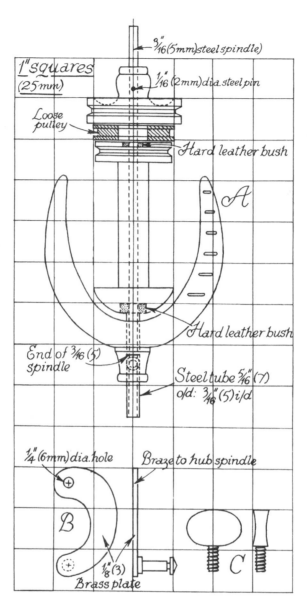

FIGURE 5

Insert the $\frac{5}{16}$ inch (8 mm) tube into the hole in the flyer so that $\frac{3}{16}$ inch (5 mm) projects as a spacer between the flyer and the hard leather bush in the spool. Push the $\frac{3}{16}$ inch (5 mm) spindle into the tube for $\frac{7}{8}$ of an inch (23 mm). Drill a $\frac{13}{64}$ inch (5 mm) dia. hole down the centre of the spool and fit hard leather bushes onto both ends.

Bore a $\frac{5}{8}$ inch (17 mm) dia. hole in the rounded end of the spool, $\frac{1}{4}$ inch (6 mm) deep, and fit a $\frac{3}{16}$ inch (5 mm) thick hard leather bush into each end; make sure that it will run smoothly on the $\frac{3}{16}$ inch (5 mm) spindle.

The outer pulley should be turned so that it has a $\frac{3}{4}$ inch (19 mm) dia. extension, $\frac{5}{16}$ inch (8 mm) long, for the loose pulley to rotate on.

Make the loose pulley $\frac{1}{4}$ inch (6 mm) thick and slip it over the outer pulley into its correct position and bore a $\frac{1}{16}$ inch (2 mm) hole through the outer pulley. Slide the pulley on to the spindle until the spool can just turn freely: drill a $\frac{1}{16}$ inch (2 mm) hole through the pulley and the spindle and insert the small steel pin.

Parts List

No. req'd	Description	Long	Wide	Thick
1	Stand (*h*)	18½ (470)	11½ (292)	$\frac{7}{8}$ (23)
1	Treadle (*i*)	12 (315)	9¼ (235)	$\frac{3}{8}$ (10)
8	Felloes	7½ (191)	3¼ (83)	$\frac{15}{16}$ (24)
1	Footman (*l*)	20 (508)	1 (25)	$\frac{3}{4}$ (19)
1	Flyer (A, Fig. 4)	5⅜ (137)	5 (127)	$\frac{7}{8}$ (23)
1	Spacer (*f*)	6½ (165)	2 (51)	$\frac{5}{8}$ (16)
2	Blocks for upright (*a*), each	6 (153)	1 (25)	$\frac{5}{8}$ (16)
1	Upright (*a*)	32 (813)	2¼ (58)	2 (51)
1	Upright (*b*)	29½ (749)	2¼ (58)	2 (51)
1	Treadle stretcher (*e*)	20½ (521)	1¼ (32)	1 (25)
1	Mother-of-all (*j*)	15 (382)	2¼ (58)	2 (51)
8	Spokes, each (*p*)	7 (178)	1¼ (32)	1⅛ (29)
1	Top piece, distaff (*g*)	4 (102)	1 (25)	$\frac{3}{4}$ (19)
1	Middle piece, distaff (*g*)	4⅝ (118)	1 (25)	$\frac{7}{8}$ (23)
1	Bottom piece, distaff (*g*)	5¾ (147)	1⅛ (29)	1 (25)
3	Legs, each (*d*)	10 (254)	1¾ (44)	1½ (38)
1	Hub (*m*)	4½ (115)	2¾ (70)	2½ (64)
2	Maidens, each (*k*)	9¼ (235)	1¾ (45)	1½ (38)
1	Distaff arm (*c*)	4 (102)	1⅛ (29)	1 (25)
1	Spool (A, Fig. 4)	4½ (115)	2½ (64)	2¼ (58)
1	End pulley (A, Fig. 4)	1⅝ (42)	3 (77)	2¾ (70)
1	Loose pulley (A, Fig. 4)	½ (13)	2½ (64)	2¼ (58)

Applied blocks to the treadle and the finials can come from scrap. Some timber can be saved by turning the neck of the flyer as a separate piece and gluing the two together although it would not be as strong as working the piece as a whole.

Allowances have been made to lengths and widths; thicknesses are net.
Millimetre equivalents in brackets.

24. BED HEAD WITH LINEN-FOLD CARVING

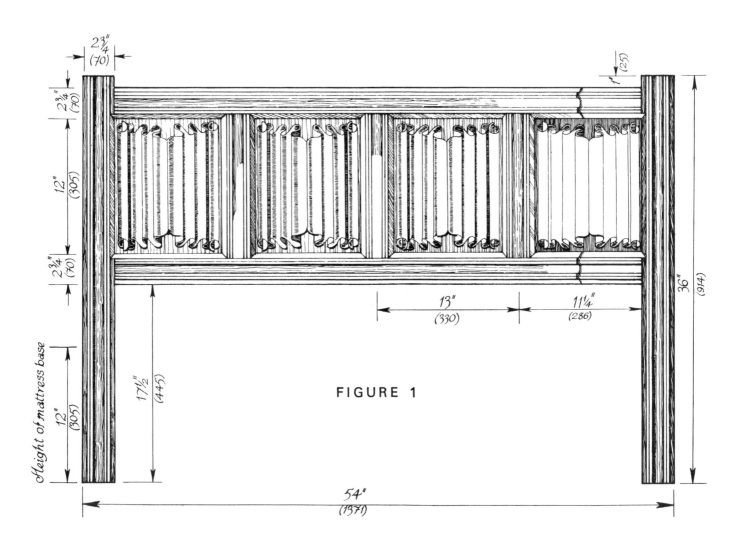

FIGURE 1

A design such as this calls for solid oak throughout, and when made up and carved it will be a really beautiful piece, well suited to be a family heirloom!

The style of linen-fold carving shown in Fig. 1 is the same as that dealt with more fully elsewhere in the book. It is, however,

quite a complicated pattern (see Fig. 2A for the one-inch squared-off drawing of the outline for marking out), so an alternative, simpler design is given at B. Note that a double line of punched dots is made round the edges as shown to simulate stitching.

General construction is straightforward,

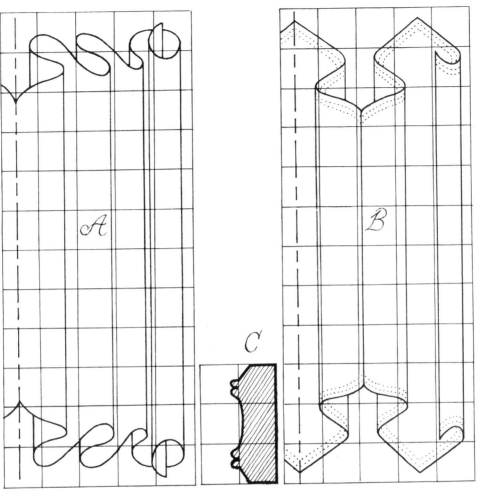

A

B

C

FIGURE 2

as mortise and tenon joints are used throughout the framing, but the mitring of the bevels
at the junctions of the rails with the vertical
posts may be tricky.

These mitres are called "mason's mitres"
because of their adaptation from stonework
and are not true mitres at all. Fig. 3 shows
details and the essential point to note is that
the joining of the two members should be
completed before the mitre itself is cut. The
bevels should, however, be formed prior to
gluing up the joint; the bevel on the rail
runs right out, but the one on the post is
stopped at a point level with the bottom edge
of the top rail (or level with the upper edge
of the bottom rail). Once the joint has been
made, the corner can be neatly carved to
resemble a mitre.

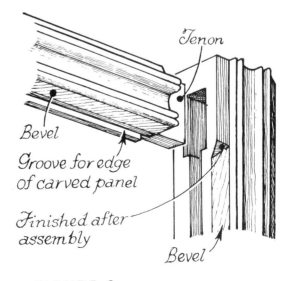

Tenon

Bevel

*Groove for edge
of carved panel*

*Finished after
assembly*

Bevel

FIGURE 3

The posts and rails have to be grooved $\frac{5}{16}$ inch (8 mm) wide by $\frac{3}{8}$ inch (10 mm) deep to accept the edges of the carved panels, which are inserted without glue so that any shrinkage can take place freely. If you wish, you could peg each tenon with a couple of dowels, and these could penetrate right through from back to front.

Fig. 2C shows a section of both the posts and the rails. The channelling and double-beads would have been worked as far as possible with moulding planes and finished off with a scratch stock with a suitably shaped cutter.

A word about the height of the headboard. This will depend on the type of bed you are using with it, and as designed it would be suitable for a spring mattress, plus a base, and plus an interior-sprung mattress.

Parts List

No. req'd.	Description	Long	Wide	Thick
2	Posts	37 (940)	3 (76)	$1\frac{1}{4}$ (32)
2	Rails	51 (1295)	3 (76)	$1\frac{1}{4}$ (32)
3	Muntins	15 (381)	3 (76)	$1\frac{1}{4}$ (32)
4	Panels	$13\frac{1}{2}$ (343)	11 (279)	$\frac{3}{4}$ (19)

Allowances have been made to lengths and widths; thicknesses are net.
Millimetre equivalents in brackets.

25. EIGHTEENTH CENTURY FOUR-POSTER BED

FIGURE 1

The four-poster bed has an interesting history, and the first designs must have been prompted by the twin desires for warmth and privacy. It must be obvious to anyone who has visited a few historic great houses or castles that the need to keep warm must have been one of the major problems of the past. What better, then, than a bed which could be totally enclosed by heavy curtainings to retain heat and keep out draughts? Further, such a bed could give some semblance of privacy in the days when the subdivision of a castle or manor house into a number of rooms was the exception rather

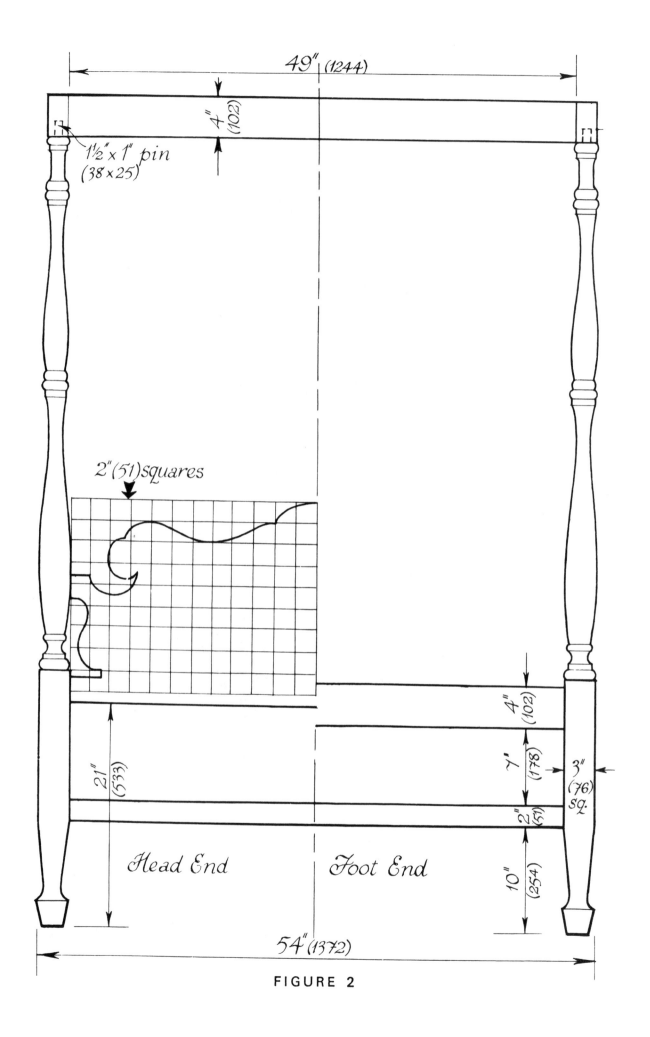

49" (1244)

4" (102)

1½" x 1" pin
(38 x 25)

2" (51) squares

21" (533)

4" (102)

7" (178)

3" (76) sq.

2" (51)

10" (254)

Head End

Foot End

54" (1372)

FIGURE 2

than the rule.

The "tester" or canopy of the traditional four poster comprised a flat framework which was fastened to the tops of the pillars. As there were often two sets of curtains — the inner ones of fine material, with an outer set of coarser "covers" to protect them from dust, the framework had necessarily to be quite wide.

We have departed from this idea in our design in favour of tester rails which are positioned vertically, as we assume that only one set of hangings will be used. No method of hanging them has been shown as there are so many different types of track on the market.

Before beginning work you must, of course, decide on the type of bed the posts are to enclose. In our design you will see from Fig. 3 that we show the section of a 4 inch (102 mm) deep base with an 8 inch (203 mm) deep interior sprung mattress on top. Both rest on a pair of mild steel side irons which either fit into "chills" (a kind of metal dovetail socket) screwed to the head and foot ends, or lap over projecting brackets to which they are bolted. In either case the overall height of 24 inches (610 mm) is the accepted level.

It is perfectly feasible to fit a divan bed between the ends but as heights vary you may have to modify the dimensions shown in the illustrations.

This is a design which really should be made up using straight-grained hardwoods for the posts. If at all possible the shaped head end should also be in solid wood; veneered man-made board could be used but you will then have the problem of masking the edges around the curved shapes. You could use one of the flexible veneer tapes sold in DIY shops for this purpose but you may have difficulty in getting such a tape to bed down nicely around the tighter curves.

The four posts are obviously the first parts to be dealt with and each one comprises three sections — the bottom one being 24 inches (609 mm) long, and the remaining two 27 inches (686 mm) each. This means that the sections should fit nicely into almost any lathe, whether professional or amateur.

Cut the spade toe feet on the bandsaw in a similar fashion to the method shown elsewhere for cutting cabriole legs. This means saving the offcut from the first cut and pinning it back on temporarily to form a flat

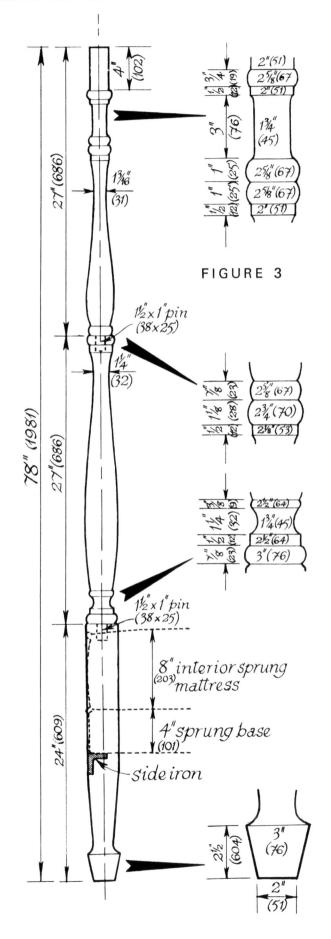

FIGURE 3

surface enabling the shape to be cut on the next face.

Joints between the sections are best made by gluing in loose dowels to the ends of each section, a suitably-sized hole having been pre-bored. Alternatively you can achieve the same result by turning a pin on one section which will fit into a hole bored in the section next to it – if you adopt this method you will have to add the length of the pin (one inch – 25 mm) to the lengths shown. The pins at the top corners fit into the square corner blocks of the tester frame. Although this sounds straightforward, you must take care to bore the holes dead-centre and truly vertical, otherwise the post will develop an unsightly kink. To ensure truth it would be worthwhile making up a simple jig to guide the bit.

Mortise and tenon joints join the rails to the posts at both head and foot ends, and are also used to fix the shaped head end. Note that the foot end has been kept simple in design, concentrating on strength rather than decoration. It is, of course, normally hidden from view by the bed covers.

The tester framework can be made up in softwood, the rails being mortise and tenoned into the corner blocks. As the length of this framework will depend on the length of the type of bed you decide on it is impossible to quote a definite length, but in any event two intermediate cross rails should be incorporated.

It is worth pointing out that there is plenty of historical precedent for constructing the design in a hardwood such as beech and painting it white. This can look very elegant, particularly if a touch of gilding is added here and there.

Parts List

No. req'd.	Description	Long	Wide	Thick
4	Posts	78 (1981)	3 (76)	3 (76)
1	Head end	50 (1270)	10 (254)	$\frac{7}{8}$ (23)
1	Head end rail	50 (1270)	$2\frac{1}{4}$ (58)	$\frac{3}{4}$ (19)
1	Foot end upper rail	50 (1270)	$4\frac{1}{4}$ (108)	$\frac{3}{4}$ (19)
1	Foot end lower rail	50 (1270)	$2\frac{1}{4}$ (58)	$\frac{3}{4}$ (19)
4	Tester corner blocks	5 (127)	2 (51)	$1\frac{7}{8}$ (48)
2	Tester end rails	51 (1295)	$4\frac{1}{4}$ (108)	$\frac{3}{4}$ (19)
2	Tester side rails	to suit	$4\frac{1}{4}$ (108)	$\frac{3}{4}$ (19)
2	Tester intermediate rails	$53\frac{1}{2}$ (1358)	$4\frac{1}{4}$ (108)	$\frac{5}{8}$ (16)

Allowances have been made to lengths and widths; thicknesses are net.
Millimetre equivalents in brackets.

26. LINEN CHEST

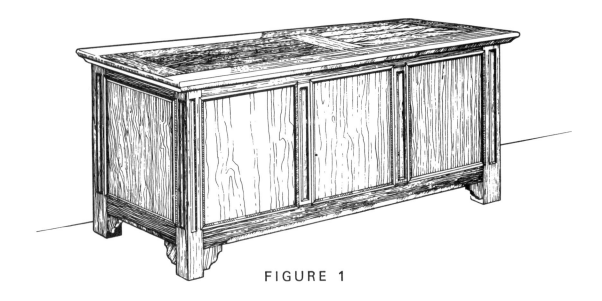

FIGURE 1

This handsome chest offers a really large storage space for household linen. Although quite restrained in its design it has a touch of the Jacobean style about it.

If a more heavily carved appearance is thought desirable then there is no reason why some diamond-shaped or linenfold panelling or carved ornamentation should not be used.

Many chests of the Tudor and Jacobean periods were, in fact, fully carved and some fine examples can be seen in the book *Shorter Dictionary of English Furniture* by Ralph Edwards.

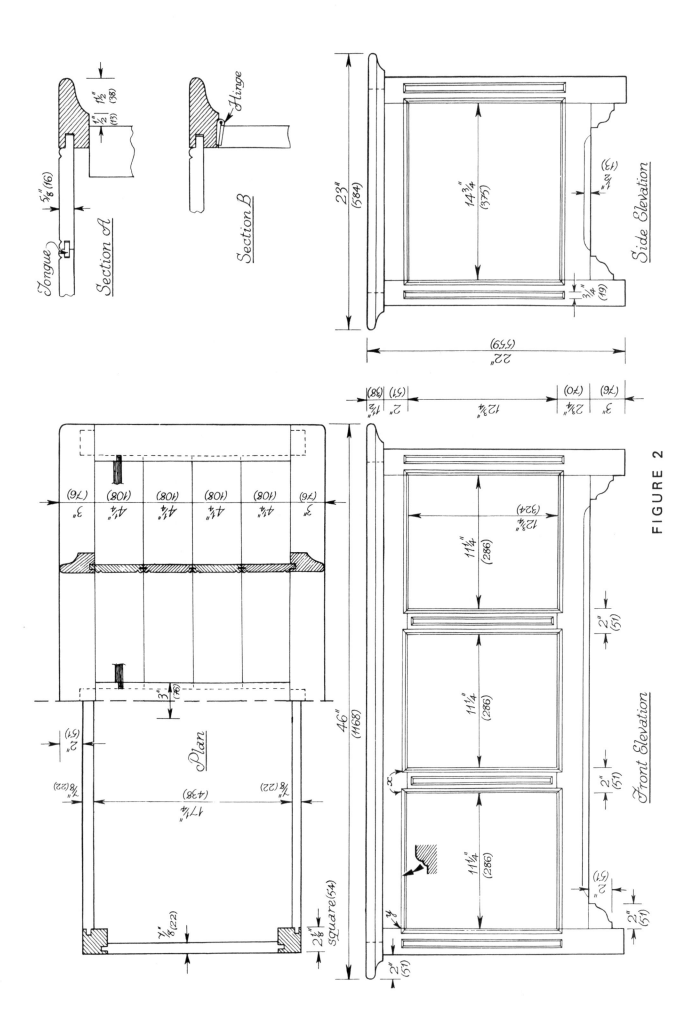

FIGURE 2

It is, of course, a matter of personal taste when it comes to the decoration of a piece such as this.

The Parts List is for the chest as illustrated and if you wish to add carving details you should make some allowance for extra depths where necessary.

Oak would be the ideal choice for making up this piece, although a good quality softwood would be a perfectly acceptable alternative.

Construction of the carcase is achieved by employing conventional mortise and tenon joints throughout, and also using the same type of joint for assembling the top frame (Fig. 2, Plan).

As the side and end panels are grooved into position into the posts, muntins, and rails, the grooves can be extended and enlarged to provide the mortises.

The long channels on the posts and muntins are recessed out by means of a router and their sides finished off by hand to a 45 degree bevel; the corners are, of course, mitred, and the total depth should be about $\frac{3}{16}$ inch (6 mm).

The edges around the panels are also moulded to the pattern profile shown in the front elevation, Fig. 2.

A point to note here is that a mason's mitre has to be used at the corners marked (x) and (y), and also at the other corresponding corners.

As has already been described, a mason's mitre is one that has to be carved by hand on the solid member to match up with the moulding which butts against it.

You will also see that the lower edge of the bottom rails has been chamfered to give a lighter appearance. The small corner blocks can be dowelled and glued in place.

As you can see from Fig. 1, the top is boarded in two panels. In the section, Fig. 2, Plan, the boards are shown with their heart sides alternating to minimize the effect of "cupping", and Section A, Fig. 2 illustrates how the boards are tongued to each other. Also, they are grooved across their ends into the cross rails at each end; a bead is worked along each long edge so that if movement does occur, any small gaps will be less noticeable.

Section B, Fig. 2, shows how the hinges are recessed into the top and the carcase rail so that the top can open without binding along its back edge. Incidentally, the profile of the moulded edge of the top rails affords a good grip for lifting the top.

The bottom can be $\frac{1}{2}$ inch (12 mm) plywood, housed into the bottom rails all round and notched around the corner posts.

PARTS LIST *See over*

Parts List

No. req'd	Description	Long	Wide	Thick
4	Posts	21 (534)	$2\frac{1}{4}$ (58)	$2\frac{1}{8}$ (54)
2	Bottom carcase rails, side	40 (1016)	$3\frac{1}{4}$ (83)	$\frac{7}{8}$ (23)
2	Bottom carcase rails, end	17 (432)	$3\frac{1}{4}$ (83)	$\frac{7}{8}$ (23)
2	Top carcase rails, side	40 (1016)	$2\frac{1}{4}$ (58)	$\frac{7}{8}$ (23)
2	Top carcase rails, end	17 (432)	$2\frac{1}{4}$ (58)	$\frac{7}{8}$ (23)
4	Muntins	$14\frac{1}{2}$ (369)	$2\frac{1}{4}$ (58)	$\frac{7}{8}$ (23)
2	Top rails, long	47 (1194)	$3\frac{1}{4}$ (83)	$1\frac{1}{2}$ (38)
3	Top rails, short cross	$20\frac{1}{2}$ (521)	$3\frac{1}{4}$ (83)	$1\frac{1}{2}$ (38)
8	Top boards	$19\frac{1}{2}$ (495)	$4\frac{1}{2}$ (115)	$\frac{5}{8}$ (16)
1	Bottom	42 (1067)	$18\frac{1}{2}$ (470)	$\frac{1}{2}$ (13)
8	Corner blocks	$2\frac{1}{2}$ (64)	$2\frac{1}{4}$ (58)	$\frac{1}{2}$ (13)

Allowances have been made to lengths and widths; thicknesses are net.
Millimetre equivalents in brackets.

27. EARLY EIGHTEENTH CENTURY CHEST OF DRAWERS

FIGURE 1

By Queen Anne's time, chests of drawers were recognized as being necessary pieces of bedroom furniture, and as in the case of this design the decoration was restrained and the appearance kept simple and dignified.

The construction is shown in Fig. 3, and the introduction of the fluted quarter-columns at the front corners makes it rather unorthodox.

However, the top is straightforward — it is shown as being solid, but it could be made up from a veneered panel with lipping around the edges. Such a lipping would

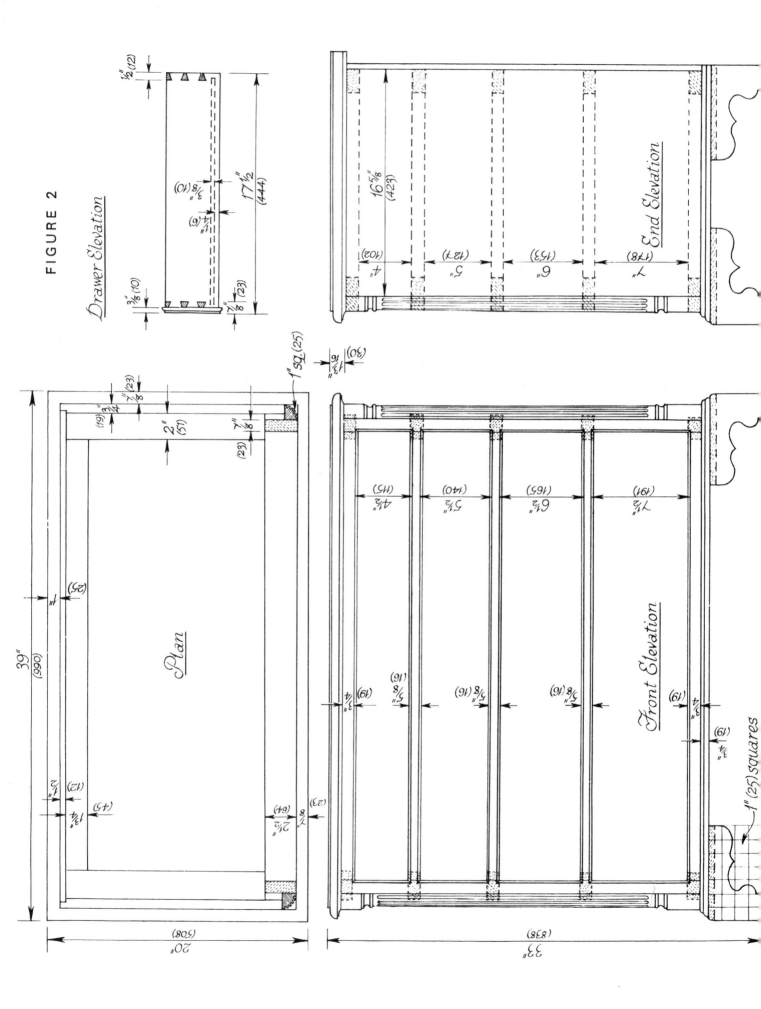

FIGURE 2

need to be 2 inches (51 mm) wide, and mitred at the front corners to avoid end grain showing.

As you can see from Fig. 3, the corner bracket feet are mitred to each other, the mitres being keyed with loose tongues. Then they are further strengthened by gluing and dowelling in triangular fillets, which will re-inforce the whole thing considerably.

They are then glued and screwed to the flat plinth framework immediately above, which has its outer edges moulded.

The carcase framing is shown best in the plan, Fig. 2 and the drawing of the end in Fig. 3. If solid timber is used for the ends,

then it must be dry and fully seasoned, other-wise it would be advisable to use veneered ply or blockboard. At the front, there is a rectangular frame with the rails arranged so that their edges show; at the corner, the top kicker and the drawer runners beneath are offset so that the fluted quarter-turning can be accommodated. The amount of offset is such that the kicker and drawer runners lie along-side the end, to which they can be glued and dowelled. A partial mortise and tenon can be used to join them to the front framing.

As can be seen, the front drawer rails are housed into the corner muntins, which makes a very strong joint. At the back, cross rails

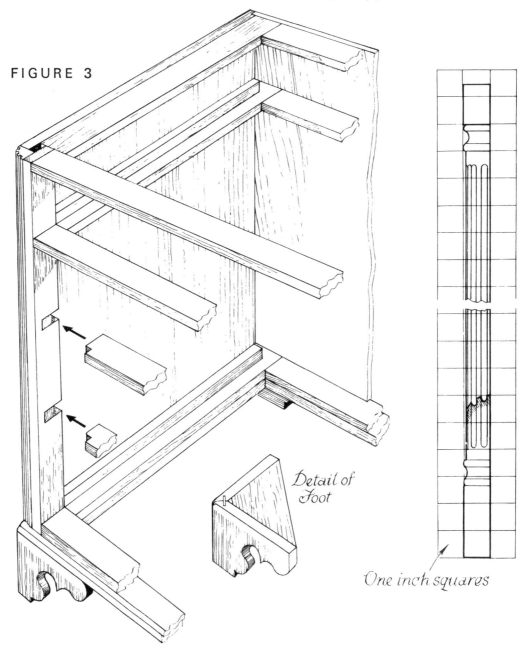

FIGURE 3

Detail of Foot

One inch squares

are mortise and tenoned into the kickers and drawer runners and are also screwed and glued to the back. The latter is rebated into the ends and laps over the bottom frame.

Loose dowels and glue will suffice to hold the quarter-turnings in place. To make these, a square block must first be turned to the measurement shown in Fig. 3, where the drawing is squared off into one inch (25 mm) squares. Then the block has to be sawn very carefully to produce the quarters.

Next comes the task of working the flutes. They could be taken out mechanically by a spindle moulder, in which case it would be easier to cut them before the square is sawn into quarters. Even so, the ends of the flutes will still need to be finished off by hand.

In fact, you will probably find that the whole job is best done at the bench, carefully marking out the flutes first and then roughing them out with a gouge. A suitably-shaped scraper can then be employed to finish them off to the correct depth and contour.

The drawers (Fig. 2) are conventional in construction and, true to the best tradition, the depth varies from top to bottom, the uppermost being the shallowest and the bottom one being deepest. Note that each drawer front has a $\frac{1}{4}$ inch (6 mm) overlap all round, and is rebated on its inside face to achieve this.

If you wish to incorporate dustboards, then you can work a $\frac{3}{16}$ inch (4 mm) groove on the inner edges of the drawer rails and runners into which sheets of plywood can be inserted These dustboards are a desirable feature, as not only do they help to prevent dust getting into the drawers but also mean that drawers cannot be overfilled with the consequent difficulty in opening the drawer because something has become jammed in the drawer aperture above!

The method of fixing the top depends on whether it is solid, or a panel which has been lipped round. If it is solid, then it can be secured along the front and back edges by means of screws driven up through the rails. To allow for shrinkage across the ends, however, it would be best to slot-screw up through the rails. In the case of a lipped top, however, it can be simply screwed on all round.

Parts List

No. req'd.	Description	Long	Wide	Thick
1	Top	40 (1016)	21 (533)	$1\frac{3}{16}$ (51)
1	Square for quarter-turnings	28 (711)	$1\frac{1}{4}$ (32)	1 (25)
8	Corner brackets	$7\frac{1}{2}$ (191)	$4\frac{1}{4}$ (108)	$\frac{7}{8}$ (23)
4	Triangular fillets for above (from 2 pcs.)	$7\frac{1}{2}$ (191)	$7\frac{1}{2}$ (191)	$\frac{3}{4}$ (19)
2	Long plinth frame rails	39 (990)	$3\frac{1}{2}$ (89)	$\frac{7}{8}$ (23)
2	Short plinth frame rails	$19\frac{1}{4}$ (489)	$3\frac{1}{2}$ (89)	$\frac{7}{8}$ (23)
2	Corner muntins	28 (711)	$2\frac{3}{4}$ (70)	$\frac{7}{8}$ (23)
2	Ends	28 (711)	$17\frac{1}{2}$ (445)	$\frac{3}{4}$ (19)

No. req'd.	Description	Long	Wide	Thick
2	Top and bottom drawer rails	34½ (876)	2¾ (70)	¾ (19)
3	Intermediate drawer rails	34½ (876)	2¾ (70)	⅝ (16)
4	Top and bottom drawer runners	16 (407)	2¼ (58)	¾ (19)
6	Intermediate drawer runners	16 (407)	2¼ (58)	⅝ (16)
2	Back drawer rails, top and bottom	34 (864)	2¼ (58)	¾ (19)
3	Back drawer rails, intermediate	34 (864)	2¼ (58)	⅝ (16)
8	Drawer guides	15 (381)	1¼ (32)	1 (25)
1	Back	37 (940)	27¾ (705)	½ (12)
1	Drawer front	34 (864)	5 (127)	⅞ (23)
2	Sides	17½ (445)	4½ (114)	⅜ (10)
1	Back	34 (864)	4½ (114)	½ (12)
1	Drawer front	34 (864)	6 (152)	⅞ (23)
2	Sides	17½ (445)	5½ (140)	⅜ (10)
1	Back	34 (864)	5½ (140)	½ (12)
1	Drawer front	34 (864)	7 (178)	⅞ (23)
2	Sides	17½ (445)	6½ (165)	⅜ (10)
1	Back	34 (864)	6½ (165)	½ (12)
1	Drawer front	34 (864)	8 (204)	⅞ (23)
2	Sides	17½ (445)	7½ (191)	⅜ (10)
1	Back	34 (864)	7½ (191)	½ (12)
4	Drawer bottoms	33½ (851)	17 (432)	⅜ (10)

Allowances have been made to lengths and widths; thicknesses are net.
Millimetre equivalents in brackets.

28. SEVENTEENTH CENTURY OAK CRADLE

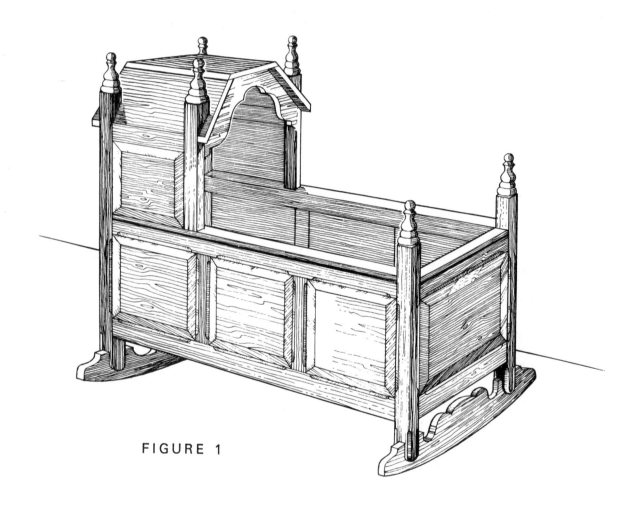

FIGURE 1

For a traditional design such as this, oak is the obvious choice and as there are no large pieces it should not be difficult to come by. If desired, the bottom could be oak-faced plywood or transverse boards of a minor hardwood, such as elm or chestnut, which would be grooved into the side and end rails, and tongued and grooved together.

Fig. 3 shows the method of construction which, as you can see, employs mainly mortise and tenon joints. There is a timesaving bonus here, as the grooves which have to be worked to accept the fielded panels can also act as mortises for the tenons, although the

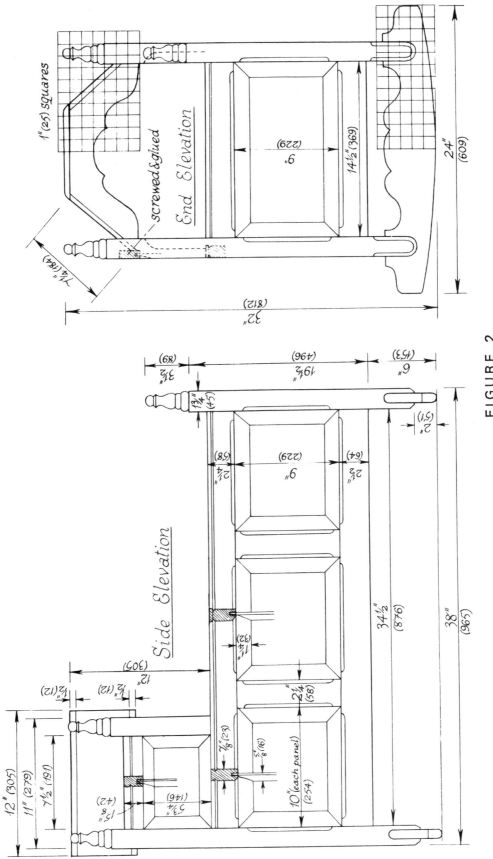

FIGURE 2

grooves may have to be eased out locally.

The two small posts (C) are, however, dowelled into the top rail (D), and this means that the rounded edges of the rail (Fig. 2) have to be stopped at the point where they are planted on. The remainder of the rail also has to be grooved to accept the panel (S).

Dowels are also used to fix the arched piece (M) into the posts (C) at either end. From the end elevation in Fig. 2, you can also see how the sloping roof pieces are screwed and glued to the rails (L). The other parts of the roof are glued and pinned together, with applied glue blocks for extra strength.

The other type of joint used is the simple form of bridle joint for fixing on the rockers,

which are housed in a slot cut in the bottom of each corner post. Further strength for the joints can be provided by driving screws through each joint assembly from the inside so that the screws are not readily visible.

If you do decide to incorporate the fielded panels it does, of course, mean that you will need solid oak for them. As an alternative, oak-faced plywood could be used, and to relieve the rather heavy and plain appearance it would be advisable to work stopped chamfers on the edges of the frame rails as shown in Figs. 1 and 2.

Lastly, note that about half the thickness of post (C) is cut away, so that the remaining thickness will be flush with the rail (D).

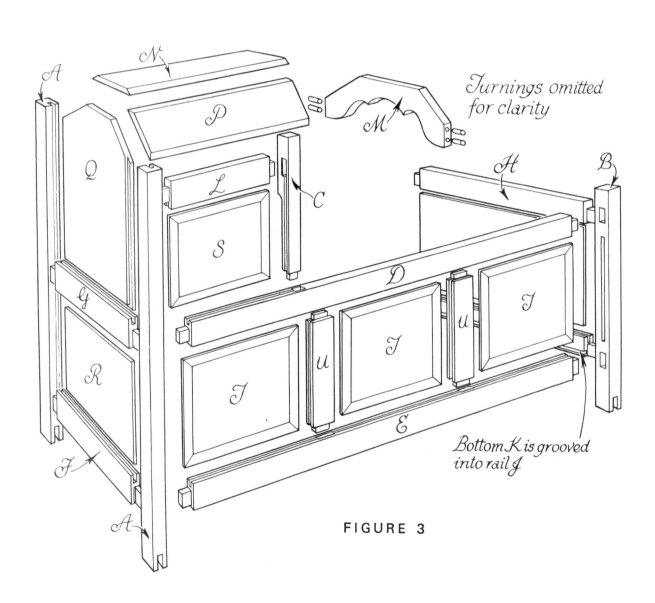

Turnings omitted for clarity

Bottom K is grooved into rail g

FIGURE 3

Parts List

No. req'd	Description	Long	Wide	Thick
2	Long posts (A)	31 (787)	2 (51)	1¾ (45)
2	Short posts (B)	28 (712)	2 (51)	1¾ (45)
2	Hood posts (C)	13 (330)	2 (51)	1¾ (45)
2	Long top rails (D)	37 (940)	2½ (64)	⅞ (23)
2	Long bottom rails (E)	37 (940)	2¾ (70)	⅞ (23)
2	End bottom rails (F) and (J)	17 (432)	2¾ (64)	⅞ (23)
2	End top rails (G) and (H)	17 (432)	2½ (70)	⅞ (23)
1	Bottom (K): oak-faced ply	35½ (902)	16 (407)	¼ (7)
2	Hood rails (L)	9 (229)	2½ (64)	⅞ (23)
1	Arching piece (M)	15 (381)	6 (153)	½ (13)
1	Top piece (N)	13 (330)	8½ (216)	½ (13)
2	Top pieces (P), sloping	13 (330)	7¾ (197)	½ (13)
1	Hood end panel (Q)	15½ (394)	12 (305)	⅜ (10)
2	End panels (R)	15½ (394)	10 (254)	⅜ (10)
2	Hood panels (S)	8½ (216)	6½ (165)	⅜ (10)
6	Side panels (T)	11 (279)	10 (254)	⅜ (10)
4	Muntins (U)	11 (279)	2½ (64)	⅞ (23)
2	Rockers	25 (635)	5 (127)	¾ (19)

Allowances have been made to lengths and widths; thicknesses are net.
Millimetre equivalents in brackets.

Bibliography

As far as possible I have only included practical books—that is, books which not only contain photographs or drawings of period pieces but also working details of construction, or which deal with a particular technique in an authoritative way.

Cabinet Making for Beginners, by C. H. Hayward
(Evans Bros, London, Drake, New York)
Although ostensibly written for beginners it nevertheless forms a very useful handbook for experienced workers.

Complete Book of Woodwork, by C. H. Hayward
(Evans Bros, London, Drake, New York)
In the nature of things it is difficult to go into too much detail on any particular subject in what purports to be a "complete" book. This book, however, manages to pack in a lot of invaluable information.

Creative Woodturning, by Dale L. Nish
(Stobart & Son, London, Brigham Young U.P., Provo)
A complete manual of the subject, written by an expert. Contains pretty well all you need to know about wood turning.

English Period Furniture, by C. H. Hayward
(Evans Bros, London)
Although primarily concerned with the development of furniture design over the centuries there are also many details of traditional construction and methods.

History and Practice of Woodcarving, by Frederick Oughton
(Stobart, London, Woodcraft Supply Corp, Woburn)
A treatise on the whole subject of woodcarving written by an acknowledged master of the art. Essential reading for serious woodcarvers.

Modern Cabinet Work, Furniture, and Fittings, by P. Wells and J. Hooper
(Batsford, London)
A book which is now, unfortunately, out of print. Although described as "modern" the methods dealt with relate to cabinet making in the early years of this century when the trade was probably at the peak of its skills. Because of this it is an indispensable book for our purpose, and it also contains a range of detailed reproduction designs. It's certainly worth the effort to get a copy.

Practical Veneering, by C. H. Hayward
(Evans Bros, London, Drake, New York)
A really exhaustive handbook on all aspects of veneering—invaluable to all serious woodworkers.

Practical Woodcarving and Gilding, by W. Wheeler and C. H. Hayward
(Evans Bros, London, Drake, New York)
Another indispensable book as it is angled towards period styles and imparts information not found in other books.

Reproducing Antique Furniture, by Franklin H. Gottshall
(Allen & Unwin, London, Crown, New York)
This deals with English and American period-style furniture. Very fully illustrated with photographs and detailed constructional drawings.

Staining and Polishing, by C. H. Hayward
(Evans Bros, London, Drake, New York)
Recognized as a standard handbook on all kinds of hand polishing, with a very full section on traditional french polishing.

The Technique of Furniture Making, by Ernest Joyce
(Batsford, London, Drake, New York)
An encyclopaedic work on the subject which has proved itself useful to many craftsmen.

Windsor Chairmaking, by Michael Dunbar
(Stobart & Son, London, Hastings House, New York)
A history of Windsor chairmaking throughout America and with instructions on how to make a bow-back design. Well illustrated.

Wood Finishing and Refinishing, by S. W. Gibbia.
(Van Nostrand, New York & Wokingham)
An American book which is notable for information on special finishes such as "distressing" and the like. Also contains many "tricks of the trade".

Woodwork Joints, by C. H. Hayward
(Evans Bros, London, Drake, New York)
The same remarks apply to this as to "Practical Veneering". An essential workshop handbook for the serious woodworker.

What Wood Is That? A Manual of Wood Identification, Herbert L. Edlin
(Stobart & Son, London, Viking, New York)
A splendid book containing 40 actual timber samples and with information needed to identify the various woods.

Glossary of Terms

No attempt has been made to include all the hundreds of terms and names of tools etc. used in woodwork and its allied crafts which most woodworkers will know, anyway. Rather, the aim has been to explain the more unusual words that you are likely to encounter in advanced work.

ACANTHUS A conventionalized representation of the foliage of the *Acanthus Spinosa*, a Mediterranean plant.

ACORN TURNING Applied to turned ornament resembling an acorn; usually found in Jacobean designs, especially on chair backs.

ADAM LEAFAGE A style of carved decoration favoured by Adam which closely resembles acanthus leafage. It is, however, more delicate in design and the ends of the lobes are rounded instead of pointed. It is also carved in low relief.

ANNULET A small moulding, usually semi-circular in section, circumscribing a column.

APRON PIECE Usually refers to a wide rail which is often curved or shaped and fixed to a piece of furniture less than three feet from the ground. Typical examples are found on Welsh dressers.

ARCHITRAVE The lowest member of the entablature in architecture; from our point of view, however, it refers to a moulding surrounding a door, window, or other opening.

ARMOIRE French term for a wardrobe or, more particularly, an old press.

ARRIS The sharp edge formed by two plane surfaces meeting at an angle.

ASTRAGAL A half-round moulding worked on an edge.

AUMBRY A small cupboard set in a wall or recess.

BALUSTER A small shaped column supporting handrailing.

BANDING A strip or band of veneer used as a decoration or to mask joints screwheads, etc. Also used around a panel or drawer front, when it is referred to as ''cross'' banding.

BANISTER A local name for Baluster. A cabinetmaker's term for a vertical splat, or splad, in the back of a chair.

BARRED DOOR A framed-up door made up with mouldings (called ''bars'') in the form of tracery.

BEAD AND BUTT A term applied when the sides of flush panels in a frame are separated from the stiles or muntins with a bead, the ends butting against the rails.

BEAD AND FLUSH Applies when the bead is worked and let in all round a panel.

BEAUMONTAGE A cabinet makers' stopping made of beeswax and resin which can be coloured to match the wood being used.

BED MOULDING Any moulding sited under the corona moulding of a cornice.

BOLECTION MOULDINGS A raised moulding with a rebate on the underside for fitting over the edges of a frame.

BOSTING-IN Term used by wood carvers to describe the roughing-out of a design.

BOTTLE TURNING A design of turned column resembling the shape of a bottle; originated in the William and Mary period.

BRACKET CORNICE Describes a cornice moulding which is supported by brackets fixed to the frieze beneath; often found in Elizabethan and Jacobean styles.

BREAK The projection on a moulding, or carcase plinth formed when it stands forward. Also called ''breakfront'' as in ''breakfront bookcase''.

BUHL or BOULE WORK Decoration formed by the inlaying of tortoiseshell, brass, silver, ivory, etc. Created by Andre Charles Boule, a French cabinet maker in the reign of Louis XV.

BURR An excrescence or growth on the bole of a tree. Much sought after for converting into veneer when a beautifully marked grain usually results.

Also, the turned-over edge of a scraper blade or, for that matter, any other blade such as that of a plane or chisel.

CABRIOLE LEG A curved leg with a projecting knee and slightly curved shaft, terminating in a shaped foot, a claw and ball foot, or a paw foot. Characteristic of the Queen Anne and Chippendale periods.

CANT Describes the sloping, slanting, or bevelling of a surface at a low angle.

CARTOUCHE A decorative feature resembling a scroll partially unrolled at top and bottom, with a central tablet. Characteristic of the French Francois 1 style.

CARYATID Stylized form of the upper half of a female body supporting an arch, entablature, or table top.

CAST Describes lengthwise twisting of timber.

CAUL A piece or block of wood or metal used to distribute pressure (and sometimes heat) evenly over the surface of a veneer.

CHOPS A special type of vice used by wood carvers.

CINQUEFOIL A Gothic motif consisting of five circles contained in a larger circle.

CLAMP A piece of wood jointed at right angles across the ends of the main members of a panel on a table top to prevent casting.

CLASH Describes the silver ''flash'' in oak.

CLAW AND BALL A carved representation of an eagle's claw clasping a ball: a characteristic of cabriole legs.

CLEFT Applies to cutting timber with an axe or adze rather than a saw: as the timber splits along the grain such cutting results in stronger pieces.

CLUB FOOT A turned foot (using off-centre turning) resembling a club and usually applied to cabriole legs.

CLUSTERED COLUMNS A Gothic detail, much favoured by Chippendale, in which columns are clustered together in groups of three or more to form a leg.

COCKED BEAD A semicircular bead which projects above an edge or a surface, especially around drawers and cabinet doors in eighteenth-century work. See also: Staff bead.

COMPO Abbreviated from the word ''composition'' and also called ''stucco''. It is a substitute for wood carving introduced by the Adam brothers and used mainly on ceilings and mantels. The chief constituents are whiting, glue and natural resin, and the mixture is cast in a mould.

CONSOLE A large bracket, usually of scroll form, supporting a table or a beam.

CONTOUR The profile of a moulding.

CONVOLUTE Rolled in the form of a scroll.

CORNICE (1) The uppermost part of a column. (2) The moulding or projection in the angle between wall and ceiling.

CORONA (1) A classical moulding design, usually a large flat projection in a cornice. It is sometimes called a ''Drip'' moulding as, in architecture, it was frequently undercut with a throating to encourage rainwater to drip off easily.
(2) Bracket fixed above a bed, from which curtains or drapes are suspended in a graceful pattern.

COURT CUPBOARD This is a design comprising cupboards and drawers in a lower carcase, with a recessed cupboard above.

COVE In furniture or interior decoration, a cove is a large concave cornice.

CURL Describes the feathery figuration of grain which occurs naturally at the crotch of a branch meeting the trunk.

CURTAIN PIECE Applied to span rails, which are frequently shaped, when they are sited above eye level.

CYMA RECTA A classical term for an ogee moulding.

CYMA REVERSA A ''reversed'' ogee moulding.

DADO The wooden framing fixed around the walls of a room to a height of about 4 or 5 feet — these days it is usually confined to public halls and the like.

DEEPING Also called ''Deep cutting''. Refers to sawing the thickest part of a plank; usually restricted to sawmill practice.

DENTIL A moulding which consists of small blocks with spaces between them, usually sited on a cornice and resembling teeth — hence the name.

DOG TOOTH A small triangular ornament repeated along the length of a moulding on Early English work.

DONKEY-EAR SHOOT A form of shooting board for mitring the edges of long boards.

DROP ORNAMENT Consists of a ''husk'' motif, plus two or three small ''drops'', often found on the knees of Queen Anne style legs.

DUSTBOARD A thin board fixed horizontally between drawers to prevent tampering with the contents and to exclude dust.

EAR PIECES The shaped bracket-like blocks fixed to the sides of the knee of a cabriole leg.

ECHINUS Egg and dart moulding.

ENTASIS The very slight swelling built into a column around the central portion of its length to correct the illusion of concavity.

ESCRITOIRE A writing desk; also applied to a bureau.

ESCUTCHEON The metal fitting (usually brass) for a keyhole.

ÉTAGÈRE A small display stand consisting of several shelves supported on columns.

EXTENDERS Types of vegetable flours such as soya, used to bulk up the volume of a synthetic resin adhesive and extend its spreading capacity.

FACING This is a thin covering of good quality timber applied to a groundwork of inferior timber for cheapness. Drawer fronts and doors were sometimes treated thus.

FALL Applied to the opening fronts of bureaux, secretaires, etc., which ''fall'' as they open.

FASCIA In a moulding, a broad band of plain wood with members above and below.

FEATHERED EDGE An edge which is tapered off almost to nothing.

FIDDLE BACK This is applied to a pattern in veneering which resembles that on the back of a violin.

FIELDED Describes a panel whose edges are canted or bevelled off to fit into grooves on a rail; also to raised or sunken panels.

FILLET A small strip of wood fixed on to a framework to support a shelf, or any small piece of wood which fills a gap.

FINIAL The terminal part of a post, especially when it is shaped or carved.

FITTING UP The final stage of work on a piece after it has been polished; usually refers to fitting handles, hinges, glass, etc.

FLASH Applied to the bright fleck in the grain of some timbers, notably oak (See also "clash").

FLITCH A parcel of squared-up leaves of veneer.

FLUTING Decoration consisting of a series of semi-circular channels running parallel to each other.

FLY RAIL The rail on a flap table which opens to support the flap.

GADROON A decorative nulling often used on Elizabethan and Jacobean furniture.

GALLERY A low rail around the top of a table or cabinet, usually pierced or consisting of a small balustrade.

GARLIC A little garlic added to Scotch glue helps to keep it fresh and increases its strength for sticking down metal inlays.

GESSO A plaster surface prepared as a ground for painted decorations. A wood panel is generally used as a base for the plaster.

GIRANDOLE A wall bracket intended for holding candles, carved or decorated and a feature of eighteenth-century interiors.

GLIDERS Small metal studs fitted with prongs which are knocked into the bottom of chair or table legs to prevent wear and tear. Also called GLIDES or DOMES OF SILENCE.

GRECIAN KEY A running-style ornament often used on mouldings; it is geometric in form.

GROUND Rough wooden framework fixed to a wall to act as a support for subsequent panelling. Also, a term used for the base on which veneer is laid, this also being called "groundwork".

GUILLOCHE A carved ornament consisting of interlaced lines and grooves, with a circular motif, arranged in one or more rows.

HANGING STILE The stile of a door on which the hinges are fixed.

HEAD The top horizontal member of a frame.

HERRINGBONE A veneered detail consisting of two narrow bands of veneer, each with the grain running obliquely and placed side by side with the grain direction opposed, thus resembling a herringbone pattern.

INCISED ORNAMENT An ornament which is cut in and afterwards filled in with coloured composition; a feature of some sixteenth century cabinet work.

INTARSIA This is a term applied to inlaid decoration which is made by cutting out the design and fitting it into matching cavities in the ground. This is in contradistinction to Marquetry, which is built up into a sheet before gluing to the groundwork.

IN THE WHITE Trade term to describe any woodwork prior to staining and polishing.

JIG A template or pattern, often capable of holding work while it is being machined.

JIGGER OR JIG SAW A vertical light treadle or motorized fret saw, used for cutting frets, pierced work and shapes.

KERF The cut made by saw teeth.

KEYING Method of strengthening a mitred joint by inserting a loose tongue of veneer or thin plywood.

KNIFE-CUT VENEER Method of slicing veneers by first softening the timber by steaming. It is then laid on a bed and a knife blade moves across to slice off the veneer.

LINENFOLD Term applied to panels carved to represent folds of linen.

LINING UP Applies to moulding or wood strip fixed to the underside of a table top (for example) for the purposes of both strengthening it and making it appear thicker.

LIPPING An edging. There are various types, ranging from strips of self-adhesive veneer to wooden beadings which are tongued into the edges they are meant to conceal.

LISTEL An alternative name for a fillet when the latter is used as a member of a piece of moulding.

LOCKING STILE The stile of a door to which the lock is fixed.

LOOSE SEAT Also called a "drop-in" seat. An upholstered frame which is not fixed in any way to the chair frame and can be removed at will.

LOPERS Also called "sliders" or "slides": supports for a bureau fall or for an extending table.

LOW RELIEF A term describing carving in wood (or in gesso) which does not protrude far above the groundwork.

LOZENGE A rectangular shape with pointed ends often used as a motif in Elizabethan strapwork and Adam-style panels.

MODILLIONS Small blocks fixed under a cornice moulding to form "dentils"

MULLET A piece of wood with a groove cut in it to test-fit panel edges and drawer bottoms.

MULLION The vertical divisions of a window frame.

MUNTINS OR MUNTINGS The inside vertical divisions of doors and framing.

NECKING A term applied to any small moulding near the top of a pillar or column.

NEWEL A main post supporting a handrail.

NULLING A carved detail, quadrant shaped in section, characteristic of Jacobean style work.

OGEE A moulding which is serpentine-shaped in cross section, correctly called "Cyma Recta". A broken ogee is an ogee moulding in which the line (in section) is broken by a square or other shape of fillet.

ORMULU Material used for casting mounts for embellishing furniture, being a composition of brass and zinc. It was often water-gilt and chased.

OVOLO A classical (Roman) moulding with a convex quadrant profile.

OYSTER SHELL A type of decorative detail made from laburnum veneer prepared by slicing obliquely through a branch.

PARALLEL STRIPS Sometimes called WINDING STRIPS, these are wooden strips which must be identical. They are placed at opposite ends of a plank and then sighted to see if the plank is twisted.

PARCHMENT PANEL A form of linenfold panelling (q.v.)

PARQUETRY A type of marquetry in which the pattern is wholly geometrical and shading is used to give striking effects. Also (in modern times) the building of a floor from wood blocks laid in geometrical patterns.

PATERA (plural PATERAE) Small turned circular disc, or ellipse, often carved, used as decoration or to hide screw heads, etc.

PEDIMENT A flat triangular or curved part placed above the cornice on tall pieces of furniture such as a bookcase.

PELLETS A small plug used to fill screwholes and hide screwheads. They are turned on the lathe in such a way that, when inserted, the grain can be aligned with the grain direction locally.

PEMBROKE TABLE Table with fixed frame (or "bed") with flaps on each side, supported with brackets.

PENDANT A hanging ornament, rather like a finial (q.v.) upside down.

PIECRUST TOP A top with the edge shaped and scalloped in a certain fashion can be circular, elliptical or rectangular.

PIER GLASS A wall mirror fixed between windows, often with a "pier" table beneath.

PIGEON HOLES Compartments in a bureau in which documents etc. can be stored.

PILASTER A flat rectangular column, often planted on a cabinet, and projecting by not more than a quarter of its width.

PILLAR AND CLAW This refers to circular tables of the eighteenth and nineteenth centuries which were fitted with a central pillar and claw feet.

PLANTED Applies to mouldings which are mitred and framed-up before being fixed to the groundwork.

PLUGGING Refers to the driving of wooden plugs into brickwork so that the grounds can be fixed to them.

POUNCE BAG A muslin bag containing very finely powdered chalk. It is dabbed on to a perforated template so that a pattern is formed on the work beneath.

PRESS A small cabinet or wardrobe used for storing linen.

PROFILE The contour of an object as shown by a cross-section.

QUATREFOIL Gothic detail comprising four circles within a larger circle.

QUIRK A small narrow groove or channel alongside a member of a piece of moulding.

REEDING Convex, semi-circular projections on a pillar, column, or pilaster, similar to inverted flutes.

REEDS Series of beads ranged alongside one another without an intervening quirk.

RIBAND DECORATION Inlaid or carved ornament simulating ribbon. Used extensively by Chippendale on his designs for Riband back chairs.

RIBAND AND STICK A Louis XVI style of ornament resembling a ribbon wound around a stick.

RIFFLER A curved file or rasp used particularly in wood carving.

ROCOCO French embellishment in Louis XIV and XV periods representing variations of shells and dripping water. Also called "pebble and splash".

ROE and ROEY Describes a certain figure of grain or veneer which has the appearance of fish roe.

ROTARY CUT A method of cutting veneers (see also "saw cut") which is used predominantly today. It involves a log being fixed with a chuck at each end and slowly revolving. As it does so, a knife blade peels off sheets of veneer.

ROTTEN STONE A soft stone used in powder form combined with oil for french polish, also polishing mother-of-pearl, Buhl and metalwork.

RUN OUT A term which applies to a moulding which "runs out" or diminishes to a point.

SALISBURY GLUE A glue made from the skins of animals rather than the bones etc. It was used for fixing tortoiseshell but has been replaced by synthetic resin adhesives.

SAW-CUT VENEER Method of sawing veneer by means of a circular saw. Necessarily this means that veneers produced by this method are much thicker.

SCALLOP Carved or machined detail simulating an escallop shell.

SCOTIA A classical moulding, the profile of which resembles an elongated parabolic curve.

SCRATCH Also called a "scratch stock". A tool made by the woodworker himself comprising a piece of sawblade filed to shape and held between two blocks of wood of convenient size and shape. Used particularly for scratching out channelling for small inlays and strings.

SCRIBING Describes the method of transferring a complicated shape or contour from an object to a template. Thus, a SCR'B'NG PIECE is a piece of stuff screwed to the back of a carcase and scribed to fit over the skirting board.

SCRIPTOIRE, SCRUTOIRE An archaic term for a writing table or cabinet.

SECTION A representation of an object as if it had been sliced through at right angles.

SETTING OUT This is the process of preparing working drawings and templates.

SETTLE A kind of seat with ends and a back.

SHADING Applied to marquetry, refers to the practice of shading veneer by scorching with hot sand.

SHOW WOOD In upholstered work refers to the parts of timber which are not covered by upholstery and, therefore, "show".

SKIVER A piece of leather used for lining table tops, usually of inferior quality.

SLIDES, SLIDERS: see "LOPERS".

SLOT SCREWING A method of fixing whereby a screw is inserted through a slot instead of a hole, so allowing movement of the timber.

SOFA TABLE A table with a small drop-flap at each end.

SOFFIT The underside of an opening: also, the underside of a wide moulding.

SOLE The bottom face of a plane.

SPADE TOE A design for the foot of a leg which tapers in a way reminiscent of a spade.

SPIRAL TURNING A special method of turning chair legs, table legs, or other members so that they resemble a solid spiral. The same result can be obtained by wood carving. Also called "TWIST LEGS".

SPLAT or SPLAD The central upright panel in a chair back: the name is, however, restricted to comparatively wide panels as are used in Queen Anne or Windsor chairs. Narrower panels (or rails) are called "Banisters" (q.v.).

SPLIT HANDLES Drop handle of Queen Anne style, usually cast hollow with a flat back, thus appearing as if the handle has been split.

SPLIT TURNING A turned ornament which, after having been turned, is sawn in half lengthwise thus giving two identical ornaments.

SPOON BACK Applied to Queen Anne dining chairs, the back legs of which are made in a sinuous curve when viewed from the side, very much resembling the curved handle of a spoon.

SPRING, TO Apart from the obvious connotation with upholstery, this describes the method of fixing a thin rail or other member in place by bending it and then releasing it so that it is held by its own tension plus, in many cases, glue, nails, or screws.

STAFF BEAD A moulding worked on a projecting edge (or "arris"), with a quirk on each side.

STILE The outermost vertical members (or rails) of a door or a frame.

STOUT-HEART PLYWOOD A three-ply board in which the central lamination is considerably thicker than the two outer ones.

STRAPWORK A carved decoration based on the motif of interlaced bands: predominantly Elizabethan or Jacobean.

STRINGS Single lines of inlay used as decoration around the edges of tops, panels, etc.

STUCK MOULDING Any moulding worked on the solid wood, as opposed to a "planted moulding" (q.v.).

STUFFOVER Applied to upholstered work where the framework is completely hidden by the upholstery.

SUNK PANEL A recessed or routed-out panel, often used on pilasters.

SWAG A type of festoon, used as carved decoration in many styles.

SWAN-NECK Describes the curved pediments on Chippendale bookcases etc.

TALLBOY A double chest of drawers, one set upon the other; the upper carcase is often set back.

TAMBOUR A flexible shutter, capable of following a curve (as in a roll-top desk), and made up of gluing thin strips (or "beads") of woods to a canvas backing.

TANG The end of a tool blade which enters the handle.

TEMPLATE (or TEMPLET) A pattern made of any convenient sheet material, e.g. cardboard, zinc, plywood, etc.

TERMINAL The finishing member or ornament on a newel, standard, or post.

TERN FEET A style of leg support for some kinds of Chippendale and Louis XV pieces, consisting of feet in a three-scroll arrangement.

TESTER Refers to the covering above a bed, being usually a canopy supported by posts. A half-tester is a canopy over the head-end only of the bed.

THICKNESSING UP Gluing a narrow strip of wood on to a panel (usually a table top), along the edges, to increase the apparent thickness; (see also "LINING").

THURMING Also called "Square Turning". A method of turning on a lathe by which only part of the wood is removed to give a square moulded appearance.

TOAT Another name for the wooden handle of a plane.

TOOTHING Accomplished by means of a Toothing plane. This has a serrated edge to its iron, and so will cut grooves in a groundwork to form a "key" for glue and thus achieve better adhesion.

TORUS A type of moulding which consists of a large bead, plus a stepped member alongside.

TRAVERSING Refers to cross-planing wide surfaces.

TREFOIL Three circles within a larger circle.

TRENCHING Cutting a wide groove.

TUDOR ROSE A stylized representation of a rose, characteristic of early Tudor work.

UNDERCUT Describes the style of carving in which the main portions of a design are made to stand out by cutting away the wood behind them.

VALANCE Fringed drapery hanging from a cornice, bed rail, or curtain rail.

VIGNETTE A detail of Gothic work consisting of a continuous ornament of delicate leaves and tendrils.

WAINSCOT Synonymous with "DADO" (q.v.). "Wainscot" oak is oak which has been specially cut to show the silver "flash".

WATER LEAF An ornamental detail which resembles an elongated laurel leaf. Found in Hepplewhite and Sheraton pieces.

Index